Muslims in Non-Muslim Lands:
A Legal Study with Applications

Other Titles on Law and Jurisprudence Published by
The Islamic Texts Society

Al-Shāfiʿī's Risāla
Principles of Islamic Jurisprudence
Islamic Commercial Law
Language & Interpretation of Islamic Law
Citizenship & Accountability of Government
The Right to Education, Work & Welfare in Islam
The Right to Life, Security, Privacy & Ownership in Islam
Freedom of Expression in Islam
Equity & Fairness in Islam
Freedom Equality & Justice in Islam
The Dignity of Man: An Islamic Perspective

Muslims in Non-Muslim Lands:
A Legal Study with Applications

Amjad Mohammed

THE ISLAMIC TEXTS SOCIETY

First published in 2013 by
The Islamic Texts Society
Miller's House
Kings Mill Lane
Great Shelford
Cambridge CB22 5EN, U.K.

British Library Cataloguing-in-Publication Data.
A catalogue record for this book is
available from the British Library.

ISBN 978 1 903682 74 6 Hardback
ISBN 978 1 903682 75 3 Paperback

CONTENTS

List of Figures

List of Tables

SYSTEM OF TRANSLITERATION

Arabic letter	English equivalent	Arabic letter	English equivalent
ء	’	ط	ṭ
ا	ā	ظ	ẓ
ب	b	ع	ʿ
ت	t	غ	gh
ث	th	ف	f
ج	j	ق	q
ح	ḥ	ك	k
خ	kh	ل	l
د	d	م	m
ذ	dh	ن	n
ر	r	و	w
ز	z	ه	-a
س	s	ي	y
ش	sh		
ص	ṣ		
ض	ḍ		

	Arabic letter	English equivalent
Long vowels	ا or ى	ā
	و	ū
	ي	ī
Doubled	يّ	iyy final form ī
	وّ	uww final form ū
Dipthongs	وَ	aw
	يَ	ay
Short vowels	َ	a
	ِ	i
	ُ	u

INTRODUCTION

The religion of Islam is one that lays down provisions for both the public and private aspects of a believer's life. Therefore a Muslim is viewed within the context of the society in which he or she lives. Since the spread of Islam, Muslims have lived in what were termed the 'lands of Islam' or, for a more up to date definition, 'Muslim-dominant' or 'Muslim-led' countries. The twentieth century, however, saw large numbers of Muslims migrate to lands that are 'non-Muslim', primarily North America and in Western Europe. As history has witnessed, Islam possesses the ability to ascribe to its adherents minority status in such situations. An example is the Muslim tradesmen who established themselves in China, to such an extent that a number of emperors declared Islam a semi-official religion of the state.[1] Thus, the notion of Muslims living in non-Muslim lands is not novel. It is the extent of the immigration of Muslims in the twentieth century, coupled with the changes in the world since the time, that the classical manuals of Islamic Law were compiled, which means that this area is in need of urgent exploration. Also, with the demographic changes caused by this mass migration, many questions have arisen for both Muslims and non-Muslims alike; questions which require answers in order for Muslims to know how to form and maintain their relationship with the 'Other'.[2]

The importance of understanding this topic is now more keenly felt because of the intense scrutiny to which Muslims in the West are being exposed. The events of 11 September 2001 brought about an unprecedented interest in Islam and Muslims, particularly of those that live as a minority in secular democratic societies. This world-changing event, and more recently the wars in Afghanistan and Iraq, has increased interest in Islam and has raised research in this field to historically unmatched levels.

[1] Dru Gladney, 'Islam in China: Accommodation or Separation?', *The China Quarterly* (vol. 174, 2003), pp. 451-67. Raphael Israeli, 'The Muslim Minority in the People's Republic of China', *Asian Survey* (vol. 21, no. 8, 1981), pp. 901-19.

[2] Syed Abedin, *Islamic Fundamentalism, Islamic Ummah and the World Conference on Muslim Minorities* (CSIC Papers Europe No. 7, Birmingham: CSIC, 1992).

In Britain, the '7/7' London bombings, together with the wider political and media discussions regarding Muslim 'integration' within a multi-cultural Britain, and the fact that Islam is now second only to Christianity in terms of numbers of adherents, makes such studies all the more urgent.

Among the accusations repeatedly addressed to Muslims since September 11 is that they—or more accurately Islam—are incompatible with living as minorities in Western countries[3] and that this incompatibility leads to 'fanatical' and 'violent' responses.[4] In addition, there is also the view that Muslims tend not to be concerned about the non-Muslim countries they live in and show little or no affiliation to them. These accusations include an underlying notion that either Muslims should assimilate and give up all their former identity within the majority state[5] or should reside in those lands where they are a majority. For proponents of this view, no middle option seems to exist, let alone one that comes from the very heart of Islam.

This study will make the argument that there is a middle option, which has been successful on numerous occasions in the past, and which avoids both isolation and assimilation, through recourse to 'classical formulations of the Islamic tradition'[6] as found in the Islamic Schools of Law.[7] The challenge now is to explore the writings and theory of the Sunni legal perspective, to which most Muslims belong, in the light of Muslim minorities in the West.

Historical Background: Economic Migrants to Citizens

The British census of 2001 has thrown up some interesting facts about the 'Muslim' population of Britain. The census results stated that there were 1,591,000 self-identified 'Muslims', which is 2.7% of the entire population. It is reported that the majority, in fact around 1 million of this total, 'originate

[3] Hisham Hellyer, *The State We Are In: Identity, Terror and the Law of Jihad* (Bristol: Amal Press, 2006), p. 96; Raphael Israeli, 'The Muslim Minority in the People's Republic of China', *Asian Survey* (vol. 21, no. 8, 1981), p. 902; Talal Asad, *The Idea of Europe: From Antiquity to the European Union* (Cambridge: Cambridge University Press, 2002), pp. 209-10.

[4] Wasif Shadid, 'The Integration of Muslim Minorities in the Netherlands', *International Migration Review* (vol. 25, no. 2, 1991), p. 370.

[5] Raphael Israeli, 'The Muslim Minority in the People's Republic of China', p. 915.

[6] Hisham Hellyer, 'Minorities, Muslims and Shariʿa: Some Reflections on Islamic Law and Muslims without Political Power', *Islam and Christian–Muslim Relations* (vol. 18, no. 1, 2007), p. 105.

[7] Whenever Law appears with a capital, we are referring to the Sharīʿa.

from South Asia (two thirds of whom are from Pakistan, under a third from Bangladesh and the remainder from India). The other 0.6 million are from North Africa, East Europe and South East Asia. More than half of all British Muslims are under the age of seventeen. The Muslims of Britain are also concentrated in older post-industrial cities and conurbations in the Southeast, the Midlands and the North.'[8]

The overwhelming majority of Muslims who migrated to Britain, in particular after the Second World War, were from low-income, poorly-educated, rural backgrounds of South Asia. Over the years, the number of Muslims in Britain increased dramatically, from 50,000 at the beginning of World War II to 100,000 in 1951, 750,000 in 1971 and 1,500,000 in 1991; with the added characteristic that approximately two-third are no longer migrants and are now British citizens.[9] Anwar[10] describes a number of 'pull' factors which he asserts brought about this mass migration and lists them as economic and social development within Britain itself as a result of the New Commonwealth and the non-existence of restrictions on migration prior to 1962. As for the 'push' factors, he lists high unemployment, lack of economic opportunities and underdevelopment within the Indian Subcontinent. Many, though by no means all, of these immigrants were motivated by economic deprivation and hence were classed as 'lower' order or 'working-class' by their own social structure.[11] A significant number of Muslims in Britain, therefore, found themselves inhabiting the 'lowest socio-economic levels within British society'.[12] They tended to settle in towns and cities that required a low-skilled labour work force, and in particular they chose the inner city due to cheap housing and accessible local amenities. The community started to grow and establish itself when wives joined their husbands and with the birth of the first generation of British Muslims.

[8] Tahir Abbas, *Muslim Britain: Communities Under Pressure* (London: Zed Books Ltd, 2005), p. 17.

[9] Mohammed Kettani, in *Political Participation and Identities of Muslims in Non-Muslim States* (Kampen: Kak Pharos Publishing House, 1996), p. 29.

[10] Muhammad Anwar, 'Muslims in Western States: The British Experience and the Way Forward', *Journal Institute of Muslim Minority Affairs* (vol. 28, no. 1, 2008), p. 129

[11] Dale Eickelman and James Piscatori, *Muslim Travellers: Pilgrimage, Migration and the Religious Immigration* (London: Routledge, 1990), p. 6. It is worth noting, however, that a minority of 'economic migrants' were highly-educated and skilled, and moved for other reasons connected with training or employment.

[12] Anthony Bradney, 'The Legal Status of Islam within the United Kingdom', in S. Ferrari and A. Bradney (eds.), *Islam and the European Legal Systems* (Dartmouth: Ashgate, 2000), p. 183.

The community's requirements needed to be fulfilled, hence mosques, *ḥalāl* butchers and Muslim funeral directors were established within those localities.[13] With these and other developments, the Muslim community distinguished itself from the rest of the population and became a Muslim minority with its own voice and distinct identity.[14] These local facilities, particularly the mosques, became the focal point and the seed of the fast growing community. Historically, cities and towns in Muslim lands were also centred on the mosque,[15] hence this development seems to be more by choice than chance.

Within a relatively short space of time, due to high immigration, a tendency to have large families and the indigenous 'white' population moving away from the districts, significant sections of certain cities became predominantly Muslim, to such an extent that some primary schools, and a significant number of secondary schools in the area, became exclusively made up of Muslim pupils.[16] Tariq Ramadan[17] describes the development of these, as he terms them, 'social microcosms', whereby Muslims live amongst themselves with little contact with the indigenous population as a means to protect their identity. Therefore, the aim, as he puts it, is to be 'at home', or 'to live in Europe but at home'. He goes on to say that this identity is not an 'Islamic' identity as such, but rather an Asian model of Islam. In it, any questioning or challenging of this identity is understood as a 'betrayal of Islam' which could jeopardise the religious identity. Deborah Phillips[18] puts forward a different suggestion. She asserts that the benefits of living together in 'ethnic clusters' need to be considered: feeling 'safe' and being relatively safe from racial harassment, mutual support of family and friends, being catered for in terms of worship, food outlets, shopping, entertainment and so forth. Finally, Nissa Finney

[13] Mohammed Kettani, in *Political Participation and Identities of Muslims in Non-Muslim States* (Kampen: Kak Pharos Publishing House, 1996), p. 18.

[14] Rachel Bloul, 'Anti-discrimination Laws, Islamophobia and Ethnicization of Muslim Identities in Europe and Australia', *Journal Institute of Muslim Minority Affairs* (vol. 28, no. 1, 2008), pp. 9-10.

[15] Baber Johansen, *Contingency in Sacred Law: Legal and Ethical Norms in the Muslim Fiqh* (Leiden: E.J. Brill, 1999), p. 153.

[16] Jorgen Nielsen, *Islamic Surveys: Muslims in Western Europe* (Edinburgh: Edinburgh University Press, 2004), p. 54.

[17] Tariq Ramadan, *To be a European Muslim* (Leicester: The Islamic Foundation, 1999), pp. 186-87.

[18] Deborah Philips, in *Housing and Black and Minority Ethnic Communities* (London: Office of the Deputy Prime Minister, 2003), pp. 36-49.

and Ludi Simpson[19] challenge some current political views and what they term as 'myths', like the idea that Britain takes in too many immigrants, that many minorities cannot be integrated, and that Britain is becoming 'a country of ghettos'. They also question the notion that Muslims move to Muslim-only areas and point to the fact that it is a growing community rather than a segregated one.[20] In this work, we shall see that the members of the Muslim community have adopted a number of different social stances with respect to the wider indigenous population and that the current geographical locations of the community are influenced both by the Muslim community's intentional choice to live together and separately from others, and by its numerical growth which gives the impression that Muslims prefer to live apart.

Relationship to the 'Other': Isolationist, Integrationist or Assimilationist?

The position Muslims, or any minority group for that matter, take with respect to the dominant community have generally been defined by the terms: 'Isolation', 'Integration' and 'Assimilation'.[21] The terms 'Secession', 'Coexistence' and 'Assimilation' have been used with respect to Muslims in Thailand and China;[22] and 'Conservative', 'Moderate Integrationist' and 'Radical Integrationist' with respect to the Muslim's voice in Indian politics.[23] More recently, 'Isolation', 'Assimilation', 'External Participation' and 'Integration' have been put forward as a means to define the Muslims of Italy.[24]

[19] Nissa Finney and Ludi Simpson, *'Sleepwalking to Segregation?': Challenging Myths about Race and Migration* (Bristol: Policy Press, 2009).

[20] Ibid.

[21] John Wolffe, in *The Growth of Religious Diversity: Britain since 1945* (vol. 1, London: Routledge and Open University Press, 1994), p. 160; Omar Khalidi, 'Muslim Minorities: Theory and Experience of Muslim Interaction in Non-Muslim Societies', *Journal of the Institute of Muslim Minority Affairs* (vol. 10, no. 2, 1989), p. 425; Tariq Ramadan, *To be a European Muslim* (Leicester: The Islamic Foundation, 1999), pp. 181-82.

[22] Raphael Israeli, 'The Muslim Minority in the People's Republic of China', *Asian Survey* (vol. 21, no. 8, 1981), pp. 901-19; Andrew Forbes, 'Thailand's Muslim Minorities: Assimilation, Secession or Coexistence?' *Asian Survey* (vol. 22, no. 11, 1982), pp. 1056-73.

[23] Gopal Krishna, 'Islam, Minority Status and Citizenship: Muslim Experience in India', *Archives Europennes de Sociologie* (vol. 27, no. 2, 1986), pp. 353-68.

[24] James Toronto, 'Islam *Italiano*: Prospects for Integration of Muslims in Italy's Religious Landscape', *Journal Institute of Muslim Minority Affairs* (vol. 28, no. 1, 2008), pp. 64-65.

In an earlier study, Robert Ezra Park,[25] when discussing race relations and immigration in the early part of the twentieth century, with regards to black and Japanese immigrants in Chicago, suggested that the three separate terms ('Isolation', 'Integration' and 'Assimilation') are actually only stages of 'Adaptation'. Sheila Patterson, influenced by Park's concept, asserted similar views when researching the immigrant-host framework in the 1960s with respect to immigrants in the UK, in particular West Indian and Asian immigrants in Brixton, London.[26] Hence, Park and subsequently Patterson, refer to the first stage as 'Accommodation' followed by 'Integration' and 'Assimilation'. Having said that, both acknowledge that some migrants can only assimilate up to a certain point. However, Werner Menski,[27] David Pearl and Werner Menski[28] and Sebastian Poulter[29] conclude that the assimilationist assumptions have not 'turned into social reality' in the case of Muslims, particularly those from South Asia. Therefore it is possible to conclude that the three positions (i.e. Isolation, Integration and Assimilation) do exist in parallel and are expected to continue to exist rather than being stages in a process that will inevitably reach completion. In other words, the immigrant community would become completely assimilated and not discernible from the host society. This is further substantiated by research, which highlights the fact that Muslims have re-ordered their lives according to their own terms rather than assimilating and adapting as theorised and expected.[30]

This present work agrees with the position and the choice of terms given above by John Wolffe, Omar Khalidi and Tariq Ramadan: Isolation, Integration and Assimilation. Let us here define these three terms further. Isolation can be due to two main reasons: cultural or pseudo-religious. 'Cultural' is self-explanatory, however, the term 'pseudo-religious' requires clarification. It refers to the

[25] Robert Park, *Race and Culture* (London: The Free Press of Glencoe, 1950).

[26] Sheila Patterson, *Dark Strangers* (Harmondsworth: Penguin, 1965) and *Immigration and Race Relations in Britain 1960–1967* (London: Oxford University Press, 1969).

[27] Werner Menski, in *Ethnicity, Identity and Migration: The South Asian Context* (Toronto: Toronto University Press, 1993), pp. 238–68.

[28] David Pearl and Werner Menski, *Muslim Family Law* (London: Sweet and Maxwell, 1998).

[29] Sebastian Poulter, *English Law and Ethnic Minority Customs* (London: Buttersworth, 1986) and *Ethnicity, Law and Human Rights: The English Experience* (Oxford: Oxford University Press, 1998).

[30] Ihsan Yilmaz, 'The Challenge of Post-Modern Legality and Muslim Legal Pluralism in England', *Journal of Muslim Minority Affairs* (vol. 20, no. 2, 2002), p. 345.

application of overly-strict rulings in order to be perceived as 'more Islamic' and hence closer to the truth. But a ruling's rigidity does not determine its accuracy; rather it is its correct derivation from the sources of the Law that does.[31] This raises an interesting point, which requires discussion as it is usually misunderstood. There are two types of Islamic ruling: one determines what is permissible and impermissible and is referred to as *fatwā* (religious-legal edict), and the other determines what is superior or praiseworthy and is referred to as *taqwā* (piety, God-consciousness) and has its source in the Qur'ānic verse, '*Inna akramakum ʿind Allāh atqākum*' ('Indeed the most honoured from amongst you in God's view are the ones superior in *taqwā*').[32] Therefore, a certain action or item may be permissible but a Muslim may still avoid it in order to act according to *taqwā*; this does not make the action or item impermissible. Furthermore, one may not apply one's piety and religious understanding to others and claim or state that a particular action or item is impermissible on the basis of personal preference. The most one can do is advise or promote piety to others.

Returning to the Isolationist perspective, one finds that it tends to dictate that the minority community should have no interest in or association with the dominant community or the state. As a result, very little interaction takes place between the two groups, minority and majority, and the consequent mutual suspicion and distrust further polarises the two communities.

In the case of Assimilation, the minority community loses most of its former identity and largely accepts the identity and way of life of the dominant society, with the possibility that personal belief survives. In other words, it is the means by which individuals and groups of individuals are 'dissolved' or 'diluted' into a much larger different group.

We shall argue below that neither Isolation nor Assimilation are models that Muslims should adopt living as a minority in Britain, and that the rejection of both these perspectives is based on Islamic theology and Law, which place a high value on social harmony.

The third perspective—Integration—is a mean between the two above and incorporates aspects of both positions. Here, the Muslim community retains its religious identity while integrating into the wider dominant community, without complete and total assimilation. Wasif Shadid[33] describes it 'as the par-

[31] Tariq Ramadan, *To be a European Muslim* (Leicester: The Islamic Foundation, 1999), p. 71.

[32] Q.XLIX.13.

[33] Wasif Shadid, 'The Integration of Muslim Minorities in the Netherlands', *International Migration Review* (vol. 25, no. 2, 1991), p. 362.

ticipation of ethnic and religious minorities, individually and as a group, in the social structure of the host society while having enough possibilities to retain the distinctive aspects of their culture and identity.' In other words, Muslims remain faithful to Islam but identify fully with Britain and adapt British structures, which will in turn support their practice of Islam.[34]

Today in Britain, Muslims have adopted all three models but these are not normally viewed as distinct, separate divisions but are more akin to a continuum with Isolation and Assimilation at the extremes and Integration in the centre.[35] The Open Society Institute[36] details the three trends among the Muslim community, and I have drawn on their findings as they provide proof of the social manifestation and application of my own interpretation:

1. A small but significant minority has become radicalised in its interpretation of Islam; it isolates itself from the wider community due to mistrust of others who are different and misunderstanding of the religion itself. This is sometimes misconstrued as extremism and a disregard for the laws of the land, however, this is not usually the case, though this group would most likely contain 'extremists'.
2. Arguably the largest group do not see their Islamic faith and their identification with it as a barrier to integrating within the wider society and to contributing positively as fellow citizens in the state. They are confident that Islam, and Muslims, can exist and can actually flourish and adapt to the new pluralistic environment with a two-way mutual engagement between Islam and British society.
3. Another significant group has now become what can best be described as 'nominal' Muslims. And in a considerable number of cases, individuals no longer feel comfortable to describe themselves as Muslims.

The way in which one community perceives another is of great importance and has an obvious and direct effect on community relations. Leaving aside the Assimilation group—as to a certain extent they now form part of the majority

[34] Ihsan Yilmaz, 'The Challenge of Post-Modern Legality and Muslim Legal Pluralism in England', *Journal of Muslim Minority Affairs* (vol. 20, no. 2, 2002), p. 346.

[35] Omar Khalidi, 'Muslim Minorities: Theory and Experience of Muslim Interaction in Non-Muslim Societies', *Journal of the Institute of Muslim Minority Affairs* (vol. 10, no. 2, 1989), pp. 425-37; Wasif Shadid, 'The Integration of Muslim Minorities in the Netherlands', *International Migration Review* (vol. 25, no. 2, 1991), p. 366.

[36] Open Society Institute, *Monitoring Minority Protection in the EU: The Situation of Muslims in the UK,* (New York: Open Society Institute, 2002), pp. 77-78.

group—the remaining two groups either engage with the wider community or desist from doing so. Abdul Bari[37] argues that communities with an open view towards fellow citizens, the view that the Integration group holds, consider them (the 'Other') as an asset rather than as a problem or worse still as a danger; whereas a closed view of society, namely the Isolation group, holds the opposite view. The same can also be said of the host-society and its relationship with the 'Other' minority community. Abdul Bari's analysis is based on the findings detailed in a recent report by the Runnymede Trust entitled *The Parekh Report*.[38] In Table 1, we refer to those points that are relevant to our argument.

Table 1: Closed and Open Views of the 'Other'

Distinction	**Closed View**	**Open View**
Separate/Interacting	The Other seen as separate: (a) not having any aims or values in common with self; (b) not affected by it; (c) not influencing it.	The Other seen as not separate: (a) having certain shared values and aims with self; (b) affected by it; (c) enriching it.
Inferior/Different	The Other seen as inferior to the self; e.g. barbaric, irrational, 'fundamentalist'.	The Other seen as different but of equal worth.
Enemy/Partner	The Other seen as violent, aggressive, threatening, to be defeated and perhaps dominated.	The Other seen as an actual or potential partner in joint co-operative enterprises and in the solution of shared problems.
Hostility towards Other seen as natural/problematic	Fear and hostility towards Other accepted as natural and 'normal'.	Critical views both of the Other and of the self for sake of fairness and accuracy.

To conclude, research has shown that the Muslim community, particularly from the Indian subcontinent has, for the most part, not assimilated in

37 Muhammad Abdul Bari, *Race, Religion & Muslim Identity in Britain* (Swansea: Renaissance Press, 2005), pp. 104-06.

38 The Runnymede Trust, *The Parekh Report, The Future of Multi-Ethnic Britain: Report of the Commission on the Future of Multi Ethnic Britain* (London: Profile Books Ltd, 2000), p. 247.

Britain as theorised and expected; instead the three models discussed above continue to exist side by side. Also, it has become apparent that of the three social stances, the Assimilationist, or at least the Integrationist view, is the one that the host society would prefer the minority community to adopt.

Hermeneutical Approaches: Liberal, Traditional and Literal

Fiqh is the system of methods and rules used by jurists to study the Qur'an and Prophetic traditions with a view of arriving at legal rulings. It is the basis for all the different interpretations of the Sharīʿa to be found in the four Sunni Schools of Law (Ḥanafī, Mālikī, Shāfiʿī and Ḥanbalī) and in the Jaʿfarī School which is followed by the majority of Shiʿi Muslims. It is our intention to explore how the Ḥanafī School of Law understands and treats the idea of a Muslim minority. Our choice of this School is because most adherents in Britain, and in fact the world, belong to the Ḥanafī School of Law[39] even if their knowledge of it may be just nominal.

Although the current trend in discussing 'minority legal considerations' is usually explored from the perspective of comparative Islamic jurisprudence across various legal Schools or through new interpretations of the revealed texts, we believe that it is important for the sake of intellectual continuity, and acceptance within religious circles, to start from the tradition of one School before branching out to other Schools. Furthermore, the principles adopted by the founders of the legal Schools are different, this obviously results in different rulings; an attempt to produce a 'generic' set of principles by mix-matching the four Schools is at best naïve and at worst simplifying a complicated set of different, in some cases contradictory, rules and methods. For instance, there are words in the Qur'ān which have both a literal and a metaphorical meaning; the Ḥanafī and Shāfiʿī Schools have different methods that they utilise in order to prioritise one meaning over the other, and hence the results they arrive at may be different. Having said this, jurists are able to adopt another School's juristic view[40] on condition that the jurist doing so possesses sufficient knowledge, experience and piety, so as to prevent

[39] Mohammed Kettani, *Muslim Minorities in the World Today* (London: Mansell Publishing Ltd, 1986), p. 41.

[40] Muḥammad Ibn ʿĀbidīn, *Radd al-muḥtār ʿalā durr al-mukhtār* (vol. 1, Karachi: Maktab Rashīdiyya, 1984), p. 55. Abdur Rahman ibn Yusuf, *Fiqh al-Imam: Key Proofs in Hanafi Fiqh* (Santa Barbara: White Thread Press, 2003).

arbitrariness when exercising *ijtihād*. The Ḥanafī School accepts the application of legal rulings from outside its own School if a major need arises within the community; therefore in the instances where the Ḥanafī School might be overly strict on a non-fundamental matter or when the School does not possess a ruling, the perspectives of other Islamic legal Schools can be explored. All hermeneutic interpretations which use the methodology of the different Schools of Islamic Law to arrive at particular rulings will be referred to as the 'Traditional' approach.

In addition to this approach, there are at least two other hermeneutic approaches of interpreting the religious sources: 'Liberal' (or 'Modernist') and 'Literal', which sit at opposite ends of the continuum with respect to source text interpretation and the accommodation of societal customs by the Law. These three approaches are discussed in broad generic terms as it is acknowledged that subgroups will exist within each trend, and therefore these interpretive models are best viewed as a continuum, with Literalism varying from absolute verbatim literalism through to significant aspects of Traditionalism, and Liberalism varying from absolute liberalist ideology to liberalism with borrowed concepts from Traditionalism (See Figure 1). Traditionalism itself inherently possesses aspects of both a literal application of the text and the consideration of the social and cultural setting.

Figure 1: The Interpretive Continuum

Literalism Traditionalism Liberalism
Lt Lt Lt/t Lt/t Lt/T lt/T lt/T T T T T T/lb T/lb T/Lb t/Lb t/Lb Lb Lb
100%------------------absolute application of text --------------------0%
0%----------------------society impacts on Law---------------------100%
Key: Lt – Literalism T – Traditionalism Lb – Liberalism

Our interpretation of the Liberal approach here is one that takes into consideration modern, to a certain extent secular, practices when interpreting the texts and when deriving principles and rulings. In some cases, it seeks to 'dilute' existing Islamic laws and precepts which do not sit well with modern practices. Nawaf Salam[41] describes it as 'interpreting Western notions in a manner compatible with the Sharīʿa precepts; and reinterpreting the latter

[41] Nawaf Salam, 'The Emergence of Citizenship in Islamdom', *Arab Law Quarterly* (vol. 12, 1997), pp. 138.

with the view of accommodating the needs generated by the challenges of the West.' Tariq Modood and Fauzia Ahmad[42] refer to this group as Modernists who 'reason from faith and first principles but doing so in ways that draw upon modernist ideas within an Islamic methodology (*Ijtihād*).' As to the Literal approach, it seeks to stick as closely as possible to the original texts and argues that there is little scope for human interpretation of God's revealed Law. Of course, other hermeneutic models may and do exist, and we shall refer to some when discussing the hermeneutic approaches in Chapter III.

It is possible to relate these hermeneutic approaches to the three social responses or positions discussed earlier.

Table 2: The Relationship between Social Stance and Hermeneutic Approach

Social position adopted with respect to Majority	**Interpretive model adopted with respect to religious source texts**
Isolation	Literal
Integration	Traditional
Assimilation	Liberal

We shall discuss in Chapter II how certain sections of the Muslim minority utilise particular interpretive models in order to justify their chosen social position. And how a hermeneutic approach could also be selected in order to produce the required social stance outcome.

In concluding this Introduction, we wish to clarify that our study is not concerned with Islamic articles of faith nor with a theological understanding of the sources. Our work is a jurisprudential one with the aim of arriving at rulings and laws; the focus is, firstly, on how the application of particular hermeneutic approaches are connected with particular social positions, and then on how the application of Traditional methodologies may result in a greater integration of Muslim minorities in Western societies.

Furthermore, we will be arguing against the idea that reducing or completely removing religious identity and its means of expression will eradicate

[42] Tariq Modood and Fauzia Ahmad, 'British Muslim Perspectives on Multiculturalism'. *Theory Culture Society* (vol. 24, no. 2, 2007), p. 194.

the process by which individuals and communities become isolated and in consequence become a cause for concern to the dominant community. As will become apparent in the latter part of this work, it is the lack of real religious knowledge and understanding which is the cause of this isolation. Individuals receiving pseudo-religious advice or limited religious teachings are more likely to take up the Isolationist position due to their lack of understanding of the breadth of Islamic scholarship. In addition, it could be argued that to remove the moral structure from a people, or to challenge a key aspect of their identity, will generate problems rather than solve them, as religion has been shown to have positive effects on its practitioners. For instance, Sara Silvestri[43] found in a recent study of European Muslim women that they felt 'empowered' due to their increased levels of education; in particular, their independent access to religious knowledge enabled them to become key individuals for 'radical transformations from within the tradition that does not need to go through radical means'.[44]

Thus, though the host community may believe that Muslims should completely assimilate into Western societies, our research will show that integration is the model Muslims can adopt in order to live as Islam permits within a multi-cultural society.

Research Design, Methodology and Structure

The research contained within this study is based on religious source texts and predominantly involves detailed textual analysis in order to demonstrate the methodology of the Traditional hermeneutic approach. A significant portion consists of the translation of Traditional scholarly texts into English, as far as we know for the first time. These texts are centuries old and were written for a Muslim audience of legal experts, and the language reflects the era and its targeted audience, hence the necessity to analyse them in depth. The final aim is to see to what extent the Traditional approach is flexible enough to provide for the minority status of Muslim, and, eventually, to arrive at traditionally sound rulings for Muslims in Britain or Muslims in similar circumstances elsewhere in the world.

We felt that it is important to give some historical background to this

[43] Sara Silvestri, *Europe's Muslim Women: Potential, Aspirations and Challenges* (Research Report, King Baudouin Foundation, 2008).

[44] Ibid., p. 7.

work and Chapter I, entitled 'Muslims Through the Ages: From Minority to Majorities to Minorities', gives a very brief history of the spread of Islam and the more recent movement to Western Europe by Muslim minorities. This will include a definition of 'Muslim' and 'minority', and a concise overview of the history of Muslims as a minority, particularly in Britain. There will also be a summary of Islam and the traditional Schools to which the majority of Muslims subscribe.

Chapter II will discuss the approaches taken by various scholars, religious and non-religious, with respect to interpretation of the source texts (Literal, Traditional and Liberal) depending on their methodology rather than their claims. Due to the competitive, rather than complementary, nature of these approaches, it will be argued that the Traditional approach is the one that is most legally accurate and 'practicable' for Muslims minorities. This chapter will also detail *fiqh al-aqalliyyāt* (*fiqh* of Muslim Minorities), a term coined by Ṭaha al-ᶜAlwānī and supported by other scholars including Yūsuf al-Qaraḍāwī, as one area of research which is striving for a complete overhaul of prior Islamic thinking and jurisprudence for Muslims living as a minority, particularly in the West.

As mentioned above, we do not subscribe to the perspective of a 'generic' School of Law derived from mix-matching the four Schools. Anyone studying Islamic jurisprudence will immediately see the precision of the scholar-jurists and the lengths they go to in reaching their legal conclusions. This is the main reason why we have decided to concentrate on only one School of Law, the Ḥanafī School. It also happens to be the School that the majority of Muslims are affiliatied with. Thus Chapter III, entitled 'The Traditional Ḥanafī Legal Approach', will bring together an overview of Islamic Law as interpreted by the Ḥanafī School. Biographies of the founders of the School will be given, and the foundational texts of the School discussed in order to highlight the transmission of knowledge from the Prophet Muḥammad to the present day. This is followed by a discussion of *ijtihād* and the legal theory and methodologies available to religious scholars to interpret the Qur'ān and the Prophet's traditions.

While Chapter III provides the background to the legal approach of the Ḥanafī school, the following three chapters concentrate on the theory and practical application of this methodology in deriving legal rulings.

Chapter IV, details the principles of Ḥanafī *fiqh* derived from the primary sources of Islamic jurisprudence; a number of classical texts have to be studied and significant sections translated and discussed in order to fully realise the principles. One particular text employed is *Uṣūl al-Shāshī* which details the explanation of language and lexical meaning from the source texts like the Qur'ān and the traditions of the Prophet Muḥammad. It also details in which order the source texts should be interrogated and in what manner. There will be an opportunity to discuss the concept of *taqlīd* and how and when it is abandoned.

Prior to the study, in Chapter VI, of the application of Ḥanafī *fiqh* to Muslim minorities in the West, we explore in Chapter V the definition of 'state' or 'political domain', *dār al-ḥarb* and *dār al-Islam* and their interpretations by the Literal, Traditional and Liberal models, with particular reference to the British legal system and its rulings. The necessity for this understanding is because the *fiqh* of minorities cannot and does not operate within a vacuum; it is directly influenced by the context in which it operates. In other words, the rulings of the legal system of a non-Muslim state affect the rulings of *fiqh* for Muslim minorities and this must be taken into consideration before tackling specific cases.

The final chapter, Chapter VI, concentrates on the application of Ḥanafī *fiqh* to the context of Muslims as a minority and details a number of examples. This section explores where it is possible for established legal principles to depart from the historically agreed-upon positions of the Ḥanafī School and to what degree they can do so. For instance, seeing how the jurisprudential ideas of 'necessity' (*ḍarūra*), 'need' (*ḥāja*), 'local societal custom' or 'culture' (*ʿurf*), 'juristic preference' (*istiḥsān*) and 'independent legal reasoning' (*ijtihād*) can lead to the Muslims of Britain receiving legal rulings that may differ from those that would be customarily issued by Ḥanafī jurists in parts of the Muslim world where Muslims are a majority and all within the framework of the Traditional rules of the School. Also, though this may be specific to Muslims as minorities it could equally be applicable in Muslim majority countries due to the effect of 'westernisation' or modernisation and the adoption of legal systems not based on Islam. A number of examples will put this into context, including examples from: private life (dealing with acts of ritual worship and medicinal treatments), social interaction (detailing employment and general interaction with the wider community), economic (considers financial transactions) and political (participation in elections and other related issues). The principles and the applications detailed in Chapters IV and V will be applied to each case in order to demonstrate how the Ḥanafī School copes with issues normally beyond those dealt with by classical jurisprudence.

In the Conclusion, we summarise the findings of the study which we hope will encourage others in further development of this research.

It is to be noted that due to the nature of this study there is an extensive use of Arabic words and terms. On their first occurrence in the text, these terms are given in transliteration followed by the translation in brackets; subsequently only the Arabic term will generally be used. A Glossary is available at the end of the book to help with the terminology employed.

Finally, as a Muslim it is recommended to mention '*ṣalla Llāhu ʿalayhi wa-sallam*' after the mentioning of the Prophet Muḥammad; it means 'May God's salutations and peace be upon him'. I have not included this within the body of the text, however I humbly ask fellow Muslims to pronounce it at the time of reading his name as it is praiseworthy to do so; in fact this can be considered as an example of *fatwā* and *taqwā* in action. Similarly, I have not always used titles like Imām, Shaykh or Muftī for the great Islamic luminaries and scholars; this is not due to lack of respect but rather to avoid repetition and to allow a natural flow in reading.

CHAPTER I

Muslims through the Ages: From Minority to Majorities to Minorities

OVER FOURTEEN CENTURIES AGO, Islam came into being with the revelation of the Qur'ān to the Prophet Muḥammad. What started with a tiny group of people—the Prophet, his family and early converts in Mecca—soon spread at an astounding speed. Today, we find the presence of Islam and its followers on every continent and in almost all countries on the face of the earth.

From the time when Islam became the predominant religion in certain geographical areas, the majority of Muslims have lived in Muslim-majority lands. However, in the last century an unusual phenomenon started to take place: it was the movement of significant numbers of people from the East to the West in order to better themselves economically. These numbers included a mass migration of Muslims who then took up permanent residence in secular, modern states and as a result becoming a 'Muslim minority'.

Definition of 'Muslim Minority'

Around one quarter of the world's population is 'Muslim', ranging from near complete majorities in some countries to virtually zero minorities in others. But before discussing Muslims as minorities around the world, definitions of the terms 'Muslim' and 'minority' are required.

The literal meaning of the word Islam is 'submission' and its interpretation is 'to submit oneself to God'. Islam is based on five principles: affirmation of belief in the Oneness of God and in Muḥammad as His messenger, prayer, almsgiving, fasting and pilgrimage. Muslims, literally 'Submitters', lay claim to all prophets from Adam to Muḥammad and believe Muḥammad to be the final link in the long line of prophets sent from God. For Muslims, the Qur'ān is the actual uncreated Word of God brought to the Prophet Muḥammad by the Angel Gabriel (*Jibrā'īl*) over a span of approximately twenty-three years. The Qur'ān consists of one hundred and fourteen chapters referred to as *Sūra* (pl. *Suwar*) and over six thousand verses (*āyāt*, sing. *āya*). These verses detail stories of previous prophets and nations, give descriptions of the Unseen, the celestial worlds and the afterlife, and includes injunctions and rulings for many aspects of the lives of Muslims. As Muslims believe that the Prophet was divinely inspired, his words and actions—the *ḥadīth*—are recorded in books of *aḥādīth* and, like the Qur'ān, are used to derive principles for everyday life. Finally, Muslims believe in Heaven and Hell, that the world will come to an end and that on the Day of Reckoning each person will account for his or her deeds.

As to the term 'minority', it is of two types: a) numerical minority when the majority are non-Muslim, e.g., Muslims in Europe and in Britain; b) minority by ruling power when the non-Muslim majority or minority is the ruling power. As Asad states, 'Minorities are defined as minorities in structures of dominant power.'[1] Under such an interpretation, the Muslims of the Mughal Empire are not considered a minority despite their numerical inferiority because they were in power.[2]

Therefore, when we employ the terminology 'Muslim minority' we refer to those individuals who profess their faith as defined above, are not in a position of dominant power and cannot establish laws within the state or decide and arrange relationships with other states of their choosing, such powers being in the hands of the 'Other'.

Muslims Living as a Minority: Examples from Around the World

In his work *Muslim Minorities in the World Today*, Mohammed Kettani observed

[1] Talal Asad, 'Muslims and European Identity: Can Europe Represent Islam?', in A. Pagden, (ed.), *The Idea of Europe: From Antiquity to the European Union* (Cambridge: Cambridge University Press, 2002), p. 223.

[2] Mohammed Kettani, *Muslim Minorities in the World Today* (London: Mansell Publishing Ltd, 1986), pp. 2-3; Taha Alwani, *Towards a Fiqh for Minorities: Some Basic Reflections*, Occasional Papers Series 10 (London: The International Institute of Islamic Thought, 2003), p. viii; Yūsuf al-Qaraḍāwī, *Fī fiqh al-aqalliyyāt al-muslima: ḥayat al-muslimīn wasṭ al-mujtamaʿāt al-ukhrā* (Cairo: Dār al-Shurūq, 2001), p. 17.

that a significant number of Muslims are living as minorities and that in 1982 the total number was nearly 40% of the world's Muslim population (representing 392 million).[3] There has been a significant increase in world population since 1982; this obviously includes an increase in the world's Muslim population and an increase in the numbers of Muslims living as minorities. Even if we assume that the figure for Muslim minorities has not increased much from what is quoted above, it still demonstrates the absolute importance of understanding the manner in which laws are promulgated in Islamic societies and how it is possible to cater for Muslims living in non-Muslim environments. A number of studies have been conducted on Muslims living as minorities, and we shall summarise some of these here as they demonstrate different understandings and approaches.

Israeli[4] and Gladney[5] have studied Muslims in China with differing, in fact completely opposing conclusions. Israeli refers to the thirty million or so Muslims as 'the Muslim problem'.[6] According to him, this 'problem' is compounded by the fact that Muslims in China are dispersed and not in one autonomous region, hence 'difficult' to manage or deal with.[7] He argues that the Muslims in China live 'outside that polity and nurture separatistic ideals,'[8] and await the opportunity to attain these goals. He argues that a greater movement of Muslims between China and Muslim countries, and a pro-Arab stance in the world will exacerbate the situation by increasing the confidence of Chinese Muslims to express their Islamic identity and that this will only increase the 'problem' for the state.

Gladney argues against the position Israeli adopts and suggests that the 'successful Muslim accommodation to minority status in China'[9] is a measure of how Muslims 'allow the reconciliation of the dictates of Islamic culture to their host culture.'[10] He acknowledges the trade pressure which Middle Eastern Muslim countries could apply on China, which he believes will naturally affect the state's treatment of its Muslim citizens in a positive manner.

3 Mohammed Kettani, *Muslim Minorities in the World Today*, p. 241.

4 Raphael Israeli, 'The Muslim Minority in the People's Republic of China', pp. 901-19.

5 Dru Gladney, 'Islam in China: Accommodation or Separation?', pp. 451-67.

6 Israeli, 'The Muslim Minority in the People's Republic of China', p. 902.

7 Ibid.

8 Ibid.

9 Gladney, 'Islam in China: Accommodation or Separation?', p. 451.

10 Ibid., p. 452.

Forbes[11] focuses on the Muslims of Thailand and estimates that in 1982 there were around two million Muslims living in Thailand, approximately 4% of the total population. He observes that the government policy of attempting to assimilate the Muslim population had produced the opposite of the desired effect, namely separatism or isolationism, and that the policy has now changed towards the greater integration of the Muslim population. The Muslims acknowledged that this change in policy requires them to re-think their attitude towards the state and to adopt a more integrative approach as they appreciate that security and influence could be better achieved as a single community. Forbes concludes that any return by the Thai government to assimilationist policies would lead to reactionary separatism on the part of the Muslim community, particularly those living in the South, 'with potentially disastrous consequences for the area as a whole.'[12]

Moving further west to India, Krishna[13] believes that an 'acute concern for power'[14] is inherent in the nature of Islam and that when Islam is not in the ascendancy the Muslim community is compelled to be wholly autonomous, 'a state within a state'.[15] He claims that 'majority' and 'minority' concepts are alien to Islam as they are based on territorial principles whereas Islam views things from the perspective of 'Muslims' and 'Others'; he further argues that 'it is a religious duty of the believers to keep the non-believers at bay and to overcome them.'[16] In his opinion, an example of this was when the Indian Constitution was being developed and Muslims argued for a retention of their personal/family law as it is an intrinsic part of their religion.

One particular area of discussion and debate which was central to the Constitutional debate in India was the definition of 'secularism' and 'integration', with a view to the removal of the direct influence of religions from the political sphere. 'Secularism, entailing separation of religion and politics and thus freeing the state from sectarian conflict, was seen by the founders of the Indian Republic as the political solution to the historical problem of religious

[11] Andrew Forbes, 'Thailand's Muslim Minorities: Assimilation, Secession or Coexistence?', pp. 1056-73.

[12] Ibid., p. 1068.

[13] Gopal Krishna, 'Islam, Minority Status and Citizenship: Muslim Experience in India', *Archives Europennes de Sociologie* (vol. 27, no. 2, 1986), pp. 353-68.

[14] Ibid., p. 353.

[15] Ibid., p. 354.

[16] Ibid.

cleavage in India. The state retained the right to regulate secular aspects of the religious institutions but guaranteed freedom of religion and protected the cultural interests of the minorities. They also expected that secularism would promote national integration, i.e., to bring about a greater increasing harmony among the different constituents of the Indian population, and over time establish a modern political community.'[17] In Krishna's opinion, the approach of the founders of the Indian Republic was misunderstood by the politically active Muslims to mean almost the complete opposite of what was originally intended. '[They] defined "secularism" to mean the state ensuring freedom of religion, equality of all religions, non-interference in religious affairs (leaving each religious community free to order its own religious life), and "integration" to mean a relatively autonomous life to each community.'[18]

In Israel, where according to Reiter[19] a sixth of the population (700,000, including occupied Jerusalem), is Muslim, there are special provisions for Muslims under the judicial system allowing for *qāḍīs* (judges) to cater for Muslims' personal/family status and *waqf* (religious endowment) affairs.

Shadid[20] has studied Muslims in the Netherlands and claims that the immigrant Turks, Moroccans, Pakistanis and Surinamers were prepared to lose the 'ethnic component of their identity in favour of the religious component.'[21] He believes that if the host society is tolerant and recognises Muslims' rights to retain their identity then the claim that their original culture will have a negative effect on their opportunities for vertical mobility would not materialise. On the other hand, in an intolerant society the preservation of the original culture would have a negative influence. He asserts that the notion of 'blaming the victim' needs to be challenged by making efforts to eradicate intolerance and discrimination. He concludes by stating 'an intolerant society always finds some characteristic to justify its intolerance of these minority groups.'[22]

From the above, it can be see that some scholars like Israeli and Krishna

[17] Ibid., p. 359.

[18] Ibid., p. 360.

[19] Yitzhak Reiter, '*Qāḍīs* and the Implementation of Islamic Law in Present Day Israel', in R. Gleave and E. Kermeli (eds.), *Islamic Law: Theory and Practice* (London: I. B. Tauris, 1997), pp. 205-31.

[20] Wasif Shadid, 'The Integration of Muslim Minorities in the Netherlands', , pp. 355-74.

[21] Ibid., p. 366.

[22] Ibid., p. 367.

have focussed on the perception of Muslim minority communities as a 'problem', while other scholars have viewed matters differently. Ahmed[23] feels that Muslim minorities may pose a 'problem' for non-Muslim countries who have an image of themselves as being plural, tolerant, secular and modern societies. These secular societies can view Muslims either as damaging or at least challenging this image because of their perceived rejectionist tendency; or as 'problem' because of historical and political factors. Asad[24] agrees with this position and suggests that many non-Muslims believe that Islam comprises values that are 'an affront to the modern Western form of life.'[25] He argues that a better understanding between secular societies and Muslims would remove this misunderstanding and allow better relationships within the state.

We shall be arguing below that when Muslims are integrated within the political and legal framework as co-citizens, then this leads to benefits for both parties, as the state has citizens who feel part of the society and hence care for its success, and likewise the citizens do not feel marginalised or overlooked. However, if attempts are made to disregard certain Islamic laws (specifically those dealing with personal or family life) which make it possible for Muslims to live according to their religious commitments, then this can lead to separatism or isolation and an increased assertion of religious identity expressed either privately or publicly.

Arrival and Establishment of Muslims in Western Europe

The presence of Muslims in Europe dates back to the dawn of Islam over 1400 years ago when tradesmen and diplomats ventured into continental Europe. With respect to established communities of Muslims in Europe there were four distinct phases. Nielsen[26] details these phases thus: the first phase was the expansion of the early Islamic empire into Spain and southern Italy, which was ended by the Normans in the eleventh century and the Spanish *Reconquista* in 1492. The second phase was a result of the Mongol invasions during the thirteenth century with the establishment of Muslim states by various Tartar groups from the Volga down to the Caucasus and Crimea; other smaller colonies were established in places like Finland and an area which currently falls

23 Akbar Ahmed, *Living Islam: From Samarqand to Stornoway* (London: BBC Books, 1993).

24 Asad, 'Muslims and European Identity: Can Europe Represent Islam?', pp. 209-28.

25 Ibid., p. 210.

26 Jorgen Nielsen, *Islamic Surveys,* pp. 1–3.

between Poland and the Ukraine. The third phase was due to the Ottoman empire's expansion into central Europe and the Balkans. Turkish settlements in Bulgaria, Yugoslavia, Romania and Greece have survived until today; the influence of the Ottomans also brought about significant Muslim populations in Albania and Bosnia.[27] The fourth phase was the establishment of migrant Muslim communities in Western Europe.

In the fourth phase, the period after the Second World War is the most significant. However, it is possible to find links between Muslims and Europe well before the end of the Second World War. For instance, the German states came into contact, or rather conflict, with Islam due to Ottoman expansion through the Balkans with two sieges of Vienna in 1529 and 1683. After the second siege many Muslims became permanent residents in Germany. King Frederick I formed the first Muslim Prussian unit, consisting of Tartar deserters from the Russian army; eventually over one thousand Muslims served in the cavalry. Further developments were the establishing of a Muslim cemetery in Berlin, followed by the building of a mosque within its grounds in 1866. As a consequence of diplomatic relations and trading treaties between Berlin and Istanbul the Muslim community grew in Germany. The recognition of this Muslim community resulted in the provision, during the Second World War, of imams and the construction of a mosque for Muslim prisoners captured from the allied armies: Tartars, Caucasians and Turks from Russia, Indians from Britain and Senegalese and Algerians from France.[28] Similarly, in the aftermath of the Second World War many soldiers and former prisoners of Soviet Muslim nationality settled in Germany.

In central Europe, Austria-Hungary occupied the Ottoman Bosnia-Herzegovina in 1878 and introduced an act 'relating to the recognition of the followers of Islam of the Hanafite rite as a religious community', hence Islamic family law was applied within its courts for Muslims.[29]

It is clear that Islam has had a relationship with Europe for centuries and that Muslims have for different reasons taken up permanent residence in European cities. However, the first major migration of Muslims into Western Europe took place after the Second World War due to a number of reasons, which will be discussed in the next section.

[27] Ibid., p. 1.
[28] Ibid., p. 2.
[29] Ibid., p. 3.

Post Second-World-War Developments in Western Europe

According to Kettani,[30] in 1991 the fifteen countries of the European Economic Community (EEC) had 10,370,000 Muslims living within a total population of 365,943,000; therefore 2.8% of the total population was Muslim. Kettani's research shows that France had the largest number of resident Muslims and also the second highest percentage of Muslims who were citizens. In addition, between 1971 and 1995, the number of Muslims in Europe tripled from 1.3% to 3.1%.[31] Both Kettani and CAIR[32] suggest that there were several reasons for this: 1) The move by local populations who had co-operated with colonial regimes to the country of the colonisers when their own countries of original gained independence; for example, the Harkis to France from Algeria and the Moluccans to the Netherlands from Indonesia. 2) In the 1950s and the 1970s, economic migration from former colonies in order to supply the demand for cheap labour in the rapidly growing economies of Western Europe. Then, in the 1970s and 80s, the expansion of Muslim communities due to the emigration of a new type of migrants: often highly trained and educated persons seeking better-paid jobs; 3) migration for personal or political reasons such as family reunions, refugees, converts and illegal immigrants.[33]

Kettani explains that the current situation of Muslims in Western Europe is partly the result of major miscalculations by all parties concerned. Those who moved at the end of colonisation, whom he calls 'collaborators', emigrated to the 'Metropole' with the idea of 'returning home when things settle down'. He further asserts that the 'Governments of the Metropole' were not expecting a Muslim community to develop in their midst but rather assumed that these people would be easily assimilated, having given their lives to the 'Metropole' and turned their backs on their own people. In fact, Kettani asserts, it was assumed that by the second generation Muslims would lose their Islamic identity and hence would be no different from other citizens, even in terms of attitudes towards religion.[34] The reality was somewhat different from the assumption;

[30] Mohammed Kettani, 'Challenges to the Organization of Muslim Communities in Western Europe: The Political Dimension', pp. 15-35.

[31] Ibid., p. 14.

[32] Council on American-Islamic Relations [CAIR], *Western Muslim Minorities: Integration and Disenfranchisement* (Washington: CAIR Policy Bulletin, 2006), p. 2.

[33] Kettani, 'Challenges to the Organization of Muslim Communities in Western Europe: The Political Dimension', p. 1.

[34] Ibid., p. 16.

the 'collaborators' never went home nor did the second generation lose Islam.

As to the second reason—the importation of labour—Kettani says that none of the four parties involved, namely, the governments of the Western European countries (receiver), the governments of the Muslim countries (sender), the Muslim workers and the Western European employers, intended to establish a Muslim community in Western Europe. Each party benefited economically in various ways: the receiver governments and employers gained much needed manpower to help solve their short-term employment needs, which when satisfied should have resulted in the return of the migrant workers to their sender governments; the sender governments solved their unemployment problems and gained economically from the monies sent home by the migrant workers; the Muslim workers also benefited financially and aspired to return home better off. What none of the parties suspected would happen was that the Muslim workers would, over time, establish a niche in the economies of the receiver countries and, therefore, their return would damage the economies of both the receiver and sender countries.[35]

With the passage of time and the arrival of spouses and families, the foreign countries started to feel like home; the finances being invested in the 'homeland' reduced and the 'myth of return' was born.[36] The growing community required various services and amenities: mosques and Islamic organisations were founded to provide religious services and to represent the Muslim minority community to the wider public.[37] Ramadan observes that Muslims have generally been free to practice their faith in Europe and can manifest their faith by establishing institutions with only occasional minor administrative hindrance from their host countries.[38] He asserts that 'by and large there is no European constitution which is anti-Islamic *per se*,'[39] and that in fact Muslims have utilised the legal system to appeal against unfair treatment. Likewise, Bloul details the relatively new anti-discrimination legislation adopted by the European Union and other specific

[35] Ibid., p. 16.

[36] Imtiaz Hussain, 'Migration and Settlement: A Historical Perspective of Loyalty and Belonging', in M. S. Seddon, *et al* (eds.), *British Muslims: Loyalty and Belonging* (Leicester: Islamic Foundation & The Citizen Organising Foundation, 2003), p.30.

[37] Wasif Shadid and P. Sjoerd van Koningsveld, *Religious Freedom and the Position of Islam in Western Europe: Opportunities and Obstacles in the Acquisition of Equal Rights* (Kampen: Kok Pharos Publishing House, 1994), p. 4.

[38] Tariq Ramadan, *To be a European Muslim* (Leicester: The Islamic Foundation, 1999), pp. 120-23.

[39] Ibid., p. 121.

legislation in various European countries which recognise faith and religion and which further assist Muslims to practice their faith and preserve their identity.[40]

The economic migrants slowly but surely became accustomed to their surroundings and grew in confidence in expressing their own cultural and religious identity. The question however arises as to how comfortable were the 'host' communities with their new-found 'residents'? One key strand which we will be investigating in this work is that Muslims are often perceived as a 'problem' due to a number of reasons which may be summed up as their 'lack of integration'. Kettani states that, as of 1991, this 'problem' had become compounded by the issue of citizenship since 40% of Muslims living in Europe were no longer immigrants but were now citizens of the European countries in which they had settled.[41]

What is, for Kettani and others, the Muslim 'problem'? John Esposito, in his book *The Islamic Threat: Myth or Reality*, elaborates by listing the opinions of a number of writers: Patrick Buchanan believes that the struggle between Christianity and Islam has 'raged for a millennium', and that the twenty-first century is no different except that the methodology has changed from outright war between the two distinct opposing sides to what he terms 'infiltration' of Muslims into the Christian heartlands: 'Patrick Buchanan could write in "Rising Islam May Overwhelm the West" that while the West finds itself "negotiating for hostages with Shiite radicals who hate and detest us," their co-religionists are filling up the countries of the West.'[42] Esposito continues: 'The Muslim threat becomes global in nature as Muslims in Europe, the Soviet Union, and America 'proliferate and prosper';[43] and he quotes Charles Krauthammer as saying that that even as the Soviet Union was unravelling, 'a global Islamic threat' was rising up and creating a new 'arc of crisis'.[44] In Britain, he continues, Charles Moore writes that 'because of our obstinate refusal to have enough babies, Western European civilisation will start to die at the point when it could have been revived with new blood. Then the hoarded hordes will win, and the Koran will

[40] Rachel Bloul, 'Anti-discrimination Laws, Islamophobia and Ethnicization of Muslim Identitics in Europe and Australia', pp. 11-13.

[41] Kettani, 'Challenges to the Organisation of Muslim Communities in Western Europe: The Political Dimension', p. 17.

[42] John Esposito, *The Islamic Threat: Myth or Reality?* (New York: Oxford University Press, 1999), p. 233.

[43] Ibid., p. 233.

[44] Ibid.

be taught, as Gibbons famously imagined, in the schools of Oxford.'[45] Clare Hollingsworth says: 'Muslim fundamentalism is fast becoming the chief threat to global peace and security as well as a cause of national and local disturbance through terrorism. It is akin to the menace of Nazism and Fascism in the 1930s and then by Communism in the 1950s.'[46]

Talal Asad[47] adds further evidence to Esposito's observations and states, 'In Europe today Muslims are often misrepresented in the media and discriminated against by non-Muslims.'[48] He quotes from an issue of *Time* magazine (19 October 1992, p. 31), when Turkey was attempting to join the European community: 'However it may be expressed, there is a feeling in Western Europe, rarely stated explicitly, that Muslims whose roots lie in Asia do not belong in the Western family, some of whose members spent centuries trying to drive the Turks out of a Europe they threatened to overwhelm. Turkish membership "would dilute the E.C.'s Europeanness," says one German diplomat.'[49]

Gilman[50] discusses a recent event when German, Italian, Polish and Slovakian delegates demanded that 'Christian heritage' be written into the new European Constitution. However, this was overruled by Valery Giscard d'Estaing, the President of the convention responsible for drafting the constitution, who thought it inappropriate, post 'September 11', and the phrase 'Christian heritage' was instead replaced by 'cultural, religious, and humanist inheritance of Europe.'[51]

Michael Wintle[52] suggests that the four key influences on Europe were: the Roman Empire, Christianity, the Enlightenment and industrialisation, and as these were not part of the experience of the Islamic world, Muslims cannot be considered as being a part of Europe. This analysis can, to a certain extent, explain why, despite its geography, some historians do not regard medieval Spain or, more relevantly, *Islamic* Spain, as part of Europe.[53]

[45] Ibid., p. 233.

[46] Ibid., p. 235.

[47] Asad, 'Muslims and European Identity: Can Europe Represent Islam?', pp. 209-28.

[48] Ibid., p. 209.

[49] Ibid., p. 211.

[50] Sander Gilman, 'The Parallels of Islam and Judaism Diaspora', *Palestine-Israel Journal of Politics, Economics and Culture,* (vol. 12, no. 2-3, 2005), pp 61-66.

[51] Ibid., p. 61.

[52] Michael Wintle, *Culture and Identity in Europe: Perceptions of Divergence and Unity in Past and Present* (Aldershot: Avebury, 1996), pp. 9-32.

[53] Asad, 'Muslims and European Identity: Can Europe Represent Islam?', p. 217.

Some writers have asserted that Islam's actual or perceived threat to Christianity has played a decisive role in developing the European identity[54]; so in a way Europe is that which is 'other than Islam'. The Enlightenment aspired to go beyond tradition and rely on universally valid dictates of reason and method in order to better understand the nature of human beings and human society,[55] whereas Islam, based on tradition, stands in stark contradistinction. And yet Europe's largest city is a Muslim city, namely Istanbul; parts of Spain were Islamic for almost as long as the country has been Catholic; the European Renaissance would not have taken place had it not been for the 'Muslim' factor; and the fact that the 'Church' does not exist in Islam means there was and is no need for the Enlightenment and no need for Islam to replay the European experience.[56]

From the above examples, it is clear that opposition exists within some European circles towards Islam and Muslims. However, recently there has been a desire to take a fresh and unbiased look at Europe's history and the Muslim role and adopt an inclusive 'shared past–shared future' view under the title of 'Our Shared Europe Project'.[57] It is also argued that Muslims should not be viewed as 'outsiders' adhering to an 'alien and foreign' religion and that the language of engagement needs to change from 'Islam vs the West' or 'Islam and the West' to more appropriately 'Islam in the West', or even 'European Islam'. [58]

Kettani predicts that by 2015 the Muslim community in Western Europe will double to 23 million, or 7% of its total population. The majority of this Muslim population will be citizens of Europe and, as these Muslims will now have a greater awareness than previous generations of their rights, the chances of assimilating Muslims into European societies is small and highly improbable. Kettani stipulates two possible scenarios: 1) integration of Muslims with a legal recognition of their rights, as for instance in Australia, so even though the community will lose some of its culture it will still retain its religious identity; 2) the

[54] Kylie Baxter, 'From Migrants to Citizens: Muslims in Britain 1950s-1990s', *Immigrants and Minorities*, (vol. 24, no. 2, 2006), p. 165.

[55] Philip Pettit, 'Liberal/Communitarian: MacIntyre's Mesmeric Dichotomy', in J. Horton and S. Mendus (eds.), *After MacIntyre: Critical Perspectives on the Work of Alasdair MacIntyre* (Cambridge: Polity Press, 1994), p. 177.

[56] Murad Hofmann, 'Muslims as Co-citizens of the West: Rights, Duties and Prospects', (see http://www.islamonline.net/English/contemporary/2002/05/article3.shtml), 2002.

[57] Martin Rose, *A Shared Past for a Shared Future: European Muslims and History Making* (UK: AMSS [Association of Muslim Social Scientists UK] and British Council, 2009).

[58] CAIR, *Western Muslim Minorities*, p. 1.

Muslim community is isolated and denied its rights, which may lead to expulsions and even genocide in some Western countries similar to the events in Bosnia during the Balkans war.[59]

Murad Hofmann[60] is somewhat more optimistic and recalls the end of the nineteenth century when German Catholics were considered disloyal citizens of the state due to their links with Rome; however with time and understanding the situation dissipated.

This greater understanding of Islam and Muslims may be facilitated if recommendations made, over twenty years ago, by the Centre for the Study of Islam and Christian-Muslim Relations[61] on how to integrate the Muslim community are acknowledged and legislation is brought about in order to bring to fruition the research group's conclusions.

Early Historical Background of Muslims in Britain

The history of Muslims in Britain is linked to the British colonial presence in Muslim countries. For example, during the late eighteenth century the East India Company recruited predominantly from Indian ports. Muslim sailors arrived in Britain and the first boarding-houses were established to house 'Asiatics, Africans and South Sea Islanders' in the Limehouse area of London.[62] Again, with the opening of the Suez Canal in 1869, many Yemeni and Somali sailors were recruited and found themselves in similar boarding-houses, in this case mostly in Cardiff and South Shields.

Some of these Muslim men married British women and settled permanently in Britain; and thus a number of communities were established and brought closer together by community centres (*zawāyā*) which met their social and religious needs. Liverpool was another area, which saw a significant Muslim presence. A number of British people also converted to Islam. Among them was Shaykh Abdullah (Henry William) Quilliam who accepted Islam in 1887 while

59 Kettani, 'Challenges to the Organization of Muslim Communities in Western Europe: The Political Dimension', pp. 15-35.

60 Murad Hofmann, 'Muslims as Co-citizens of the West: Rights, Duties and Prospects' (see http://www.islamonline.net/English/contemporary/2002/05/article3.shtml), 2002.

61 Churches' Committee on Migrant Workers in Europe [CCMWE], Expert Group on Islam, Nielsen, Jorgen, *Islamic Law and its Significance for the Situation of Muslim Minorities in Europe* (Research Papers, Muslims in Europe Birmingham: Centre for Study of Islam and Christian-Muslim Relations, 1987).

62 Nielsen, *Islamic Surveys*, p. 4.

travelling in the Ottoman Empire and Morocco. He was appointed Shaykh al-Islam of Britain by the Ottoman sultan and Vice-Consul to Liverpool by the Shah of Persia. He had a significant congregation in Liverpool where he converted a row of terraced houses to be used for regular prayers, festivals, weddings and funerals; these premises were also utilised as a boys' day school, evening classes, hostel, library and printing press. With his departure from Britain towards 'Muslim lands' in 1908 all that he had set up gradually disappeared. [63]

In London, Dr Gottlieb Wilhelm Leitner, a Hungarian orientalist, established in 1889 the Shah Jahan Mosque in Woking, with the financial assistance of Her Highness Begum Shah Jehan of Bhopal. Much was expected from this project but only a hostel was realised before Dr Leitner's death in 1899. It was not until 1913, when Khwaja Kamal al-Din, supported by an English convert, Lord Headley, bought the hostel and utilised it for missionary work for the Lahori branch of the Ahmadi sect. It was now referred to as the Woking Muslim Mission and it concentrated its efforts on welfare work, particularly providing assistance to the widows and orphans of Indian soldiers during the Second World War. The Mission also supported a Muslim Literary Society which had distinguished members such as the two early translators of the Qur'ān, Muhammad Marmaduke Pickthall and Abdullah Yusuf Ali. The Mission faced political opposition from Indian Sunnis who rejected the claim by Ahmadis that their founder, Mirza Ghulam Ahmed, was a prophet. After the quick successive demise in 1932 and 1933 of both Kamal al-Din and Lord Headley, the Mission cut all ties with the Ahmadi sect. [64]

The 1914 British Nationality and Aliens Act gave all individuals born within the Empire the status of a British subject; 'Britishness' was henceforth recognised as loyalty to the Crown.[65] This Act, combined with a number of other factors, foremost amongst which was the demand for labour after the Second World War, catalysed a mass migration of Muslims, in particular from the Indian subcontinent, which had never occurred before or since.

[63] For more details about early Muslim communities, see Philip Lewis, *Islamic Britain. Religion, Politics and Identity among British Muslims* (London: I. B. Tauris, 2002); Jorgen Nielsen *Islamic Surveys: Muslims in Western Europe* (Edinburgh: Edinburgh University Press, 2004) Mohammed Seddon, *British Muslims between Assimilation and Segregation* (Leicester: The Islamic Foundation, 2004.

[64] Lewis, *Islamic Britain*, p. 65; Nielsen, *Islamic Surveys*, p. 5.

[65] Baxter, 'From Migrants to Citizens: Muslims in Britain 1950s-1990s', p. 166.

Muslims in Britain: Post Second World War

The largest groups of Muslims to arrive on British shores soon after the Second World War were from certain areas in Pakistan, Bangladesh and India. The Indian Gujaratis from the districts of Baroda, Surat and Broach came from relatively well-educated and professional backgrounds compared with the remainder of their Indian Subcontinent counterparts. Pakistani immigrants mostly came from poorer agricultural areas of the Mirpur district in Kashmir, due to the building of the Mangla Dam, which eventually flooded 250 villages, and from the Cambellpur district of Punjab. Sylhet district and the areas around Chittagong were the main sources of Bangladeshi emigration.[66] Smaller groups also arrived from across the Arab world, Iran, Turkish Cyprus, Malaysia, West Africa and Morocco. Given the significantly larger numbers of Muslim migrants from the Indian subcontinent, theirs has had the most profound impact on the public sphere in Britain[67] and explains the particular importance they hold in this present work.

Even though there are concentrations of Muslims in a number of cities in the South East, across the Midlands and Yorkshire, Muslim communities are to be found throughout Britain.[68] According to the 2001 national census, London has the highest number of Muslims in the country (607,083; 8.5% of its population). Of the London boroughs, the borough of Tower Hamlets has the highest concentration of Muslims (36.4%), followed by Newham (24.3%). After London comes Birmingham, with 140,017 Muslims (14.3%), and Bradford, with 75,201 Muslims (16.1%). The Muslim population is unusual as it is younger than the national average: 33.8% of British Muslims are aged between 0-15 years (the national average 20.2%) and 18.2% are aged between 16-24 (the national average 10.9%).[69]

The most visible mark of Muslims on the British landscape is in the form of the mosque from renovated terraced houses to multi-million pound purpose-built structures.[70] This is a good measure of both the religiousness

[66] Nielsen, *Islamic Surveys*, p. 41.

[67] Steven Vertovec, 'Muslims, the State, and the Public Sphere in Britain', in G. Nonneman, T. Niblock and B. Szajkowski (eds.), *Muslim Communities in the New Europe* (Reading: Ithaca Press, 1996), p. 170.

[68] Kettani, *Muslim Minorities in the World Today*, p. 42.

[69] Muhammad Abdul Bari, *Race, Religion & Muslim Identity in Britain* (Swansea: Renaissance Press, 2005), p. 96.

[70] Shadid and van Koningsveld, *Religious Freedom and the Position of Islam in Western Europe*, pp. 23-59.

and the organisation of the community along religious lines throughout the years. Within forty years, the number of mosques has increased phenomenally from around ten in 1963 to around 1000,[71] (this is based on a conservative estimate as many are not registered).[72] In Bradford there are an estimated fifty mosques within a five-mile radius of the city centre.[73]

There are several issues and challenges which on the face of it are particular to British Muslims as opposed to the remainder of the population: education, employment, housing, political representation, religious discrimination and insecurity.[74] Much of the research which has been conducted on Muslims over the years has postulated that Muslims of South Asian descent are living impoverished lives in ethnic ghettos, are involved in non-mainstream religion, and align themselves culturally and politically on ethnic and religious lines.[75] Politically, Muslims are often portrayed as giving loyalty to transnational Muslim leaders and causes rather than to the British state and to core British values of freedom, tolerance, democracy, sexual equality and secularism. For the general British public, the question that must be asked here is how are these opinions of Muslims arrived at and what part does the British media play in defining the portrait of Muslims to the wider non-Muslim community?

A recent study carried out by Cardiff University[76] on the media coverage of British Muslims between the years of 2000 to 2008 made significant findings. The researchers found that coverage of Muslims had increased significantly over the years the study was conducted peaking in 2006. The explanation for this is certain world events and the increase in the coverage of terrorism; 36% of stories involving British Muslims were about terrorism. The study discovered that the emphasis in the coverage was changing; the difference between British culture and Islam was being highlighted (32% of stories in 2008) and was overtaking coverage of Muslims and terrorism (27% by 2008). In fact, two

[71] Nielsen, *Islamic Surveys*, p. 45.

[72] Centre for the Study of Islam and Christian-Muslim Relations [CSIC], *British Muslims Monthly Survey* (Birmingham: Selly Oak Colleges, 1997), p. 1.

[73] Seán McLoughlin. 'Mosques and the Public Space: Conflict and Cooperation in Bradford', *Journal of Ethnic and Migration Studies* (vol. 31, no. 6, 2005), p. 1046.

[74] Anwar, 'Muslims in Western States: The British Experience and the Way Forward', pp. 130-33.

[75] Robert Leiken, 'Europe's Angry Muslims', *Foreign Affairs* (vol. 84, no. 4, 2005), pp. 120-35.

[76] Kerry Moore, Paul Mason and Justin Lewis, *Images of Islam in the UK: The Representation of British Muslims in the National Print News Media 2000-2008* (Cardiff: Cardiff School of Journalism, Media and Cultural Studies, 2008).

thirds of the reporting focused on Muslims in a negative way by either describing them as a 'threat (in relation to terrorism), a problem (in terms of differences in values) or both (Muslim extremism in general).'[77] The study goes on to report that, 'The language used about British Muslims reflects the negative or problematic contexts in which they tend to appear. Four of the five most common discourses used about Muslims in the British press associate Islam/Muslims with threats, problems or opposition to dominant British values. So for example, the idea that Islam is dangerous, backward or irrational is present in 26% of stories.'[78] The conclusion the report reaches is condemning to say the least: 'Decontextulisation, misinformation and a preferred discourse of threat, fear and danger, while not uniformly present, were strong forces in the reporting of British Muslims in the UK national press.'[79] It is our view, that this simplistic, sensationalist and even biased reporting of Muslims is a contributing factor in the perception of Muslims as a 'problem' and in the perpetuation of this perception, and that this needs to be challenged by both Muslims and non-Muslims.

Aside from the general image of Muslims propogated by the media, one area which has defined Muslims in Britain is their involvement in the education and working environments. Research suggests that Muslims are perceived as consistently under-performing in both the educational and labour contexts.[80] The question has been asked as to whether this is due to the religion they profess. In our opinion, it is a combination of the former rural, under-educated background of the majority of first-generation British Muslims, and social deprivation, rather than religious belief, which is the cause for this under-achievement. In addition, there is also the issue of racism in employment which can be a factor, but the effects of racism are beyond the scope of this study.

In recent years, a response to and a means of escaping from social

[77] Ibid., p. 3.

[78] Ibid.

[79] Ibid.

[80] For further information on this, see Angela Dale, Nusrat Shaheen, Virinder Kalra and Edward Fieldhouse, 'Routes into Education and Employment for Young Pakistani and Bangladeshi Women in the UK', *Ethnic and Racial Studies* (vol. 25, no. 6, 2002), pp. 942-68; Tariq Modood, Richard Berthoud, Jane Lakey, James Nazroo, Patten Smith, Satnam Virdee and Sharon Beishon, *Ethnic Minorities in Britain: Diversity and Disadvantage* (London: Policy Studies Institute, 1997); Performance and Innovation Unit [PIU], *Ethnic Minorities and Labour Markets: An Interim Analysis,* (London: Cabinet Office, 2002).

deprivation and limited economic opportunities has been an increased affirmation of Islamic identity. Part of the appeal of this Islamic identity is a certain moral superiority.[81] However, this Islamic identity does not necessarily have to be in competition with British identity but can be complementary to it. This becomes apparent when analysing the Home Office Citizenship Survey conducted in 2003. Rahsaan Maxwell[82] asserts that the arguments regarding the alienation of Muslims are exaggerated and summarises the findings of the Survey by stating that in reality Muslims are 'almost as likely as whites to identify themselves as British.'[83] Another study conducted by Choudhury for the Department for Communities and Local Government came to similar conclusions. These are the first four points of the Executive Summary:

> 'A growing body of research since the 1990s has noted the increasing prominence of religion as a marker of identity among Muslims. It is important to understand the complex and diverse reasons for the foregrounding of religion in their identity.
>
> The public devaluation and disparagement of Muslims and Islam are among the external factors that have led to increased in-group solidarity and identification on the basis of religion. Muslim identity can also be important in defining a sense of masculinity among young Muslim men, who construct a "strong" Muslim identity as a way in which to resist stereotypes of "weakness and passivity".
>
> The discourse of religion and identity is also used for internal empowerment. Studies of young Muslim women show how religious discourse plays an important role in negotiating and resisting parental and community restrictions. Similarly, research among young Muslim men finds that Muslim identity provides a positive role model, compared to their parents' unemployment and as an alternative to the street and drug cultures in their neighbourhoods.
>
> Muslim identity can support and encourage integration. Action around demands for the accommodation of religious needs have played an important role in the initial mobilisation of Muslim communities for

81 Sarah Glynn, 'Bengali Muslims: The New East End Radicals?', *Ethnic and Racial Studies* (vol. 25, no. 6, 2002), pp. 969-88.

82 Rahsaan Maxwell, 'Muslims, South Asians and the British Mainstream: A National Identity Crisis', *West European Politics* (vol. 29, no. 4, 2006), pp. 736-56.

83 Ibid., p. 736.

civic and political engagement. These campaigns indicate affection rather than disaffection; they show a commitment to Britain and a wish, by Muslims, to make themselves more at home in Britain.'[84]

A point raised by Choudhury whilst discussing how radicalisation takes place is relevant to our study and partially answers the hypothesis we raised in the Introduction. His research found that it is the lack of religious education which appears to be a common feature amongst those individuals who adopt the isolation model, and as a result are drawn towards extremist views.[85]

If we now turn to the Muslims' view of the British state, the Islamic Human Rights Commission produced a report[86] suggesting that most Muslims in Britain thought that the British legal system was unfair and cited reasons such as 'double standards', that the legal system was 'biased', and even more so in recent times; and that Muslims felt 'unprotected' by the law and felt that their needs were not recognised. This is not the place to explore further whether these are only perceptions or whether there is a basis of truth in the matter. What is significant for us is that it shows that there exists a lack of understanding of the 'other' both by British society and the Muslim minority.

Anwar[87] echoes the findings of the Commission's report and suggests a number of changes that could help transform the situation: anti-discrimination laws protecting Muslims; including better representation in the political arena, greater sensitivity from employers, service providers and the media.

Muslims in Britain have come a long way from the deprived backgrounds the majority originated from in order to seek a better way of life in Britain. With each new generation, they have shown a keenness and willingness to develop as a community but not at the expense of key aspects of their faith. Our argument is that if Muslims feel confident that their religious identity can be preserved and protected, then, rather than feeling threatened

84 Tufayl Choudhury, *The Role of Muslim Identity Politics in Radicalisation (A Study in Progress)* (London: Department for Communities and Local Government, 2007), p. 5.

85 Ibid., p. 6

86 Saied Ameli, Beena Faridi, Karin Lindahl and Arzu Merali, *Law & British Muslims: Domination of the Majority or Process of Balance?* (British Muslims' Expectations Series, No. 5, Islamic Human Rights Commission), see http://www.ihrc.org.uk/file/BMEG_VOL5.pdf, 2006.

87 Anwar, 'Muslims in Western States: The British Experience and the Way Forward', p. 135.

and opting for an isolationist reaction, the community can open up and integrate into the wider society. In order for this to take place, we suggest that certain allowances or accommodations are made within the British legal system to meet a number of Islamic religious requirements. As we shall see below, allowances have already been granted to Muslims with regard to aspects of their religious law; we are suggesting that extending these allowances to other essential requirements will be beneficial for both Muslims and wider British society.

The Case for Legal Pluralism

Very often when the Sharīʿa is invoked, the impression that is given is of an antiquated and monolithic system that has to be applied as it is without any change or consideration for circumstances, etc. What most people who are not familiar with Islamic Law (*fiqh*) do not recognise is that Islamic law is itself profoundly pluralistic and this pluralism can be clearly found in the multiple schools of interpretation of the Sharīʿa, known as the Schools of Law or the *madhāhib* (sing. *madhhab*). Under Islamic Law, there are six main Schools of interpretation; four belonging to Sunnism and two to Shiʿism. The four Sunni *madhāhib* are: the Ḥanafī, Mālikī, Shāfiʿī and Ḥanbalī; while the two Shiʿi Schools are: the Jaʿfarī and the Ismāʿīlī. Most Muslims belong to one or other of these Schools of Law either by educated choice, or more usually because it is the School of the legal system in the country he or she lives in, or because it is the School that his or her forefathers belonged to. This is a brief description of each of the Schools:

1. The Ḥanafī School was founded by Imām Abū Ḥanīfa (d. 150/772) and his two students Abū Yūsuf (d. 182/804) and Muḥammad al-Shaybānī (d. 189/811); they were all based in present-day Iraq. It is the School which a number of Islamic empires, including the last Islamic empire—the Ottoman empire—applied and ruled by. Today, it has the largest number of adherents who are predominantly based in the subcontinent, Central Asia and large parts of the Arab world. The Ḥanafī School will be discussed in greater detail below as it will be the reference for what we call the Traditional approach.
2. The Mālikī School takes its name from its founder Imām Mālik b. Anas (d. 173/795) and was based in Medina. One of the principles which differentiates it from the other Schools is that it takes the custom of the

Medinan population as evidence when forming laws; it now has followers predominantly in northern and western Africa.

3. The Shāfiʿī School was founded by Imām Muḥammad b. Idrīs al-Shāfiʿī (d. 198/820) in the western part of the Arabian Peninsula. The Shāfiʿī School continues to have adherents in north and east Africa and southern Arabia.
4. The Ḥanbalī School was founded by Imām Aḥmad b. Ḥanbal (780-855) and has followers in present-day Saudi Arabia where it is the juristic view of the state.
5. The two Shiʿi Schools of Law—the Jaʿfarī and the Ismāʿīlī—differ from the Sunni Schools concerning the principle of who can interpret the Law. While in the Sunni Schools the Law is interpreted by jurists, the Shiʿi Schools believe that the Imāms are the only ones who are capable of interpreting God's Law. The Jaʿfarī School goes back to Imām Jaʿfar al-Ṣādiq (d. 143/765), the sixth Imām and great-great grandson of Caliph ʿAlī. As according to Shiʿism, the twelfth and last Imām, Abū'l-Qāsim Muḥammad, went into occultation in 252/874 and will only appear again close to the end of time, Shiʿi scholars must interpret the Law to the best of their ability. The Ismāʿīlīs differ from the Jaʿfarīs in that they believe the Imām continues to exist from generation to generation. The Jaʿfarī School has the greater following and can be found in Iran, Iraq, Lebanon and parts of the subcontinent and Arabian Peninsula.

We have included the above in order to demonstrate that legal pluralism is a fundamental aspect of Islamic Law and a considerable asset for Muslims living as minorities. The differing opinions held by the Schools on legal issues shows how there can potentially be collaboration with other legal systems. Historically, the application of Muslim law in non-Muslim states can be found in India, China and Spain; in these situations the Muslim minorities 'exercised considerable autonomy in judicial matters.'[88] Today, the combining of two legal systems and the acknowledgement of the value of legal pluralism can be seen in action in the Philippines. Here, the Moro Muslims make-up 5% of the total population; and yet, Muslim Personal Law co-exists alongside the state's Family

[88] Bustami Khir, 'Who Applies Islamic Law in Non-Muslim Countries? A Study of the *Sunnī* Principle of Governance of the Scholars (*wilāyat al-ʿulamā*)', *Journal of Muslim Minority Affairs* (vol. 27, no. 1, 2007), p. 79.

and Civil Codes and has become part of the law of the land. This Personal Law covers those issues 'pertaining to status, marriage and divorce, matrimonial and family relationships, and property between spouses.'[89] Similar to this is the Israeli-Islamic judicial system for the Muslim citizens of the Israeli state.[90]

In Britain, there are a number of Islamic religious legal issues that have been successfully implemented with little difficulty, hence reflecting the multicultural philosophy of Britain. The dietary requirement of *ḥalāl* meat, which requires animals not to be stunned before slaughter, has been acknowledged; Muslims, alongside Jews, have been granted an exception to slaughter animals according to their religious requirements.[91] In terms of education in schools, uniforms, and religious and sex education have also been modified in order to take Muslim concerns into account.[92] Local authorities have mostly met the demands of Muslim citizens in terms of planning permissions for mosques and the allocation of burial grounds.[93] Similarly, employers have also had to take into consideration Muslim employees' requests for certain dress codes, time to pray during the day and annual leave for celebrating religious festivals.[94]

Despite the above, a perceived view in Britain today is that only British law should be applied in the UK and there is no place for Islamic or any other law. This is a misunderstanding, for legal pluralism is identified as an attribute of the social field rather than of 'law' or a 'legal system'; it can be defined as the

[89] Michael Mastura, 'Legal Pluralism in the Philippines', *Law and Society Review* (vol. 28, no. 3, 1994), p. 464.

[90] Reiter, '*Qāḍīs* and the Implementation of Islamic Law in Present Day Israel', pp. 205-31.

[91] Shadid and van Koningsveld, *Religious Freedom and the Position of Islam in Western Europe*, p. 82.

[92] See Vertovec, 'Muslims, the State, and the Public Sphere in Britain', p. 178; Shadid and van Koningsveld, *Religious Freedom and the Position of Islam in Western Europe*, pp. 77-98; Anthony Bradney, 'The Legal Status of Islam within the United Kingdom', pp. 187-90.

[93] Shadid and van Koningsveld, *Religious Freedom and the Position of Islam in Western Europe*, p. 98-101.

[94] Ibid., pp. 101-05; Bradney, 'The Legal Status of Islam within the United Kingdom', pp. 191-93. For more detailed discussions on the application of Islamic Law in Europe, see Michael King, *God's Law versus State Law: The Construction of Islamic Identity in Western Europe* (London: Grey Seal, 1995), pp. 1-15. Similarly, Maleiha Malik, *Muslim Legal Norms and the Integration of European Muslims*, EUI Working Papers, RSCAS 2009/29 (San Domenico di Fiesola: European University Institute, 2009), details the advancement of Muslim Legal norms within the European context. As for a discussion specific to Britain, see Robert Gleave, 'Elements of Religious Discrimination in Europe: The Position of Muslim Minorities', in N. Konstadinidis (ed.), *A Peoples' Europe: Tuning a Concept into Content* (Aldershot: Dartmouth Ashgate, 1999), pp. 95-107.

presence of more than one legal order in a social space.[95] According to Yilmaz,[96] legal pluralism allows unofficial and official laws to co-exist. Thus, even though there is no doubt that British Law is the official law of the United Kingdom, it is not the only one that governs and regulates the personal and family relations of all British citizens.[97] Islamic law is found in various aspects of Muslims' lives either on an official level, when given recognition by the legal system, and unofficially when that recognition is absent.[98] According to Yilmaz, the majority of Muslims in Britain today, still prefer to apply Islamic law alongside British law in the area of personal and family life such as marriage, divorce, matters of inheritance and the resolution of disputes.[99] This attitude towards British law is not because Britain is a non-Muslim state; the same attitude applies in Muslim countries that do not follow Sharīʿa law.

Let us now consider an aspect of family law—marriage (*nikāḥ*) and divorce (*ṭalāq*)[100]—which will demonstrate the practicalities of how Muslims adopt a pluralistic approach in family and personal law: according to Islamic law a marriage can take place in any venue but it will not be recognised under British law unless a civil ceremony takes place. Therefore, an unregistered Muslim marriage will not be recognised by the state but will be recognised by the Muslim community. Another point is the attendance of the bride and bridegroom; according to Islamic law the couple do not have to be present but can send representatives instead. However, this would not be a legal marriage under British law as both parties have to attend in person and use a standard form of words to exchange their vows.

One aspect of marriage which most definitely causes a conflict between Islamic and British law is polygamy; or in particular polygyny (multiple wives) rather than polyandry (multiple husbands), as the latter is also prohibited under

95 John Griffiths, 'What is Legal Pluralism?', *Journal of Legal Pluralism* (vol. 24, no. 1-2, 1986), p. 8.

96 Ihsan Yilmaz, 'The Challenge of Post-Modern Legality and Muslim Legal Pluralism in England', *Journal of Muslim Minority Affairs*, (vol. 20, no. 2, 2002), pp. 343-50.

97 Ibid., p. 343.

98 See David Pearl and Werner Menski, *Muslim Family Law*; Ihsan Yilmaz, 'Muslim Law in Britain: Reflections in the Socio-Legal Sphere and Differential Legal Treatment', *Journal of Ethnic and Migration Studies* (vol. 28, no. 2, 2000), pp. 343-54.

99 Yilmaz, 'The Challenge of Post-Modern Legality and Muslim Legal Pluralism in England', pp. 343-50.

100 For actual cases, see David Pearl, 'The 1995 Noel Coulson Memorial Lecture: The Application of Islamic Law in the English Courts', *Arab Law Quarterly* (vol. 12, 1997), pp. 211-19.

Islamic law. One way in which British laws on polygamy have been circumvented by Muslims is when a man is already married in a country to which he has ethnic ties either by birth or through his parents. He then marries for a second time in Britain, by Islamic law (*nikāḥ*), without divorcing his first wife.[101] This allows the husband to bring his first wife into Britain. There have been drives to acknowledge the legal rights of the second wife as she (and any children she may have) is the weaker party with no protection under British law.[102]

Marriage under Islamic law is a civil contract rather than sacrament and a contract can be terminated, in this case by divorce. Divorce can be achieved in a number of ways: *ṭalāq,* which is the verbal or written statement of the husband; *khulᶜ*, where the wife divorces her husband by returning her *mahr* (dowry) to him; *liᶜān,* which is mutual cursing if the husband suspects his wife of being unfaithful but cannot provide the four witnesses required by Islamic law and the wife accuses her husband of lying; and dissolution of the marriage contract by a Sharīᶜa court due to inadequacies on the husband's part. Divorce according to British law can only be gained through a decree granted by a court which recognises that a marriage has 'irretrievably broken down'.[103] Again, efforts are being made between Muslim imams and the relevant public bodies to bring the two legal systems together in order to protect a second wife in a Muslim marriage with respect to divorce.

There is a growing demand for a separate family law for Muslims in Britain. Legal pluralism would be a further step in fully integrating Muslims into the British social and legal system. It would ensure that the state can properly administer the law and that, in particular, weaker parties are afforded greater protection. Having said this, even if, in future, there is an acceptance of a pluralistic approach to law, it will always be possible for Muslims to continue to apply Islamic family law 'unofficially' within their communities, whether alongside the British legal system or independently of it.

[101] Alison Shaw, *A Pakistani Community in Britain* (Oxford: Basil Blackwell, 1988), p. 64.

[102] See Ihsan Yilmaz, 'Muslim Alternative Dispute Resolution and Neo-*Ijtihad* in England', *Alternatives: Turkish International Relations* (vol. 2, no. 1, 2003), pp. 117-39; Ahmad Thomson, *Dissolution of Marriage: Accommodating the Islamic Dissolution of Marriage Law within English Law* (Regents Park Mosque: Lecture Proceedings, 2006).

[103] Yilmaz, 'The Challenge of Post-Modern Legality and Muslim Legal Pluralism in England', p. 350.

CHAPTER II

Hermeneutic Approaches to Religious Texts

As WE HAVE SEEN in the chapter above, the majority of Muslims in Britain today still prefer to apply Islamic law either on its own or in combination with British law. The main reason for this is that Islam does not recognise a division between the secular and the sacred; each act of the Muslim, no matter how small, can be transformed into an act of worship. This absence of separation explains the attachment of Muslims to a sacred law, the Sharīᶜa, which guides all their actions. Our aim in this work is to find means by which the Sharīᶜa can be applied by Muslim living as minorities. Given that the majority of Islamic laws are interpretations of religious source texts, we now propose to look at the hermeneutical approaches that predominate today in the interpretation of these texts. We will then look at these approaches when applied to the Islamic source texts of the Qur'ān and the Prophet's Traditions referred to as the *aḥādīth*. But before we embark on this, we would like to give a brief outline of discourse analysis and the aims and goals of this analysis.

Introduction to Discourse Analysis

The analysis of discourse is in reality the analysis of language in use; therefore this analysis cannot be restricted to the description of the linguistic forms independent of the 'purposes or functions which those forms are designed to serve in human affairs'; thus the discourse analyst investigates what the language is used for.[1] Hence, a balance must exist between literalism and purposes or intentions behind the actual words.

In analysing texts the context will also require consideration in order

[1] Gillian Brown and George Yule, *Discourse Analysis* (Cambridge: Cambridge University Press, 1983), p. 1.

to obtain a relevant and accurate understanding; this area of language study is referred to as 'pragmatics'. Having said that, primarily the analyst must focus on the speaker/writer and the utterance on that particular occasion of use. There are a number of terms such as *reference*, *presupposition*, *implicature* and *inference* which the analyst must appreciate and then subsequently utilise in order to describe the speaker/writer and potentially the audience without focussing on the relationships between sentences or statements.[2] This is a concise definition of the four: reference, the relationship between words and things is the relationship of reference, words refer to things;[3] presupposition, the assumptions the speaker makes about what the hearer is likely to accept without challenge;[4] implicature, what the speaker may imply, suggest or mean, as distinct from what the speaker literally says;[5] and inference, 'the analyst's or audience's process of inference to arrive at an interpretation for utterances or for the connections between utterances.'[6] What we wish to demonstrate through these basic definitions is that an exclusively literal approach is not sufficient and can be misleading; this point will be essential when we come to discuss the literalist Islamic approach.

Aside from the four considerations above, *cohesion* too is essential for a passage of speech or writing to function as a text; a particular feature is that it contains 'the property of signalling that the interpretation of the passage in question depends on something else. If that "something else" is verbally explicit, then there is cohesion.'[7] Therefore, when interpreting the text one must take the whole into consideration rather than a particular line or sentence on its own. However, where the speaker is clearly speaking about a specific subject one cannot ignore or devalue it and instead search for other texts which are more general and therefore open to misinterpretation. Again, these points will be crucial to later discussions of hermeneutical approaches and are useful in demonstrating that understanding a text is not a straightforward simplistic process, but rather requires rules and procedures.

Now, discourse analysis and, in particular, the analysis of sacred texts is not an exercise in and for itself. Normally, it has a purpose; and the

2 Ibid., pp. 26-31.
3 Ibid., p. 28.
4 Ibid., p. 29.
5 Ibid., p. 31.
6 Ibid., p. 33.
7 Ibid., p. 195.

purpose in religious and ethical discussions is the search for the truth or the search for what is good. In Islam, the search for truth concentrates on what God requires from mankind, both as individuals and as a collective. Islam acknowledges the role of human intelligence, rational thought and observation; it also acknowledges that all these can grant humans beings an understanding of the world and the ability to build on this understanding. However, rational and empirical observations are not considered sufficient in determining what God requires from humanity. God reveals His wishes in the revelations that He sends through His messengers. The revelation of Islam is the Qur'ān brought by the Prophet Muḥammad. Thus it is in the Qur'ān, and in the *aḥādīth* or the words and example of the Prophet who is the pre-eminent interpreter of the Qur'ān, that the wishes of God are directly to be found; together they are the sacred texts to which all hermeneutical approaches in Islam must return.

Hermeneutical Approaches

A review of literature on hermeneutics makes it apparent that religious scholars and academics are today mostly adopting three approaches when engaging with religious source texts. These methodologies can broadly be summarised as: literalist, liberal/modernist and traditionalist.

The literalist approach permits only the bare minimum of interpretation of the sacred texts or, even, no interpretation at all. For it, God's Words are not open to deliberation and conjecture but rather have to be accepted at face value; it is only God who can explain what it is that He means by the Words He reveals. Since little to no hermeneutic methodology exists according to this view, we will focus on the two remaining interpretive models in order to detail their foundations, their theoretical basis and how they are utilised to obtain the 'truth', which, in our study, is to determine the intentions in and behind God's Words.

Traditionalism and Liberalism/Modernism

When religious source texts are interrogated with a view of arriving at answers to moral and ethical questions and determining the validity of certain actions, then the problem of 'authority' has to be tackled. Simply put, traditionalists believe in the authority of revelation and liberal/modernists in the authority of reason. Though there are overlaps between the two parties in the use of reason to arrive at certain interpretations, usually these two camps are mutually exclusive and each believes that it, and it alone, possesses the only correct interpretive method in order to determine the truth. Very often, traditionalism is perceived by liberals/modernists to be 'backward', a kind of elastic band holding back society and not allowing it to progress and reach its highest destined potential.[8] Whereas traditionalists argue that a more traditional approach has the benefit of being tried and tested, that it is arguably more reliable and predictable, and that it is not susceptible to the fleeting whims and desires of societies. In addition, traditionalists, or in this case established religions, argue that, as opposed to liberals/modernists who are only concerned with this life, their beliefs in a 'Day of Reckoning' and an afterlife affect both their premise and the conclusions they arrive at in the formation of positive laws.

The moral philosopher Alasdair MacIntyre has written in detail regarding tradition; he explains it as: 'An argument extended through time in which certain fundamental agreements are defined and redefined in terms of two kinds of conflict: those with critics and enemies external to the tradition who reject all or at least part of those fundamental agreements, and those internal, interpretive debates through which meaning and rationale of the fundamental agreements come to be expressed and by whose progress a tradition is constituted.'[9] He further states that a living tradition is an 'historically extended socially embedded argument...through many generations'; when an individual searches for good, in our case what God intends, it is 'conducted within a context defined by those traditions of which the individual's life is a part.'[10]

MacIntyre explains that liberals claim to provide a political, legal and economic framework which is based on a set of rationally justifiable principles which would allow people of incompatible conceptions of a good life to live together peacefully enjoying equal rights.[11] This would come about

[8] Louay Safi, 'The Creative Mission of Muslim Minorities in the West: Synthesising the Ethos of Islam and Modernity', presented at *Fiqh Today: Muslims as Minorities* (AMSS UK, Westminster University, London, February 21st 2004). See also Yūsuf al-Qaraḍāwī, *Fī fiqh al-aqalliyyāt al-muslima: Ḥayat al-muslimīn wasṭ al-mujtamaʿāt al-ukhrā*, Cairo: Dār al-Shurūq, 2001.

[9] Ibid., p. 12.

[10] Alasdair MacIntyre, *After Virtue: A Study in Moral Theory* (London: Gerald Duckworth & Co. Ltd, 1985), p. 222.

[11] Alasdair MacIntyre, *Whose Justice? Which Rationality?* (London: Gerald Duckworth & Co. Ltd, 1988), pp. 335-36.

due to the claim of inherent neutrality of the model. However, if we were to interrogate this further by investigating the case where a number of groups reach opposing conclusions of what is good in a particular matter due to their different views, MacIntyre argues that the only rational way would be to resolve these disagreements 'by means of a philosophical enquiry aimed at deciding which out of the conflicting sets of premises, if any, is true.'[12] However, the liberal approach does not set out to do that but rather proposes its own principles, attitudes and views. The liberal model he argues is a tradition with its own 'authoritative texts and its disputes over their interpretation' and is 'no more and no less than the continued sustenance of the liberal social and political order;'[13] it, therefore, cannot be positioned as a neutral tool which can be utilised to measure and assess other attitudes.

Furthermore, MacIntyre asserts that the intellectual positions adopted by the adherents of a tradition can only be understood within its context. As he holds liberalism to be a tradition and since traditions are 'incommensurable' he believes that applying so-called universal principles of rationality and justice is a liberal myth, which he feels is a major characteristic of modernity.[14] Liberal critics have challenged MacIntyre's view of liberalism as a tradition and his view of incommensurability and feel that, 'MacIntyre is in the grip of a world view promulgated by authority rather than reason [and]... is using this view to justify perpetuating authority at the heart of human life and, indeed at the heart of human reason.'[15] However, MacIntyre's main argument is that liberal rationalism is not a neutral, independent process that allows an individual to determine the truth, but that it is a tradition like any other tradition with its own views and attitudes.

If we now turn to definitions of Islam, Talal Asad,[16] while drawing on MacIntyre's work, defines Islam as a 'discursive tradition': 'A tradition consists

[12] Ibid., pp. 342-43.

[13] Ibid., p. 345.

[14] Alasdair MacIntyre, *Three Rival Versions of Moral Enquiry: Encyclopaedia, Genealogy, Tradition* (London: Gerald Duckworth & Co. Ltd, 1990), p. 5 and 'A Partial Response to My Critics', in J. Horton and S. Mendus (eds.), *After MacIntyre: Critical Perspectives on the Work of Alasdair MacIntyre* (Cambridge: Polity Press, 1994), p. 294.

[15] Jean Porter, 'Openness and Constraint: Moral Reflection as Tradition-Guided Inquiry in Alasdair MacIntyre's Recent Works', *Journal of Religion*, (vol. 73, no. 4, 1993), p. 522.

[16] Talal Asad, *The Idea of an Anthropology of Islam* (Washington: Center for Contemporary Arab Studies, Georgetown University, 1986).

essentially of discourses that seek to instruct practitioners regarding the correct form and purpose of a given practice that, precisely because it is established, has a history. These discourses relate conceptually to a *past* (when the practice was instituted, and from which the knowledge of its point and proper performance has been transmitted) and a *future* (how the point of that practice can best be secured in the short or long term or why it should be modified or abandoned) through a *present* (how it is linked to other practices, institutions, and social conditions). An Islamic discursive tradition is simply a tradition of Muslim discourse that addresses itself to conceptions of the Islamic past and future, with reference to a particular Islamic practice in the present.'[17] Hence, Islam should be approached as a 'discursive tradition' with the Sharīʿa as the basis of this tradition.

Messick refers to the Sharīʿa as a 'total discourse' which has a set of institutions and practices that have shaped many aspects of people's lives, particularly in pre-modern Muslim societies.[18]

Omar, in the third part of his detailed papers titled 'Reasoning in Islamic Law',[19] arrives at a different understanding. He states that in terms of renewing Islamic jurisprudence there are three approaches: the traditional, the innovative and the renovative. With respect to traditional jurisprudents, he describes them as individuals who give 'disproportionate attention to trivial details and pay only lip service to the ends and purposes of the Sharīʿah.'[20] The innovators, he argues, demand a complete break with the past and request that 'new ideas and institutions [be] based directly on the Qur'ān and the Sunnah.'[21] While, in his opinion, the renovative approach is that jurisprudence should be renovated with due regard to the 'immutable values and precepts of the Sharīʿah and the variable concepts and rules which are derived therefrom', but must also facilitate the adoption of new concepts and systems.[22] In our view, Omar has misunderstood the traditional approach as it inherently possess the ability to renovate, hence we will argue that, what we have referred to as

[17] Ibid., p. 14.

[18] Brinkley Messick, *The Calligraphic State: Textual Domination and History in a Muslim Society* (Berkeley: University of California Press, 1993), p. 3.

[19] Mohammed Omar, 'Reasoning in Islamic Law: Part Three', *Arab Law Quarterly* (vol. 23, 1998), pp. 23-60.

[20] Ibid., p. 24.

[21] Ibid., p. 25.

[22] Ibid.

the traditional approach is in fact the traditional and renovative approaches. We accept the definition for the innovative approach; however we choose to refer to it as liberalist/modernist, as innovative is more general than the definitions and methodology Omar applies. We believe the end of the continuum is missing in Omar's description and can only be completed by a virtually non-interpreting model, namely literalism, which seems to be his understanding of the traditional approach.

Wael Hallaq,[23] when explaining the methodologies Islamic scholars have applied throughout the twentieth century in developing Islamic law (*fiqh*), reaches a slightly different conclusion. He divides the community, with respect to the interpretive models they adopt, into 'secularists' and 'puritan traditionalists' at the two extremes and those holding the middle ground he splits into two: 'religious utilitarians' and 'religious liberals', the task of the latter is to develop legal theory in order to correlate the foundational values of Islam with substantive law so that the needs of modern societies can be addressed. He further explains that the difference between the liberals and utilitarians is that the former develop new methodologies whilst the latter only propose slight modifications.[24] We have found it difficult to differentiate between religious liberals and religious secularists. In addition, can a secularist be described as 'religious'?

In our study, we share William Graham's[25] disagreement with the modernists and his argument that traditionalism is a key feature of Islam and that it is 'not in some imagined atavism, regressivism, fatalism or rejection of change and challenge', but that it facilitates 'a personally guaranteed connection with a model past, and especially model persons, offers the only sound basis...for forming and reforming one's society in any age.'[26] Therefore, Islamic traditionalism, as Graham describes it, is a template or a model for a society to emulate; it can be utilised by the religious scholars of any time and place in order to compare and contrast the societies that they live in, and in order to bring about the required legal rulings. In other words, tradition is 'an inherited scholastic methodology and set of paradigms', a transmission of knowledge

[23] Wael Hallaq, *A History of Islamic Legal Theories* (Cambridge: Cambridge University Press, 1997), pp. 213-14.

[24] Ibid., p. 231.

[25] William Graham, 'Traditionalism in Islam: An Essay in Interpretation', *Journal of Interdisciplinary History* (vol. 23, no. 3, 1993), pp. 495-522.

[26] Ibid., p. 522.

by individuals with 'deep roots in scholarship'.[27] In Islam, this transmission is referred to as *isnād* (chain of transmission, i.e. the narrators who transmit the *ḥadīth*) and connects those within it to the Prophet Muḥammad who is the first link in the chain. Since the death of the Prophet, this chain provides a 'guarantee' of authenticity and a blueprint for how to best live their lives, individually and collectively.

We conclude this review of literature on hermeneutics by affirming that, despite a few differences, the majority of scholars have summarised the methodologies as: literalist, liberal/modernist and traditionalist, and that these are the three methods that we shall be adopting and applying throughout the remainder of this study. We also conclude that, each party claims to propose legal, social and political systems, which in the case of literalists relies solely on what exists in the sacred texts, while modernists based themselves in liberal rationalism that places the human at the centre, and traditionalists place God at the centre and derive their structures from a form of revelation. Therefore, each model has its own views of truth and knowledge and, in our view, it is not possible to consider any as a neutral independent model applicable across the board to all matters that are sources of disagreement.

The Applications of Literalism, Liberalism/modernism and Traditionalism to the Islamic Context

If we now look in more detail at the three methodologies from an exclusively Islamic perspective, we find that there are similarities between those who espouse the liberal/modernist approach to Islamic thought and literalists/Islamists. Generally speaking, the aims of both liberal Islamic scholars and Islamists are to find ways of making Islam compatible with the challenges of the modern age. Both claim to wish to retrieve the 'true' teachings of Islam from the mist, dust and cobwebs that centuries of 'sterile' scholasticism and 'blind' imitation of earlier authorities has brought about. For this to take place, a fresh but 'authentic' reading of the foundational texts, especially the Qur'ān, should be undertaken, and that this would facilitate the clarification of Islamic teachings and, in the case of the liberals/modernists, bring them closer to a liberal rationalism understanding.

[27] Aftab Malik, *The State We Are In: Identity, Terror and the Law of Jihad* (Bristol: Amal Press, 2006), pp. 27-28

For the modernists to warrant the move from traditionalism to liberal rationalism which 'must furnish a solution to the problems which had previously proved intractable' due to the sterility or incoherence of the traditional model,[28] an epistemological crisis has to exist within the Islamic tradition. A number of questions have to be posed: have Islamic modernists fully understood the traditionally accepted principles and hermeneutical methods practiced for centuries in the Islamic world? As their approach to interpreting religious texts is alien to historical Islam, is it a legally sanctioned development or an illegitimate innovation (*bidʿa*)[29]? We argue that those who advocate this view have no legitimate reason to turn towards another approach as they tend not to be traditionally-trained scholars and are therefore not versed in the dynamic nature of the traditional approach nor are they in a position to advocate a completely different model as the current traditional model has not been thoroughly investigated. Putting it another way, an epistemological crisis has not occurred as the model is still applicable; ignorance of it does not negate its validity. Also, if we adopt Alasdair MacIntyre's concept of incommensurability, then modernist scholars are not in a position to apply their views to a different method of ascertaining truth.

Like Islamic modernists, Islamists—many of whom are affiliated to modern, secular educational institutions—aim to radically alter their societies and states through means they regard as 'true' Islam.[30] However, when their ideas are analysed, these tend to be nothing more than rhetoric with little substance, and in most cases 'true' Islam is actually modern politics with an Islamic veneer rather than Islamic jurisprudence. While traditional jurists from the Islamic legal Schools continue applying the traditional hermeneutic principles, the Islamists tend to adopt interpretive methodologies which are utilised in the social and natural sciences in which they are trained and hold expertise.[31]

[28] Alasdair MacIntyre, *Whose Justice? Which Rationality?* (London: Gerald Duckworth & Co. Ltd, 1988), p. 362.

[29] *Bidʿa* is a technical legal term meaning illegitimate innovation, or an illegal development or introduction of practice which is not sanctioned by the Sharīʿa.

[30] Muhammad Zaman. *The Ulama in Contemporary Islam: Custodians of Change* (Princeton: Princeton University Press, 2002), pp. 7-8.

[31] Wael Hallaq, *Sharīʿa: Theory, Practice, Transformations* (Cambridge: Cambridge University Press, 2009), pp. 475-76.

There is scant relevant literature in the area of Islamic hermeneutical methodologies. We will, however, now attempt to outline these methodologies in more detail basing ourselves in the available literature of classical and contemporary Muslim scholars. Though scholars' names have been identified with the various positions, this does not mean that they are the only ones to hold these views nor is it our aim to target any particular individual.

The Literal Approach

This view tends to emanate from religious scholars living in Muslim-majority states who view non-Muslim lands as *dār al-ḥarb* (domain of war). The scholars who tend to adopt this approach do not claim affiliation to any of the four traditional Sunni Schools of Law and believe that they are thus free to interpret source texts directly without reference to earlier scholars and interpretations. Two prominent advocates of this viewpoint were the scholars ʿAbd al-ʿAzīz b. Bāz and Muḥammad b. Ṣāliḥ al-ʿUthaymīn; Bin Bāz was—between 1993 and his death in 1999—the Grand Mufti of Saudi Arabia. Among the statements issued by these scholars is: 'It is incumbent upon the whole Muslim community to adhere to the Book of their Lord and to the authentic Sunna of their Prophet (Allah send peace and salutations upon him),'[32] a statement which cannot be contradicted by any Muslim, but which does not constitute a methodology. However, it is in their use of emotive language—for example, in describing non-Muslims as 'enemies',[33] which makes clear their view of the 'Other'—that some of the methods they use are revealed.

Generally speaking, Islamic scholars of this school rely on a literal understanding of the source texts and their presentations tend to be simplistic, many in the form of questions and answers as in the above mentioned scholars' *Muslim Minorities*. Their approach has been likened to that of the Khawārij—an early Islamic sect which was separate from the Sunnis and the Shīʿa and which tended towards fanaticism, recognising only their own interpretation of Islam and even turning on the fourth Caliph, ʿAlī bin Abī Ṭālib, and murdering him as they considered his decision to accept arbitration with Muʿāwiya contrary to their beliefs.[34]

[32] Abdul-Aziz Ibn Baz and Muhammad Uthaymeen, *Muslim Minorities: Fatawa Regarding Muslims Living as Minorities* (Middlesex: Message of Islam, 1998), p. 11.

[33] Ibid., p. 15.

[34] Khaled Abou El-Fadl, *Islam and the Challenge of Democracy* (Boston: Boston Review, 2003), p. 2.

From the perspective of the literalist ideology, Muslims should practice their religion as documented in the source texts. And yet, literalists tend to select individual Qur'ānic verses and *aḥādīth* and to concentrate on these rather than on the entire corpus. Their choice of verses and *aḥādīth* is used to emphasise that the literal interpretation is the only one without 'dispensations' or 'flexibility'. If the application of this interpretation proves too difficult for Muslims living as a minority then these Muslims should emigrate to a Muslim-majority country. Thus the opinion of certain literalist Islamic scholars is in fact no different from what seems to be the far right-wing view within the West, along the lines of, 'If you cannot live in this culture, then emigrate to a Muslim country.'

The literalist approach thus manifests itself by a complete isolation of the Muslim minority community from the wider society and their viewing of all non-Muslims with hostility, which results in the disengagement of the minority from the socio-political and educational spheres. This isolation and disengagement from the majority non-Muslim society is not sanctioned in the source texts or in the derived practical laws of the main Schools of Islamic jurisprudence. Critics of this perspective have thus deemed it as not lawful as it makes religion difficult—especially for those who live as minorities—and this is in direct conflict with certain verses of the Qur'ān and a number of *aḥādīth*. It also puts a stop to development in all spheres of life and, in some severe cases, regresses the community, who may then become viewed by the majority non-Muslim community with resentment and fear; the latter may even act upon this fear by restricting the rights of Muslims and the expression of their Muslim faith and eventually by persecuting the minority Muslim community. This perspective is also contrary to the way that Islam spread all over the world, where, in places, it has existed exclusively in minority status but in complete harmony with its majority neighbours. Had the literalist perspective been applied in all situations and context from the beginning of Islam, then this would have significantly impacted on the spread of Islam; this in itself further suggests that the literalist perspective is detrimental to Islam and Muslims in general, and especially in the case of minority-status.

Another group of individuals who adopts this literalist approach is the Islamists. Before detailing their viewpoint, however, we shall define what we mean by Islamist as this term is vague and includes a wide number of positions with varying aims and methods.[35] Our definition of Islamists are those individuals who desire an Islamic political solution to the world's problems and who call for the re-establishment of the Caliphate, with one leader presiding over the Muslim *umma* (the worldwide Muslim community). This view tends to be supported by graduates of 'western' educational institutions rather than graduates of traditional theological schools. Traditional Islam also supports the concept of the Caliphate and particularly looks to the model applied by the four first Caliphs. The difference with the Islamists is that traditional scholars have usually remained aloof from the political sphere. This will be explored further in Chapter V discussing political domains.

Islamists advocate a form of Sharīᶜa which existed in the first decades of Islam and which has not existed since.[36] Frank Griffel argues that they believe that corruption came about and has subsequently existed within the Islamic world after the era of the first four Caliphs, and therefore all legal developments subsequent to 40/661 (the year in which the fourth Caliph ᶜAlī was killed) are considered irrelevant.[37] This dismissal of centuries of legal development is a modern understanding of the Sharīᶜa and its applications.

An example of this Islamist viewpoint is Asif Khan's attack on the '*fiqh* or law of minorities' (*fiqh al-aqalliyyāt*) in his book *The Fiqh of Minorities: The New Fiqh to Subvert Islam*.[38] We shall be returning to discuss this title in more detail later on in our study. Khan, who is not a traditionally-trained religious scholar, asserts that *fiqh al-aqalliyyāt* is a relatively new development which 'has led to the neglect of certain Shariah rules to the contradiction of what has been established with certainty from the Qur'an and Sunnah.'[39] While refuting *fiqh al-aqalliyyāt*, he continually urges 'to go back to legal texts and study them in order to acquire the Islamic ruling.'[40] His main argument seems to be against Muslim political participation in non-Muslim countries as he

[35] Knut Vikor, *Between God and the Sultan: A History of Islamic Law* (London: Hurst & Company, 2005), p. 257.

[36] Frank Griffel, 'Introduction', in A. Amanet and F. Griffel (eds.), *Sharīᶜa: Islamic Law in the Contemporary Context* (Stanford: Stanford University Press, 2007), p. 12.

[37] Ibid., p. 14

[38] Asif Khan, *The Fiqh of Minorities: The New Fiqh to Subvert Islam* (London: Khilafah Publications, 2004).

[39] Ibid., p. 6.

[40] Ibid., p. 16.

holds it to be un-Islamic and unbeneficial.[41] His concluding remarks clearly express his position: '[The *Fiqh* of Minorities]...is a symptom of a corrupted thought process, which looks to the dominant West for its solutions...The aim of participating in the political life of the West...is to achieve a set of benefits...However, contrary to what is said by them, these aims can be achieved by following the Shariah path permitted by Islam, without the need to commit haram or trying to legitimise it by the deviant use of the rules of necessity (daruraat), benefit (masalih) and repelling the evils (mafaasid).'[42]

The Liberal/Modernist Approach

As we have mentioned above, a liberal approach to the interpretation of source texts takes into consideration modern, to a certain extent secular, practices and consequently derives principles and rulings based on that framework or 'dilutes' existing Islamic practices which do not sit well with modern practices. There are a number of individuals and organisations that adopt this approach, for example, the group called 'Progressive Muslims' who look to 'challenge' traditional concepts of justice, gender and pluralism based on modern liberalism.[43] However our study is more concerned with those individuals and groups who 'reason from faith and first principles but doing so in ways that draw upon modernist ideas within an Islamic methodology (*Ijtihād*).'[44]

As the only real area which requires new applications of the law (*fiqh*) is the area of the *fiqh* of minorities (*fiqh al-aqalliyyāt*), this is the field that has concerned most of the liberal/modernist Islamic scholars. The two key individuals who are particularly active in this area are Yūsuf al-Qaraḍāwī and Taha Jābir al-Alwani (the latter has been credited with coining the term),[45] and their respective organisations: the European Council for Fatwa and Research (ECFR) and the International Institute of Islamic Thought (IIIT). Another organisation which has been active in this area, particularly since 2004, is the Association of Muslim Social Scientists who organise an annual conference

[41] Ibid., pp. 26-28.

[42] Ibid., p. 42.

[43] Omid Safi, *Progressive Muslims: On Justice, Gender and Pluralism* (Oxford: Oneworld Publications, 2003).

[44] Tariq Modood and Fauzia Ahmad, 'British Muslim Perspectives on Multiculturalism', p. 194.

[45] Shammai Fishman, *Fiqh al-Aqalliyyat: A Legal Theory for Muslim Minorities*, Research Monographs on the Muslim World, Series No. 1, Paper No. 2, (Washington: Hudson Institute, Center on Islam, Democracy, and the Future of the Muslim World, 2006), p. 1.

and bring together many researchers within this area.[46]

Initially, the concept of *fiqh al-aqalliyyāt* was welcomed as it was assumed that it was a new name for an old area of jurisprudence, namely *al-nawāzil* (the occurrences). However, once specifics started to filter out, that initial welcome changed to confusion and, for some, even outright objection and ridicule.[47] The main ideas and arguments of the two above-mentioned scholars are contained in two works which will be interrogated extensively in order to draw out an understanding of their position and the position of those who subscribe to this approach: *Fī fiqh al-aqalliyyāt al-muslima: Ḥayat al-muslimīn wasṭ al-mujtamaʿāt al-ukhrā* (Islamic Jurisprudence for Muslim Minorities: Life of Muslims in the Midst of Other Societies) by Yūsuf al-Qaraḍāwī, and *Towards a Fiqh for Minorities: Some Basic Reflections* by Taha Alwani. The aim of this project is to bring about structures for the development of Muslim thought, 'in all areas bearing on theology, law and even history.'[48]

The basic argument behind this project is that the global situation has changed over time and Muslims and non-Muslims are now living, working and socialising together, especially those Muslims who live as minorities. Furthermore, it is argued that classical Islamic law is inadequate[49] as one of the two fundamental source texts for Islamic jurisprudence—namely the corpus of the *aḥādīth*—is no longer valid because it is linked to a different time and context; only the Qur'ān should be referred to due to its eternal nature.[50] The conclusion is that the minority status of Muslims has created a vacuum and that research into a 'new' *fiqh* is required.[51] There is a similarity here between the scholars who espouse this perspective and the Literalists in that neither party admits connections to any of the four Sunni traditional Schools of Law.

Alwani claims that, to date, an unscientific and illogical approach has been

[46] The Association of Muslim Social Scientists, *Fiqh Today: Muslims as Minorities* (Conference Booklet), 5th Annual AMSS (UK) Conference, 21st–22nd February 2004 (London: University of Westminster, 2004).

[47] Nuh Keller, 'Which of the Four Orthodox Madhhabs Has the Most Developed Fiqh for Muslims Living as Minorities?' (see, http://www.sunnah.org/fiqh/usul/fiqh4.htm, 1995) and 'Modernism and Fiqh al-Aqaliat', (see, http://al-miftah.blogspot.com/2007/09/islam-not-cereal-shaykh-nuh-keller-uk.html, 2007).

[48] Alwani, *Towards a Fiqh for Minorities*, p. vii.

[49] Safi, 'The Creative Mission of Muslim Minorities in the West: Synthesising the Ethos of Islam and Modernity', p. 1.

[50] Alwani, *Towards a Fiqh for Minorities*, p. viii.

[51] Ibid. See also Qaraḍāwī, *Fī fiqh al-aqalliyyāt al-muslima*, p. 30.

applied in the deduction of *fiqh* and insists that the background of the query, the enquirer and the underlying social factors which brought about that query need to be taken into consideration.[52] He continues by arguing that the tone of legal queries should be modified from a negative to a positive one so that there is a change from questions such as: 'Can Muslim minorities participate in the political life of a host country where non-Muslims form a majority and where the political system is non-Islamic?' to: 'What is Islam's view regarding a group of Muslims who find themselves living among a non-Muslim majority whose system of government allows them to observe and exercise all Islamic obligations that do not threaten public order?'[53]

Fiqh al-aqaliyyāt is based on three fundamental premises: the immutability of the Qur'ān which is regarded as the 'overriding source of all legislation, the absolute criterion and final reference', the territorial principle of *ʿālamiyyat al-Islām* (Islam as a global religion), and the juristic principle of *maqāṣid al-Sharīʿa* (ruling according to the intentions of the Islamic Law).[54]

In the application of the first premise—that of actually interpreting Qur'ānic verses—traditional methods, such as the use of *aḥādīth* to explain Qur'ānic verses and the consensus of scholars' opinion (*ijmāʿ*), are disregarded completely. The elimination of traditional methods of interpretation thus allows other, and new, interpretive models to be applied; in this case a modernist one is applied. The view that these scholars hold is that Muslims need to 'liberate themselves from traditionalism by deepening the commitment to the universal values of Islam.'[55] In particular, the traditional concept of *taqlīd*, i.e., adhering to a School's teachings, is regarded as the cause of Muslims not facing today's challenges by hiding their heads in the past due to an excessive paranoia of deviation or 'western' influence on Islam and Muslims,[56] and to a lesser extent because of literalist reductionism.[57] This misunderstanding of traditional Islam in which rulings cannot be changed and are considered 'eternal', even though circumstances and times may change, is—in the opinion of

[52] Alwani, *Towards a Fiqh for Minorities*, p. 4.

[53] Ibid., pp. 5-6.

[54] Qaraḍāwī, *Fī fiqh al-aqalliyyāt al-muslima*, pp. 36-37.

[55] Safi, 'The Creative Mission of Muslim Minorities in the West: Synthesising the Ethos of Islam and Modernity', p. 10.

[56] Tariq Ramadan, *Radical Reform: Islamic Ethics and Liberation* (New York: Oxford University Press, 2009), pp. 257, 293 and 317.

[57] Ibid., p. 293.

modernists—a major drive for the need for a different methodology.[58] The new methodology thus allows modernist religious scholars to directly derive 'principles' from the Qur'ān and to reject all *aḥādīth*, even *mutawātir* and *mashhūr* ones, and all other evidence that contradicts their interpretation of the Qur'ān.[59] It prioritises a religious scholar's own interpretation; a sort of subjectivism, which will be explored later. Its aim is to adapt the law to the necessities of Muslim communities in the West, thus allowing legal leniencies so that these communities can be both true to their faith and flourish within non-Muslim societies.[60] Furthermore, it is argued that the whole *fatwā* process should cease to be rulings delivered by *muftī*s to the public, but should be one of debate and discussion, as the 'ultimate testing ground' has gone beyond establishing the intention of God in sacred texts to 'how appropriate and practical the fiqh really is.'[61] From the point of view of *maqāṣid al-Sharīʿa*—the third premise used by modernists—there is a contradiction here. Shāṭibī, the 'father' of *maqāṣid al-Sharīʿa*, makes rational derivations subservient to the source texts when they are mutually supportive, and even more so when the former contradicts the latter. In his *Muwāfaqāt* he states: 'If textual and rational evidence are mutually supportive concerning legal questions, then the text is given priority as it is to be followed and the rational evidence is deferred as it is the follower. Reason is not restrained except in the manner the textual evidence itself restrains it.'[62] Thus, if there is an explicit text regarding a matter and a rational derivation which contradicts it, then the text has to be given priority.

The second premise of *fiqh al-aqaliyyāt*—the territorial principle of *ʿālamiyyat al-Islām* (Islam as a global religion)—provides the rationale for permitting the very existence of permanent Muslim communities in non-Muslim lands, as it is asserted that *fiqh al-aqalliyyāt* is the only successful way of managing the 'conflict' between liberal democracies and Muslims who choose to practice Islamic Law.[63]

58 Jasser Auda, *Maqasid al-Shariah as Philosophy of Islamic Law: A Systems Approach* (London: IIIT, 2008), p. 111.

59 Qaraḍāwī, *Fī fiqh al-aqalliyyāt al-muslima*, p. 38; Alwani, *Towards a Fiqh for Minorities*, p. 20.

60 Fishman, *Fiqh al-Aqalliyyat: A Legal Theory for Muslim Minorities*, p. 2.

61 Alwani, *Towards a Fiqh for Minorities*, p. 23. See also, Salah Soltan, 'Methodological Regulations for the Fiqh of Muslim Minorities' (see, http://www.salahsoltan.com/main/index.php?id=16,64,0,0,1,0), 2005.

62 Abū Isḥāq al-Shāṭibī, *al-Muwāfaqāt fī uṣūl al-sharīʿa* (Beirut: Dār al-Kutub al-ʿIlmiyya, 2003), vol. 1, p. 21.

63 Maleiha Malik, 'Accommodating Muslims in Europe: Opportunities for Minority Fiqh', *Law and Society* (ISIM Newsletter 13, 2003), p. 10

The third premise of *maqāṣid al-Sharīʿa* is actually a traditional model developed between the eleventh and fourteenth centuries by scholars such as Abū al-Maʿālī al-Juwaynī (d. 478/1085), Abū Ḥāmid al-Ghazālī (d. 505/1111), Al-ʿIzz b. ʿAbd al-Salām (d. 606/1209), Shihāb al-Dīn al-Qarāfī (d. 684/1285), Shams al-Dīn b. al-Qayyim (d. 748/1347) and, most significantly, the above-mentioned Abū Isḥāq al-Shāṭibī (d. 790/1388). The International Institute of Islamic Thought has been active in researching and publishing in this area over the last several years conducting translations and analysis of key traditional texts the main ones being by Raysuni,[64] Ibn Ashur,[65] Attia,[66] Auda,[67] Chapra[68] and Kamali.[69] As it is not our purpose in this study to go into the details of *maqāṣid al-Sharīʿa*, we recommend Raysuni's discussion on Imām Shāṭibī's texts.

Islamic modernists generally accept the traditional concept of determining 'the objective behind any revealed law' (this is the literal translation of *maqāṣid al-Sharīʿa*). However they criticise this concept for a number of reasons which include the following: traditionally the objectives or *maqāṣid* are limited to five and they believe that this number should be increased; the objectives are too much focussed on the individual rather than paying attention to groups such as families, societies and humans in general; the objectives do not include universal and basic values such as justice and freedom; and, finally, it is argued that traditional *maqāṣid* are derived from legal literature rather than directly from the Islamic source texts.[70] Despite these criticisms, there is an acknowledgement by some scholars that *maqāṣid al-Sharīʿa* can be developed further without the need for a new discipline, and that it can be a part of the existing traditional *uṣūl*

64 Ahmad al-Raysuni, *Imam al-Shatibi's Theory of the Higher Objectives and Intents of Islamic Law* (London: The International Institute of Islamic Thought, 2005).

65 Muhammad Ibn Ashur, *Ibn Ashur: Treatise on Maqāṣid al-Sharīʿah* (London: IIIT, 2006).

66 Gamal Attia, *Towards Realization of the Higher Intents of Islamic Law:* Maqāṣid al-Shariʿah*: A Functional Approach* (London: IIIT, 2007).

67 Jasser Auda, *Maqasid al-Shariah as Philosophy of Islamic Law: A Systems Approach* (London: IIIT, 2008) and *Maqāṣid al-Sharīʿah: A Beginner's Guide* (Occasional Papers Series 14, London: IIIT, 2008).

68 Muḥammad Chapra, *The Islamic Vision of Development in the Light of Maqāṣid al-Sharīʿah*, Occasional Papers Series 15 (London: IIIT, 2008).

69 Mohammed Kamali, *Maqāṣid al-Sharīʿah Made Simple*, Occasional Papers Series 13 (London: IIIT, 2008).

70 Auda, *Maqasid al-Shariah as Philosophy of Islamic Law*, pp. 3-5; Attia, *Towards Realization of the Higher Intents of Islamic Law*, pp. 87-90.

al-fiqh (legal theory or principles of *fiqh*) included under the study of *istiṣlāḥ*,[71] or the Ḥanafī variant *istiḥsān*. Auda argues for this because: 'It is a methodology from "within" the Islamic scholarship that addresses the Islamic mind and Islamic concerns. This approach is radically different from projects for Islamic "reform" and "renewal" that come from "without" the Islamic terminology and scholarship;'[72] thus it will be more acceptable to Muslim scholars and laypersons alike.

Of the two above-mentioned scholars, Qaraḍāwī adopts a relatively more traditional approach than Alwani.[73] This may be due to the more scholarly and detailed investigation he has conducted, as opposed to Alwani who has focussed more on the actual need for a *fiqh* of minorities. Hence, there seems to be a difference of opinion between those who advocate this new *fiqh* as to what it *actually* is. The European Council for Fatwa and Research [ECFR] has developed a coherent body of rulings based on their understanding of the principles of *fiqh al-aqaliyyāt*. Qaraḍāwī argues for principles which earlier traditional scholars have used; for example, *taysīr* (seeking ease), changing of *fatwā* due to changing times, and *ḍarūra* (need).[74] However, he also asserts that moving away from following the four Schools of Law or, as he describes it, 'from the prison of restricted traditionalism towards the spacious permissible sharīʿa', is what is required in order to best serve Muslims living as minorities.[75] For instance, he puts forward an example that according to the four traditional Schools a non-Muslim cannot inherit from a Muslim and vice versa based on an authentic *ḥadīth*. Therefore, all those who adhere to the Schools of Law will have to abide by this ruling; and yet a reliable view exists that this is only when one party is at war with the other.[76] Qaraḍāwī also holds the view, which from a traditional perspective is considered an innovation, that Muslim minorities are in a state of *tadrīj* (transience) similar to the first Muslims at the birth of Islam, for whom impermissibility of certain items and issues were brought about gradually rather than in an abrupt and immediate manner.[77]

This idea of *fiqh al-aqaliyyāt* has been criticised because of two main issues:

[71] Attia, *Towards Realization of the Higher Intents of Islamic Law*, p. 168.

[72] Auda, *Maqasid al-Shariah as Philosophy of Islamic Law*, pp. 8-9.

[73] Qaraḍāwī, *Fī fiqh al-aqalliyyāt al-muslima*, pp. 40-44.

[74] Ibid., pp. 48-52 and pp. 55-56.

[75] Ibid., p. 57.

[76] Ibid., pp. 58-59.

[77] Ibid., pp. 53-55.

firstly, there are those who categorically reject the concept that Muslims who choose to live as a minority should have a special system of *fiqh* for them alone as this may divide Islam and transform it into 'various territorial Islams'.[78] Secondly, and this is even more serious, is that this interpretation of *fiqh* is a *bidʿa* (an illegitimate or illegal innovation) as it is a manipulation of God's religion,[79] which can act like a Trojan horse at the heart of Islam and which could result in the infiltration of the religion and an 'enlightenment' of restructuring for the whole of Islam.

While it can be argued that legally *fiqh al-aqaliyyāt* may theoretically be possible, the problem of the doctrine of juristic consensus (*ijmāʿ*)—a foundational tenet of *fiqh*—and the concept that the community of Muslims cannot agree on an error have to be addressed. As, for centuries, there has been a consensus of scholars and of the community on matters of *fiqh*, to assert that some of these laws were at best dubious implies that the community must have agreed on errors and this would have serious ramifications for the whole of Sunni Islam.[80]

The Traditional Approach

Over the past few decades, there has been an erosion of traditional Islam worldwide. This has come about for numerous reasons. According to Aftab Malik, traditional Islam today is perceived by many Muslims to be irrelevant, as it does not answer questions pertinent to current times.[81] Due to this perceived absence, many Muslims, in particular the young, prefer to search for immediate answers. Their approach is that there is no need to study at the feet of traditionally-trained scholars for years of theological, legal and spiritual training; that there is no need even to consult traditional scholars for a legal ruling as one can go directly to the sources and draw one's own conclusions.[82] What this approach ignores is that the source texts provide general principles and that it has been

[78] Saʿīd Bouti, 'It Is Not a Coincidence that the Call to the Jurisprudence of Minorities Meets with the Plot Aiming at Dividing Islam', (see http://www.bouti.net/en/article.php?PHPSESSID=fa65d3e34ef946bad316aa05e5a67840&id=336), 2001.

[79] Fishman, *Fiqh al-Aqalliyyat: A Legal Theory for Muslim Minorities*, pp. 12–13; Nuh Keller, 'Modernism and Fiqh al-Aqaliat' (see http://al-miftah.blogspot.com/2007/09/islam-not-cereal-shaykh-nuh-keller-uk.html, 2007.

[80] Wael Hallaq, 'Considerations on the Function and Character of Sunnī Legal Theory', *Journal of the American Oriental Society* (vol. 104, no. 4, 1984), p. 682.

[81] Malik, *The State We Are In*, p. 14.

[82] Ibid., p. 15.

jurists throughout the centuries who have used the methodologies of their different schools to interpret and derive the legal rulings from the principles.

In order to understand this crucial position of traditional scholars and jurists, we need to differentiate between the Sharīʿa—the infallible commandments of God which are to be found in the Qur'ān and the Sunna of the Prophet—and the *fiqh* which is the jurists' interpretation of the Sharīʿa.[83] Most aspects of *fiqh* have been extensively explored and have reached a conclusive end and are not era-, context- or people-related; for example, the number of prayers in the day. However, one area in particular which requires a fresh look is that dealing with social affairs (*muʿāmalāt*), as within the last sixty years or so many Muslims have moved from a dominant political/social position to a minority one. Until the last century, there has been no requirement, except in a small number of cases, for this area of *fiqh* to develop, as jurists were more concerned in concentrating on Muslim-dominant situations; now however the need demands this *ijtihād*.

In the following chapters, we will discuss in detail the traditional hermeneutic approach and the legal applications it makes possible for Muslims living as minorities. For now, we will give a brief review of the literature available on this subject from the traditional perspective. The immediate conclusion is that there is a serious dearth of literature on traditional hermeneutics. One essay that will be interrogated later, in fact the only one we believe which elaborates the traditional approach is Abou El-Fadl's 'Islamic Law and Muslim Minorities'.[84] However, this essay is predominantly, if not exclusively, about political abodes, namely *dār al-ḥarb* and *dār al-Islām*, rather than a detailed methodology of how to derive rulings for minority Muslims; as its focus is mostly political, we will discuss it further in the chapter on politics (Chapter V). The only other essay we have found is by Kathryn Miller, who translates and discusses two *fatwā*s by jurists from the Mālikī law School regarding emigration of Muslims in areas of al-Andalūs that had been conquered by Christian forces.[85] Again due to the

[83] Tariq Ramadan, *Islam, the West and the Challenges of Modernity* (Leicester: The Islamic Foundation, 2001), p. 324.

[84] Khaled Abou El-Fadl, 'Islamic Law and Muslim Minorities: The Juristic Discourse on Muslim Minorities from the Second/Eighth to the Eleventh/Seventeenth Centuries', *Islamic Law and Society* (vol. 1, no. 2, 1994, pp. 141-87).

[85] Kathryn Miller, 'Muslim Minorities and the Obligation to Emigrate to Islamic Territory: Two *Fatwās* from Fifteenth-Century Granada', *Islamic Law and Society* (vol. 7, no. 2, 2000, pp. 256-88).

contents of this essay it is more appropriate to detail it in the political domains chapter. Aside from these two articles, we could not locate a single academic piece of work applying traditional Islamic hermeneutic methodologies and processes with a view of helping minorities derive legal rulings. This we believe is due to the specialist nature of the task which requires expertise in both traditional Islamic Law and western academic principles. We hope that this present work will provide a step forward in this area.

Finally, before moving on to the next chapter, in which we will discuss how traditional Islamic Law, with a particular emphasis on the Ḥanafī School, can be applied to minority-status Muslims both in private and public matters, we would like to conclude this section with a summary. The literature review shows that in terms of engaging with the Islamic religious sources three hermeneutic models have been and are applied by Islamic scholars: literalism, liberalism/modernism and traditionalism. All three interpretive models claim to interpret God's Words and to explain what He intends by them. Literalists claim that no interpretation is required nor is it permissible, whereas liberals/modernists assert that one must interpret the sources until they comply with current social demands and principles. The remaining model, the traditional, adopts the middle path and argues for a rational system not subject to change but which has an inherent flexibility to allow it to be relevant for all times and all peoples. In addition, it is claimed that its robustness can be verified by the fact that it has existed for 1400 years and is still going strong, and—to this day—continues to influence the lives of the majority of Sunni Muslims worldwide.

Ontologically there is agreement across the three views in that God is the source of the Law. Their differences lie in their epistemology, which is scriptural in its pure and absolute form for the literalists, society-focused in the case of the liberals and a combination of the two for the traditionalists.

Our position is that Islam—or more accurately its sources—is considered to be a tradition and more specifically a discursive tradition, which must apply its historically tried and tested principles and methodologies in order to ascertain God's will. The view that liberal rationalism is required as an interpretive model instead of traditionalism, because the latter is not suited to the modern world, is flawed in at least three ways: firstly, liberal rationalism is in itself a tradition; it cannot claim neutrality and it cannot be given exceptional status but must be regarded as a tradition amongst traditions. Secondly, traditions are incommensurable which means that the premises and views within liberalism cannot be applied to religious traditionalism and neither can it claim unbiased accuracy and exclusive truthfulness. Thirdly, incommensurability does not permit modernist scholars the legal or philosophical position of assuming and declaring an epistemological crisis within traditionalism as they are not traditionally trained and only know the model superficially.

We believe that traditionalism has been applied throughout the history of Islam up to, and including, the present day by diverse ethnic groups in wide-ranging geographical, political and social situations. Muslims, however, have tended to live in Muslim-majority states. This situation has changed over the last century due to mass migration to Western Europe and North America. To date, it has been mostly assumed that traditional methods will no longer be applicable nor flexible enough for this new environment and hence a new hermeneutic model is required. According to our knowledge, the application of the traditional model within a minority context has not been sufficiently investigated and it is our aim in this work to explore the application of the traditional hermeneutical model to the situation of Muslims living as minorities.

CHAPTER III

The Traditional Ḥanafī Legal Approach

THE VIEW OF THIS STUDY is that the traditional hermeneutical model has not been sufficiently investigated in order to determine its applicability and usefulness in a new era and environment, namely the twenty-first century and Western countries where Muslims are in a minority. In order to examine this traditional model, we need to take as an example one of the traditional Schools of Law. As all the traditional Schools of Law have had similar developments and modus operandi, focusing on one School will be sufficient for our purpose. We have chosen the Ḥanafī School as it has the most adherents in the world. This chapter will give the history of the Ḥanafī School through the biographies of its founders and through its foundational texts. We will then introduce a number of processes and procedures to demonstrate how Ḥanafī *muftī*s (legal experts) arrive at answers to legal questions and will follow this with a general discussion of the Islamic legal theory or the principles of *fiqh* (*uṣūl al-fiqh*). We shall argue that these processes and procedures are still valid and can be applied to Muslims in any era or place.

Founders of the Ḥanafī Legal School

Abū Ḥanīfa Nuʿmān b. Thābit: Nuʿmān b. Thābit b. Zūta b. Mah, better known by his agnomen Abū Ḥanīfa, was born in Kūfa, Iraq, in 80/699. Abū Ḥanīfa initially worked as a trader and established a silk-weaving factory;[1] but after mistakenly being taken for a student by the *fiqh* scholar Imām Shaʿbī of Kūfa, he turned to an educational career.[2] He devoted a significant number of years

[1] Muḥammad Sulaymān, *al-Mu'taṣar al-ḍarūrī: sharḥ lī al-mukhtaṣar al-qudūrī* (Karachi: Idārat al-Qur'ān wa'l-ʿUlūm al-Islāmiyya, 2004), p. 7.

[2] Muḥammad Ṣiddīqī, *Rawḍat al-azhār: sharḥ lī kitāb al-āthār* (Karachi: Zam Zam Publishers, 2001), pp. 106-07.

to the study of theology (*ʿilm al-kalām*) until he realised that the Companions of the Prophet did not spend as much time on *kalām* as they did on *fiqh*. It is said that the need for *fiqh* was crystallised in his mind when a woman asked him how a man divorces his wife according to the Sunna. He told her to go to Ḥammād b. Abū Sulaymān al-Ashʿarī's school and to ask the imam there; and he requested that she tell him the answer on her return. After hearing the answer and realising his lack of knowledge of *fiqh*, Abū Ḥanīfa joined Ḥammād's classes until the latter's death in 120/737. Ḥammād had been the last surviving representative of the legal school of the Companion ʿAbd Allāh b. Masʿūd (d. c. 30/650). He had studied Law with Ibrāhīm al-Nakhaʿī (d. 97/714) and Shaʿbī, who had both studied with Shurayḥ (d. 76/695), ʿAlqama b. Qays (d. 62/681) and Masrūq b. al-Ajdaʿ (d. 62/681). Both Shurayḥ and Masrūq had studied in the teaching circles of the two Companions ʿAbd Allāh b. Masʿūd and ʿAlī b. Abū Tālib.[3] Although Abū Ḥanīfa had other teachers of Law, Ḥammād had a lasting impression on him.

In terms of Abū Ḥanīfa's teachers of *ḥadīth* it is reported that they exceeded ninety in Kūfa alone; some of them were Shaʿbī Salama b. Kuḥayl, Muharrib b. Dithār, Abū Isḥāq Sabʿi, Aʿmash, and ʿAlqama b. Murthid. The second city in Iraq where he received education in *ḥadīth* was Baṣra, where he studied under Shuʿba and Qatāda. He also travelled to the two holy sanctuaries of Mecca and Medina in search of *ḥadīth* knowledge. In Mecca, he studied under ʿAṭā' b. Abū Rabāḥ and ʿIkrima; and in Medina he studied under Sulaymān and Salīm b. ʿAbd Allāh.[4]

During Ḥammād's life, Abū Ḥanīfa did not—out of respect for his teacher—have his own circles of teaching. However, after the death of his teacher, Abū Ḥanīfa set up his own school and became famous far and wide for his piety, intellect, and deep understanding of jurisprudence. His school spread throughout the Islamic empire due to his students, especially Qāḍī Abū Yūsuf, Muḥammad al-Shaybānī and Ẓufar b. al-Huẓayl.

After a disagreement with the Abbasid Caliph Mansūr over Abū Ḥanīfa's

[3] Asʿad Saʿīd, *al-Fiqh al-ḥanafi wa-adillatu*, vol. 1 (Karachi: Idārat al-Qur'ān wa'l-ʿUlūm al-Islāmiyya, 2003), p. 19.

[4] Hadi Hussain, *Imam Abu Hanifah: Life and Work*, English translation of Allahmah Shibli Nuʿmani's *Sirat-i-nuʿman* (New Delhi: Idārat Ishāʿāt-e-Dīnīyat, 1995), pp. 32-39.

suspected sympathy for the Zaydī[5] rebels and his refusal to accept an official legal position within the court, Abū Ḥanīfa was sent to prison in 146/763.[6] But, even in prison, he continued with his teaching. (In fact, it was in prison that Muḥammad b. al-Ḥasan al-Shaybānī received his education.) Abū Ḥanīfa died in prison in 150/767 of suspected poisoning. He was buried in the graveyard at Khayzrān and funeral prayers were performed for him for twenty days.[7]

Abū Ḥanīfa left no actual books, but the books of his students contain his dictations or notes taken down during the lessons he gave.[8] Part of his importance lies in his closeness to the earlier generation of Muslims; he is considered to be a *Tābiᶜ*, i.e., of the generation that came directly after the Companions of the Prophet.[9]

Qāḍī Abū Yūsuf Yaᶜqūb b. Ibrāhīm: Qāḍī Abū Yūsuf Yaᶜqūb b. Ibrāhīm b. Ḥabīb al-Anṣārī was born around 113/731 in Kufa to a poor family. He was fond of learning from an early age but his father needed him to earn a living and removed him from Abū Ḥanīfa's classes. Abū Ḥanīfa found out about this and personally took on the financial responsibility for Abū Yūsuf's education until the latter acquired mastery of all the taught sciences and became an acknowledged authority.[10] Abū Yūsuf was appointed as *qāḍī* in 166/783 by the Abbasid Caliph[11] a role he retained until eventually he was made *Qāḍī al-Quḍāt* (Chief Justice) of the whole realm; the first ever occurrence of this position in Islam.[12] He is thought to have memorised one hundred thousand *ḥadīth* and was granted the title of *Ḥāfiẓ al-Ḥadīth* (Memoriser of *Ḥadīth*).[13] Abū Yūsuf died in 182/804.

Muḥammad b. al-Ḥasan al-Shaybānī: Abū ᶜAbd Allāh Muḥammad b.

[5] Zaydis were followers of Zayd ibn ᶜAlī, the grandson of Ḥusayn ibn ᶜAlī, who is considered as the fifth Imam in Shiᶜism. Zaydī *fiqh* is similar to the *fiqh* of the Ḥanafī School. Abu Ḥanīfa was suspected of supporting their cause by issuing a *fatwā* in their favour.

[6] Abdulwahab El-Affendi, *Who Needs an Islamic State?* (London: Malaysia Think Tank London, 2008), p. 72.

[7] Hussain, *Imam Abu Hanifah: Life and Work*, pp. 39-40.

[8] Saᶜīd, *al-Fiqh al-ḥanafīwa-adillatu*, p. 22.

[9] Abdur Rahman Yusuf, *Fiqh al-Imam: Key Proofs in Hanafi Fiqh*, pp. 22-23.

[10] Hussain, *Imam Abu Hanifah: Life and Work*, pp. 210-11.

[11] Baber Johansen, *Contingency in Sacred Law*, p. 25.

[12] Abd al-Ḥayy al-Laknawī, 'Introduction' in Shaybānī's *al-Jāmiᶜ al-ṣaghīr maᶜ sharḥ al-nāfiᶜ al-kabīr* (Karachi: Idārat al-Qur'ān, 2004), p. 29.

[13] Sulaymān, *al-Mu'taṣar al-ḍarūrī*, p. 9.

al-Ḥasan b. Farqād[14] al-Shaybānī was born in 132/750 in Wāsiṭ[15] and subsequently raised in Kūfa.[16] He studied for approximately two years under Imām Abū Ḥanīfa. Most of his education in *fiqh* was with Abū Yūsuf in Iraq, Mālik in Ḥijāz, Awzāᶜī (d. 157/774) in Shām (Greater Syria) and Thawrī in Iraq 161/778. Through his studies with these and other great scholars, Shaybānī was able to combine the various legal schools of the time.[17] He was appointed as *Qāḍī* by Caliph Hārūn al-Rashīd in al-Raqqā. Shaybānī passed away in 189/811.[18] One of his students was Imām al-Shāfiᶜī, the founder of the Shāfiᶜī School of law.

Ẓufar b. al-Huẓayl: Though Ẓufar b. al-Huẓayl b. Qays al-Baṣrī (110/728-158/775) is reported to have been a greater master of *fiqh* than Shaybānī, little is known of him and none of his writings survive. Originally his interests were in *ḥadīth*, to such an extent that he was known as *Ṣāḥib al-Ḥadīth* (Master of *Ḥadīth*). Later he turned to *fiqh*. He was particularly skilled in analogical reasoning and Abū Ḥanīfa held him in high esteem in this field. Wakīᶜ b. al-Jarrāḥ (d. 198/814), a renowned expert in *fiqh* and *ḥadīth*, used to regularly consult him due to his recognised expertise.[19]

Foundational Texts of the Ḥanafī Legal School

A number of books have been ascribed to Imām Abū Ḥanīfa, however, there is much debate about whether he actually authored any books. Ibn Nadīm, Kawtharī, Tash Kubrā, Bazzāzī state that Abū Ḥanīfa authored books. Shiblī Nuᶜmānī states that he did not; however, Nuᶜmānī does not preclude that Abū Ḥanīfa may have dictated works to his students. In our opinion, Abū Ḥanīfa may not have physically written any books; however, he would have certainly dictated to his students, which makes him an author. Some of the titles ascribed to him are *al-Fiqh al-akbar*, *Kitāb al-ᶜalim wa'l-mutaᶜallim*, *Kitāb al-athār* and *Kitāb al-rad ᶜalā al-qadariyya*. The latter text is no longer extant.[20]

Abū Yūsuf did author a number of books, for example *Kitāb al-kharāj*.

[14] Abd al-Ḥayy al-Laknawī states his grandfather to be Farqād whilst Muḥammad Sulaymān believes it to be Waqīd. We agree with the former.

[15] Saᶜīd, *al-Fiqh al-ḥanafī wa-adillatu*, vol. 1, p. 31.

[16] Hussain, *Imam Abu Hanifah: Life and Work*, p. 10.

[17] Saᶜīd, *al-Fiqh al-ḥanafiwa-adillatu*, vol. 1, p. 31.

[18] Ibid.

[19] Hussain, *Imam Abu Hanifah: Life and Work*, pp. 218-19.

[20] Ṣiddīqī, *Rawḍat al-azhār*, pp. 115-16.

However, it is Imām Muḥammad al-Shaybānī who was the most prolific writer of the Ḥanafī School, to such an extent that his books are the ones used by the School today. The following is a list of his works in which he cites Abū Ḥanīfa's expositions—either directly or through the link of Abū Yūsuf—and which are therefore considered as the foundational texts of the Ḥanafī Law School:[21]

1. *Al-Mabsūṭ*: Although originally written by Abū Yūsuf, Shaybānī revised it, making the exposition clearer; this was his first work. It contains over ten thousand questions and answers on legal issues. *Al-Mabsūṭ* was memorised by Imām Shāfiʿī, the founder of the Shāfiʿī School of Law, who based his book *al-Umm* on it.[22]
2. *Al-Jāmiʿ al-ṣaghīr:* This was written after *al-Mabsūṭ*. In this text, Shaybānī quotes the dicta of Abū Ḥanīfa on the authority of Abū Yūsuf, dealing with five hundred and thirty-three questions; over a third of these questions had a number of different responses to them. The questions fall into three categories: i) those mentioned only in this book, ii) those mentioned in other books of Shaybānī, but not explicitly taken from Abū Ḥanīfa's rulings, iii) and those mentioned in other books of Shaybānī, but included here in words that give them a new significance.
3. *Al-Jāmiʿ al-kabīr*: This was written after *al-Jāmiʿ al-ṣaghīr* and is a voluminous work which contains quotations of the dicta of Abū Ḥanīfa, Abū Yūsuf and Ẓufar. On every question the methods of argumentation have also been stated. Later Ḥanafī scholars formulated their legal theory or principles of *fiqh* (*uṣūl al-fiqh*) on the basis of the method of reasoning followed in this work. Many eminent jurists wrote commentaries on it, of which forty-two have been mentioned in Ḥajjī Khalīfa's *Kashf al-ẓunūn*.
4. *Al-Ziyādāt*. As its name suggests, this is a supplement to *al-Jāmiʿ al-kabīr*.[23]
5. *Al-Siyar al-ṣaghīr.*
6. *Al-Siyar al-kabīr*: *Al-Siyar al-ṣaghīr* (the Lesser *Siyar*) was Shaybānī's penultimate work. Upon its completion, Awzāʿī commented that the

[21] Hussain, *Imam Abu Hanifah: Life and Work*, pp. 217-18.

[22] Ṣiddīqī, *Rawḍat al-azhār*, p. 102.

[23] Ibid., p. 104.

Iraqi scholars were in no position to write on the subject of *Siyar*.[24] When this remark reached Shaybānī, he started to write *al-Siyar al-kabīr* (the Greater *Siyar*). When completed, it consisted of sixty chapters.

Ḥanafī jurists refer to the above six books as *Ẓāhir al-riwāya* (the Evident Narration or Clear Transmission). Aside from the *Ẓāhir al-riwāya*, Imām Shaybānī authored other books of *fiqh* mostly on judicial issues; among these are *Kitāb al-nawādir*,[25] *al-Jurjāniyyāt*[26], *al-Kaysāniyyāt*[27], *al-Raqqiyyāt*[28] and *al-Hārūniyyāt*.

The *Ẓāhir al-riwāya* became the foundational texts upon which later scholars built the Ḥanafī School of Law. In fact, these books gained such popularity that they became *the* reference works for judicial rulings consistent with the Ḥanafī School. In order to make it easier for students to gain mastery of the contents of these books and thereby understand the underlying principles of Ḥanafī law, a jurist of the fourth Hijri century, Imām al-Ḥākim al-Shāhid Muḥammad al-Marwazī, produced a summary which he named *al-Kāfī fī furūᶜ al-ḥanafiyya*; it is often referred to by its shorter name *al-Kāfī*. In the fifth Hijri century, another great scholar, Muḥammad b. Aḥmad al-Sarakhsī wrote a thirty-volume commentary on *al-Kāfī*. This treatise titled *al-Mabsūṭ* is considered one of the most popular and authoritative expositions of Islamic Law as understood and expounded by the Ḥanafī jurists.

After the early period, numerous summaries—referred to as *al-mutūn al-muᶜtabara* (texts which are relied upon)—which contain the most reliable legal positions of Imām Abū Ḥanīfa and his School were written. Among these are:[29]

1. *Al-Mukhtaṣar al-qudūrī* by Imām Abū al-Ḥasan Aḥmad al-Qudūrī (d. 428/1037). A very popular *matn* that is employed worldwide to introduce students to Ḥanafī *fiqh*.
2. *Tuḥfat al-fuqahā'* by Imām Muḥammad b. Aḥmad al-Samarqandī (d.

[24] *Siyar* is the conduct of state affairs, especially within an international context. Awzāᶜī's view was that Iraq, had little to no contact with the non-Muslim world, especially in matters of trade, warfare and general political relationship, whereas the Syrians regularly came into contact with the Christians through the Crusades and the neighbouring European states.

[25] Transmitted by Ibrāhīm b. Rustum.

[26] Transmitted by ᶜAlī b. Ṣāliḥ al-Jurjānī.

[27] Also called *al-Amānī*, transmitted by Shuᶜayb b. Sulaymān al-Kaysānī.

[28] This is a collection of the judicial rulings that Shaybānī gathered during his time as a *qāḍī* in *Raqqat*.

[29] Muḥammad Manṣūrpūrī, *Fatāwā nawaysī kay rahnumā uṣūl* (Karachi: Maktaba Nuᶜmāniyya, 2001), p. 164; Imran Nyazee, 'Introduction' in A. Marghīnānī's *Al-Hidāyah: The Guidance* (Bristol: Amal Press, 2006), pp. ix-xxxii.

538/1143). This *matn* also has a commentary on it by Kasānī called *Badāiᶜ al-ṣanāiᶜ*.

3. *Kitāb bidāyat al-mubtadī* by Imām Abū al-Ḥasan ᶜAlī al-Marghīnānī (d. 593/1196). This includes the *masā'il* (transmitted legal opinions) from Abū Ḥanīfa's *al-Jāmiᶜ al-ṣaghīr* and Qudūrī's *al-Mukhtaṣar al-qudūrī*. Marghīnānī also wrote a commentary called *al-Hidāya*.[30]
4. *Wiqāyat al-riwāya fī masā'il al-hidāya* by Imām Tāj al-Sharīᶜa Maḥmūd al-Sharīᶜa (d. 673/1274) is a summary of *al-Hidāya* by Marghīnānī.
5. *Al-Mukhtār lī al-fatwā* by Imām Abū Faḍl ᶜAbd Allāh al-Mawsilī (d 683/1284). This text is used at al-Azhar University as a standard Ḥanafī law textbook.
6. *Majmaᶜ al-baḥrayn* by Imām Aḥmad b. ᶜAlī Saᶜatī al-Baᶜlabakkī (d. 694/1295).
7. *Kanz al-daqā'iq* by Imām Abū al-Barakāt Hāfiẓ al-Dīn ᶜAbd Allāh al-Nasafī (d. 710/1310). It has two commentaries on it: *al-Baḥr al-rā'iq* by Ibn Nujaym and *Tabyīn al-ḥaqā'iq* by Zayla'ī.
8. *Al-Niqāya* by Imām Ṣadr al-Sharīᶜa ᶜUbayd Allāh al-Ḥanafī (d. 745/1344). A summary of his grandfather's book *Wiqāyat al-riwāya*.
9. *Multaqā al-baḥr* by Imām Ibrāhīm b. Muḥammad al-Ḥalabī (d. 956/1549). This text is based on the *Mutūn al-muᶜtabara*.

Imām Ibn ᶜĀbidīn in his *Sharḥ rasm al-muftī* describes the *mutūn*: 'It is obvious that what is intended by *al-Mutūn* is *al-Mutūn al-muᶜtabara* like *al-Bidāya*, *Mukhtaṣar al-qudūrī*, *al-Mukhtār*, *al-Niqāya*, *al-Wiqāya*, *al-Kanz* and *al-Multaqā*; for indeed they contain the *madhhab* [the School of Law].'[31] Other jurists have allocated a different ranking for these, and other, texts. According to one view the most reliable are three: *Mukhtaṣar al-qudūrī*, *Kanz al-daqā'iq* and *Wiqāya*. Others include *al-Mukhtār lī al-fatwā* and *Majmaᶜ al-baḥrayn*.[32]

Aside from the above groupings, Ḥanafī textbooks have, more recently, been divided into three according to historical divisions: ancient, classical

[30] Ya'akov Meron, Research Note: Marghīnānī, his Method and his Legacy', *Islamic Law and Society* (vol. 9, no. 3, 2002), p. 414.

[31] Muḥammad Ibn ᶜĀbidīn, *Sharḥ ᶜuqūd rasm al-muftī* (Karachi: Qadīmī Kutub Khāna, no date), pp. 29-30.

[32] Manṣūrpūrī, *Fatāwā nawaysī kay rahnumā uṣūl*, p. 164; Laknawī, 'Introduction' in Shaybānī's *al-Jāmiᶜ al-ṣaghīr*, p. 23; Sulaymān, *al-Mu'taṣar al-ḍarūrī*,p. 15.

and post-classical;[33] and sometimes according to the geographical locations of the authors. The texts that are said to belong to the ancient period are: Shaybānī's *al-Aṣl* (a collective noun for Shaybānī's six books), Ṭaḥāwī's (d. 321/933) *Mukhtaṣar* and Abū al-Layth al-Samarqandī's (d. 375/983) *Khizānat al-fiqh*. It is argued that in this period there was a certain lack of order and a lack of justification for the reasons that underlie the legal solutions; the last of the above mentioned texts saw the beginning of a change in this. Ya'akov Meron argues that this era reflected 'a young system of law, started chaotically and developing with an increasing measure of systemisation.'[34]

Following Meron's classification, the classical period starts with Qudūrī's (d. 428/1037) *Mukhtaṣar*, Sarakhsī's (d. 490/1097) *Mabsūṭ* and ʿAlā' al-Dīn al-Samarqandī's (d. 539/1144) *Tuḥfat al-fuqahā'*. Within this period Ḥanafī *fiqh* is said to have reached its pinnacle with Kāsānī's (d. 587/1191) *Badāiʿ al-ṣanāiʿ*. Meron argues that the development in *fiqh* during this period and the utilisation of *ijtihād* (independent reasoning by jurists to obtain legal rulings) clearly challenges and refutes the assertion that the doors of independent reasoning were closed at the beginning of the fourth century.[35] Finally, for Meron the post-classical period was initiated by Burhān al-Dīn al-Marghīnānī's (593/1197) *Hidāya*. He asserts that in the post-classical period a slavish approach is adopted in contrast to 'the spirit of independence which animates the Classical texts', that in the classical period, Samarqandī and Kāsānī introduced new terminology and brought about a new systemisation, and that none of this is seen in Marghīnānī's and his successors' works.[36]

Figure 2 opposite displays the various texts during the three eras, described with modifications from Meron's thesis (based on Baber Johansen)[37] as Sarakhsī was located in Transoxania (roughly corresponding to modern day Uzbekistan) and never left for Syria (as Meron suggests) and as Kāsānī was a mature jurist before he travelled from Transoxania to Syria.

[33] Professor Chafik Chehata first suggested this division. See also Ya'akov Meron, 'The Development of Legal Thought in Hanafi Texts', *Studia Islamica* (vol. 30, 1969).

[34] Ibid., pp. 73-75.

[35] Ibid., pp. 90-91.

[36] Ibid., p. 93.

[37] Baber Johansen, 'Casuistry: Between Legal Concept and Social Praxis', *Islamic Law and Society* (vol. 2, no. 2, 1995), p. 139.

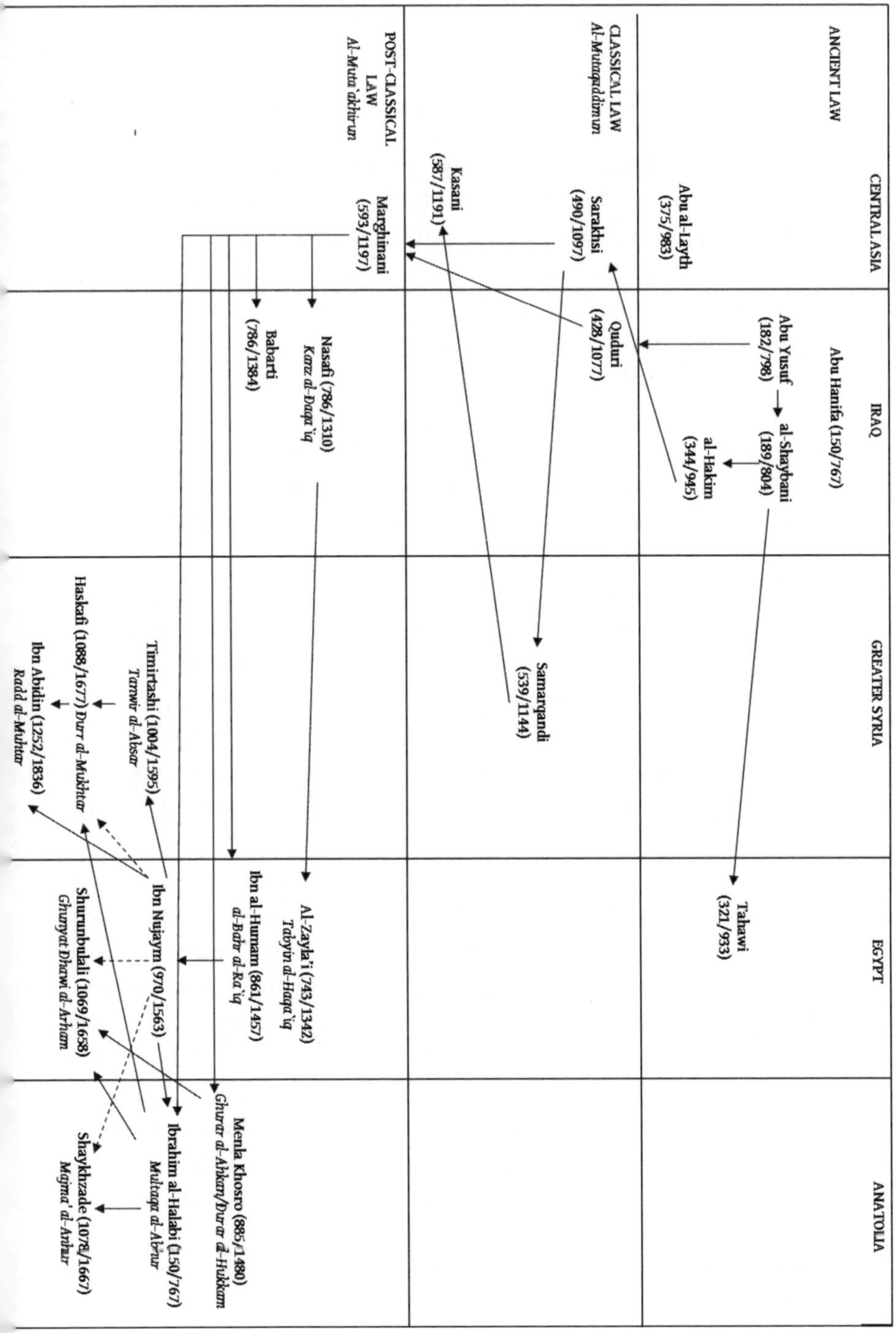

Figure 2: Historical and Geographical Representation of the Key Jurists of the Ḥanafī Law School

The Divisions of Legal Opinions

The titles we have listed above deal mostly with legal opinions (*masāʾil*) or are collections of legal opinions. Legal opinions, however, are of different rank; so when there is a conflict between two views there must be a way to prioritise one over the other. Imām al-Kūfī states in *al-ᶜĀlam al-akbar*:

> The legal opinions of the first rank (*masāʾil al-uṣūl*) are the *masāʾil* found in *Ẓāhir al-riwāya*: the *masāʾil* of *al-Mabsūṭ* by Muḥammad [Shaybānī] which is also referred to as *al-Aṣl*, the *masāʾil* of *al-Jāmiᶜ al-ṣaghīr* and *al-Jāmiᶜ al-kabīr* and *al-Siyar* [both *al-Ṣaghīr* and *al-Kabīr* are inferred] and *al-Ziyādāt*; all of these have been authored by Muḥammad b. al-Ḥasan [Shaybānī]. Included also…are the *masāʾil* of *Kitāb al-muntaqā* of al-Ḥākim al-Shāhid—this is also a foundational text of the School after the books of Muḥammad b. al-Ḥasan.
>
> The second rank of legal opinions are the *masāʾil* found in other than the *Ẓāhir al-riwāya* or quoted from leading scholars in other than the above-mentioned books; either in the other books of Muḥammad [Shaybānī] like *al-Kaysāniyyāt, al-Raqqiyyāt, al-Jurjāniyyāt* and *al-Hārūniyyāt*, and other books like *al-Mujarrad* by al-Ḥasan b. Ziyād; or those books dictated by the founding scholars which were written down by students and which are called *al-Nawādir*, like the *Nawādir* of Ibn Samāᶜ, *Nawādir* of Hishām and *Nawādir* of Ibn Rustum.
>
> The legal opinions of the third rank are called *al-wāqiᶜāt* and they are those *masāʾil* that were arrived at by later scholars from among the companions of Shaybānī or the companions of his companions. The first book that was authored on this subject was by Abū al-Layth al-Samarqandī, called *al-Nawāzil*. He gathered in it the legal edict (*fatāwā*) of the later *mujtahidūn* (scholars qualified to give legal opinions) from his teachers and the teachers of his teachers, like Muḥammad b. Muqātil al-Rāzī, Muḥammad b. Salama and Nusayr b. Yaḥya. Then this process of collation and addition continued with the likes of *al-Jāmiᶜ* by Qāḍī Khān and *Kitāb al-khulāṣa*, etc.[38]

Ibn ᶜĀbidīn, in his book *Radd al-muḥtār ᶜala'l-durr al-mukhtār*, says:

> The legal opinions of the first rank are also referred to as *ẓāhir al-riwāya*. They are the *masāʾil* quoted from the founders of the School (*aṣḥāb*

[38] Laknawī, 'Introduction' in Shaybānī's *al-Jāmiᶜ al-ṣaghīr*, pp. 17-18. See also, Hallaq, 'From Fatwās to Furū: Growth and Change in the Islamic Substantive Law', *Islamic Law and Society* (vol. 1, no. 1, 1994), p. 39.

> *al-madhhab*), namely: Abū Ḥanīfa, Abū Yūsuf and Muḥammad [Shaybānī], Ẓufar, al-Ḥasan b. Ziyād and others who took from the Imām [Abū Ḥanīfa] are also included, however it is widely understood and accepted that it is the opinion of the [first] three. The books of *Ẓāhir al-riwāya* are the six books of Muḥammad [Shaybānī].
>
> The second rank of legal opinions are *masā'il al-nawādir*; they are quotations of our companions mentioned above, but not in the [six] mentioned books [of Shaybānī].[39]

The third rank of *masā'il* are identical to those of Kūfī above.

This distinction between the three ranks was somewhat blurred after ᶜAlā' al-Dīn al-Samarqandī's *Tuḥfat al-fuqahā'*, whereby the collections of *fatāwā* were mixed with the collections in *Ẓāhir al-riwāya* and in those of the *Nawādir*; two such works are *Fatāwā Qāḍīkhān* and *al-Khulāṣa*. One can conclude that it would have been preferable to maintain the initial order and divisions; however, the increasing importance of the *fatāwā* overrode this desirability,[40] as they brought about a balance between the theoretical *Ẓāhir al-riwāya* based on the sources and the pragmatic rulings based on the practical application of the law.

The evidence for the fact that *fatāwā* became a significant part of the foundational texts can be seen in *Kanz al-daqā'iq*, an authoritative work which has attracted many commentaries. In it, Ḥāfiẓ al-Dīn al-Nasafī acknowledges that he included in his work '*masā'il al-fatāwā wa'l-wāqiᶜāt*.' Furthermore, Ibn Nujaym (d. 790/1563), commenting on Nasafī's work, states that he drew on approximately twenty *fatwā* collections some of which were *al-Muḥīt* (Raḍī al-Dīn al-Sarakhsī), *al-Dhakhīra* (Ibn Māza), *al-Badā'iᶜ, al-Ziyādāt, Fatāwā qāḍīkhān, al-Ẓahīriyya* (Muḥammad b. Aḥmad al-Ḥanafī), *al-Walwālijiyya* (Isḥāq b. Abū Bakr al-Walwāliji), *al-Khulāṣa* (Sirāj al-Dīn b. al-Mulaqqīn), *al-Bazzāziyya* (Ibn Bazzāz al-Kurdarī) and *al-Sirājiyya* (Sirāj al-Dīn al-Awshī).[41] Ibn ᶜĀbidīn in his *Ḥāshiya ᶜalā radd al-muḥtār* also relied heavily on *fatwā* literature and he constantly referred to those who were 'committed to the study and issuance of *fatāwā*', including Ibn al-Humām, Ibn Amīr al-Ḥajj, Ramlī, Ibn Nujaym, Ibn Shalabī, Ismāᶜīl, al-Ḥa'ik and Ḥanūtī.[42]

39 Laknawī, 'Introduction' in Shaybānī's *al-Jāmiᶜ al-ṣaghīr*, pp. 18-19.

40 Hallaq, 'From Fatwās to Furū: Growth and Change in the Islamic Substantive Law', p. 40.

41 Zayn al-ᶜĀbidīn Ibn Nujaym, *al-Baḥr al-rā'iq: sharḥ kanz al-daqā'iq* (Cairo: al-Maṭbaᶜa al-ᶜIlmiyya, 1893).

42 Hallaq, 'From Fatwās to Furū: Growth and Change in the Islamic Substantive Law', p. 42.

The fact that the order of priority from *masā'il* to *fatāwā* is being challenged, and to some extent the third level is being amalgamated with—and even taking priority over—the first two, means that some instructions are required for those who are in a position to issue *fatāwā* (the *muftīs*) so that they can discern between the various levels of legal opinions and issue *fatāwā* according to the School's position. Awzajandī states that if the case is found in *Ẓāhir al-riwāya* without disagreement between the founders of the School then it must be accepted, if it is with disagreement then it is Abū Ḥanīfa's view, not that of his two main students', that must be accepted. However, if the disagreement is related to the needs of a later age, then the view of his two students must be accepted on the premise that 'conditions of people do change.' The reason for this is because Abū Ḥanīfa was issuing legal opinions approximately half a century before his two main students and Awzajandī recognised that culture and society had changed since that time, therefore, the latter's view was more accurate as the context had to be taken into consideration. This same principle is applied when selecting between differing views of the early and later centuries. For example, Ibn ᶜĀbidīn asserts that a substantial segment of Ḥanafī law was formulated in the later centuries by jurists who on occasions held different views than those of the founders. Furthermore, Khayr al-Dīn al-Ramlī (d. 1082/1671) followed the Ḥanafī methodology of issuing *fatāwā* and he included opinions of jurists who had modified 'the earlier doctrines due to the difference in time or to the changing conditions of society.'[43] Thus, the new legal literature—in the form of *shurūḥ* (commentaries) and *fatāwā* (religious-legal edicts)—which departs from the *mutūn* (foundational texts) became the basis for the issuing of *fatāwā*. Having said that, both remain valid. The *mutūn* are utilised for teaching purposes and are applied in some cases, whilst the *shurūḥ* and *fatāwā* are applied in the judicial process.[44]

The argument for the above was that the questioner's circumstances need to be taken into consideration and changing conditions justify changing certain rules in order to bring them into conformity with the needs of the society in question. Ramlī, when referring to this procedure, states that the texts have been altered; in fact he states in stronger terms that they are 'corrected (*ṣaḥḥaḥa*) by the main jurists of the School due to the changing times or the changes of the conditions of the people.'[45] This method of 'correction' became known as *taṣḥīḥ*. *Tarjīḥ*

[43] Ibid., pp. 49-50.

[44] Johansen, *Contingency in Sacred Law*, p. 463.

[45] Hallaq, 'From Fatwās to Furū: Growth and Change in the Islamic Substantive Law', p. 53.

is another method brought about for the same reasons; it is a method of prioritising a view when there are a number of apparently conflicting views.[46] The argument that is usually levelled against individuals who today strive to obtain an answer different from former scholars, especially from the founders of the School, is that they are deviating from the sources or the authoritative position of the School. This is incorrect, as both *taṣḥīḥ* and *tarjīḥ* illustrate that the School acknowledged the possibility of change and established methods by which this could be achieved. Therefore, new rulings cannot be considered as going contrary to the School's view and deviating from legally sound and accepted opinions. Raḥamānī re-emphasises what has already been stated and gives an example:

> In India, in the recent past if one investigates the *fatāwā* of Mawlānā Muftī Kifāyat Allāh Ṣāḥib, Mawlānā Ashraf ʿAlī Thānwī and Mawlānā Muftī Muḥammad Shāfiʿī Ṣaḥib one will see that they were very careful and strove courageously with intellect and wisdom to answer the questions submitted. An accusation levelled against them is that they were short sighted in their thinking or that whenever something new arose then they preferred to adopt a strict line; this is not correct. The answer is that experts in every field change their view depending on circumstances and developments. A good example is hearing the prayer via the loud speaker. Initially, after thorough research it was agreed that the voice form the speaker was not the actual voice of the Imām but rather like an 'echo'. Then, later research showed it to be his original voice; hence it is obvious that initially one fatwā was issued and then subsequently another.[47]

With changing social, medicinal and technological developments, or with the changes in social and political systems, Muslims find themselves in new situations. In many cases, the books of Islamic jurisprudence are silent about these new situations. However, traditional methodologies do exist to equip the scholar to deliver Islamic rulings on these developments. This is the realm of what is called *ijtihād*. But in order for us to discuss *ijtihād*, we need to return briefly to the source materials of Islamic law—the Qur'ān and the *Sunna*—we need to discuss three other concepts central to Islamic law and we need to introduce the principles of Islamic legal theory or *uṣūl al-fiqh*.

46 Ibid.

47 Khālid Raḥamānī, *Jadīd fiqhī masā'il* (Karachi: Zam Zam Publishers, 2005) vol. 1, pp. 38-39.

Qur'ān, Sunna, Ijmā^c, Qiyās and ^cUrf

As we have mentioned above, the source materials—which will also be referred to occasionally below as the 'text'—for Islamic Law are the Qur'ān and the *Sunna* of the Prophet. With reference to the Qur'ān, it is those verses which detail rulings. Linguistically they can be divided into two categories: the first are verses that are clear and which can have only one meaning; the second are verses that are polysemous and capable of various interpretations.[48] Thus, the rulings derived from the first category require no interpretation and the law is clear and applied, for example, in the verses that state that the eating of pork is prohibited to Muslims. As for those verses that are not self-evident, they must be interpreted in order to derive as sound opinion as possible, which then becomes law.[49]

In order to derive rulings from the *Sunna*, jurists must first discern in which capacity the Prophet spoke: whether as a prophet, as a *muftī*, as a judge, or as a head of state. Qarāfī—who was the first scholar to differentiate these roles—defines the results as: verbatim communications from God, as *fatāwā*, as judicial rulings (*aḥkām*)[50] and as injunctions promulgated by the head of state. With the passing of the Prophet, the roles that were united in him became divided between various individuals of the Islamic community (*umma*): those who memorised of the Qur'ān and the *aḥādīth* continued to preserve the Message, the *muftī*s issued *fatāwā*, the *qāḍīs* passed judgements, and the caliph became the head of state.[51] To the above, Ibn Ashūr adds guidance, conciliation, advice to those seeking his opinion, counselling, spiritual uplifting of people, teaching high and lofty truths, disciplining and non-instructive ordinary statements.[52]

The Qur'ān and *Sunna* do not specify law as is found in law manuals but rather contain instructions and various indications from which the causes of particular rulings (*ᶜilal*) can be effectively deduced. Therefore, the Qur'ān and

[48] Wael Hallaq, 'Non-Analogical Arguments in Sunni Juridical Qiyas', *Arabica* (vol. 36, 1989), p. 287.

[49] Weiss, 'Interpretation in Islamic Law: The Theory of *Ijtihād*', *American Journal of Comparative Law* (vol. 26, 198), p. 203.

[50] While *fatāwā* are legal edicts, *aḥkām* are legally binding judicial rulings expressed by judges and are applied to individuals in a court of law.

[51] Sherman Jackson, 'From Prophetic Action to Constitutional Theory: A Novel Chapter in Medieval Muslim Jurisprudence', *International Journal of Middle East Studies* (vol. 25, no. 1, 1993), p. 74.

[52] Ibn Ashur, *Ibn Ashur: Treatise on Maqāṣid al-Shariᶜah*, p. 34.

Sunna are sources of law not the actual law.[53] While the Qur'ān and the *Sunna* are regarding as divine and divinely-inspired, the actual Law relies on 'human' tools or means to interpret the immutable sources and to ensure that the interpretations are sound and not arbitrary. The means that were arrived at to achieve this are: *ijmāᶜ* (consensus), *qiyās* (analogical reasoning) and *ᶜurf* (culture/customs). We will only give brief definitions for these here as they are discussed in detail in Chapter IV.

Ijmāᶜ is understood to mean the consensus of legal opinion and is based on a number of *aḥādīth* which state that the community of Muslims will not agree on an error.[54] It acts as a safeguard for the Law, in that a majority opinion is more certain than an individual opinion. The feasibility of achieving consensus by all the traditional scholars on all matters is clearly not what is intended nor claimed except on matters which are explicit in the Qur'ān and *mutawātir aḥādīth*.

Qiyās is a methodology used by the four Schools of Law. It is a method of reasoning based upon Aristotelian logic, causal demonstration and non-causal (indicative) demonstration,[55] and it can be applied in three ways: firstly, analogical reasoning which is the application of a known case to a new case;[56] secondly, *a minore ad maius* (*al-tarraqī min al-adnā ilā al-aᶜlā* [i.e. from the smaller to the larger]) and thirdly, *a maiore ad minus* (*al-tarraqī min al-aᶜlā ilā al-adnā* [i.e. from the larger to the smaller]). The first is for cases similar to when the Qur'ān speaks of reward for an atom's worth of good (Q.XCIX.7-8), therefore more than an atom's worth would bring about more equivalent reward, and the second, is for cases when the Qur'ān permits the killing of non-Muslims when in war with Muslims, therefore the taking of their property would also be permissible; the third type of *qiyās* is *reduction ad absurdum* (*al-mafhūm al-mukhālif*) which is to argue the absurdity of a case on the basis of the ruling for another one, however this type of *qiyās* tends not to be adopted by the Ḥanafī School.

Finally, *ᶜurf* is the particular customs and culture of a society. In their edicts and rulings, jurists take into consideration both the customs of a particular society—obviously when these do not contradict the immutable

[53] Weiss, 'Interpretation in Islamic Law: The Theory of *Ijtihād*', p. 199.

[54] Mohammad Hashim Kamali, *Principles of Islamic Jurisprudence* (Cambridge: The Islamic Texts Society, 2003), pp. 240-44.

[55] Wael Hallaq, 'Logic, Formal Arguments and Formalization of Arguments in Sunni Jurisprudence', *Arabica* (vol. 37, no. 3, 1990), pp. 315-57.

[56] Hallaq, *Sharīᶜa: Theory, Practice, Transformations*, p. 105.

sources—and the changing circumstances of societies. This sometimes results in the changing of earlier legal opinions out of consideration for specific circumstances and changing conditions. Abū Ḥanīfa, Shaybānī and Abū Yūsuf differed regarding its applicability. Abū Yūsuf was of the view that a current custom would be preferred to an older one, whereas the former two disagreed. Ibn ᶜĀbidīn quotes a number of cases in which older *ᶜurf* were eventually superseded by new ones: 'Earlier jurists did not allow the permissibility of hiring somebody for teaching the Qur'ān... [For them,] the Qur'ān was to be taught free of charge because teachers were paid by the state.'[57] [As Qur'ān teachers are no longer paid by the state, this situation has changed and requires a modification in the law.]

Brief Introduction to Islamic Legal Theory (Uṣul al-Fiqh)[58]

As we have mentioned above, the source materials for Islamic Law are the Qur'ān and the *Sunna* of the Prophet. But, in reality, there are only a relatively small number of issues that have a clear judgement in either the Qur'ān or the *Sunna*. The founders of the different Schools of Law realised that principles and methods had to be established in order to be able to interpret the source materials. This methodology they called *uṣūl al-fiqh,* or principles of jurisprudence, and it had two purposes: firstly, to understand the contents of the sources; and secondly, to draw conclusions from them.[59] Metaphorically speaking, the 'roots' (*uṣūl*) are what is granted by God, and through human husbandry the 'branches' (*furūᶜ*) or 'fruit' (*thamara*) are what are made to appear.[60]

For Ḥanafī scholars, this methodology was extracted from the foundational texts, in particular from *al-Jāmiᶜ al-kabīr*. It is appropriate at this stage, in order to bring about a better understanding, to introduce *uṣūl al-fiqh*. Mohammad Hashim Kamali states in his *Principles of Islamic Jurisprudence*:

'*Uṣūl al-fiqh* is concerned with the sources of Islamic law, their order of

[57] Mohammed Othman, '*ᶜUrf* as a Source of Islamic Law', *Islamic Studies* (vol. 20, 1981), pp. 345–47.

[58] Research has been carried out on *uṣūl al-fiqh* but in reality, according to Hallaq, 'we have not scratched the surface of this important subject', to which I agree wholeheartedly (Hallaq, 'Considerations on the Function and Character of Sunnī Legal Theory', p. 679). An article that gives an overview of this subject is Hallaq, '*Uṣūl al-fiqh*: Beyond Tradition', pp. 172-202.

[59] Hallaq, 'Considerations on the Function and Character of Sunnī Legal Theory', p. 680.

[60] Weiss, 'Interpretation in Islamic Law: The Theory of *Ijtihād*', p. 199.

priority, and the method by which legal rules may be deduced from the source materials of the *Sharīʿah*. It is also concerned with regulating the exercise of *ijtihād*. The sources of the *Sharīʿah* are of two kinds: revealed and non-revealed. Whereas the former provide the basic evidence and indications from which detailed rules may be derived, the latter provide the methodology and procedural guidelines to ensure correct utilisation of the source evidence. *Uṣūl al-fiqh*, or the roots of Islamic law, thus expound the indications and methodology by which the rules of *fiqh* are deduced from their source evidence. The rules of *fiqh* are thereby derived from the Qur'ān and *Sunnah* in conformity with a body of principles and methods, which are collectively known as *uṣūl al-fiqh*.[61]

Uṣūl al-fiqh is distinctly clear and separate from *fiqh* itself. The former is the methodology employed to achieve the latter. In other words, *fiqh* is the technical juristic details of the law, whereas *uṣūl al-fiqh* is the methodology of the law.[62] The difficulty, for some, to distinguish between *fiqh* and *uṣūl al-fiqh* can partly explain the differing views as to which came first. The two Schools that have developed *uṣūl al-fiqh* most and are specialists in the field are the Ḥanafī and Shāfiʿī Schools. In fact, Imām Shāfiʿī is usually acknowledged as being the founder of *uṣūl al-fiqh*; though it has been argued that *uṣūl al-fiqh* also pre-dates him; references have been made to Companions who deduced rules from *fiqh*. It is well known that Abū Ḥanīfa and his colleagues used analogical reasoning and juristic preference (*istiḥsān*),[63] and likewise Imām Mālik employed *ijmāʿ*, all of which are aspects of *uṣūl al-fiqh*. ʿAbd al-Ḥayy al-Laknawī states that Abū Yūsuf was the first to write a book regarding *uṣūl al-fiqh* according to the *madhhab* of Abū Ḥanīfa.[64] Having said this, it is generally agreed that Shāfiʿī was the one who first developed *uṣūl al-fiqh* into a coherent science by modifying and refining existing rational arguments and adding details to others. His *Risāla* is acknowledged as the first work solely dedicated to *uṣūl al-fiqh*.

Aside from the difference between *fiqh* and *uṣūl al-fiqh*, a distinction must be drawn between *uṣūl al-fiqh* and *al-qawāʿid al-fiqhiyya* (legal maxims)[65]. The legal maxims are general abstract rules derived from the *fiqh* sources in order

[61] Mohammed Hashim Kamali, *Principles of Islamic Jurisprudence*, p. 1.

[62] CCMWE, *Islamic Law and its Significance for the Situation of Muslim Minorities in Europe*, p. 10.

[63] Hallaq, 'Considerations on the Function and Character of Sunnī Legal Theory', p. 682.

[64] Laknawī, 'Introduction' in Shaybānī's *al-Jāmiʿ al-ṣaghīr*, p. 38.

[65] For more details on *al-qawāʿid al-fiqhiyya*, see Chapter IV.

to assist the *faqīh* (jurist). Ibn Nujaym al-Ḥanafī has gathered many in his book *al-Ashbā wa'l-naẓā'ir*, as has Abū al-Ḥasan al-Karkhī in *Uṣūl al-karkhī* and Abū Zayd al-Dabūsī in *Uṣūl al-masā'il al-khalafiyya*; and one hundred of them can be found at the beginning of the Ottoman manual[66] *Majallat al-aḥkām al-ʿadliyya*.[67]

Generally speaking, the Ḥanafīs take a more deductive approach with respect to *uṣūl al-fiqh*, in comparison to what we can justifiably call the more theoretical or inductive approach that the Shāfiʿīs employ. The Ḥanafī approach manifests itself by being more closely related to matters pertaining to the *furūʿ al-fiqh* (branches of law) rather than exclusively to the theoretical principles. Some of the earliest Ḥanafī works on *uṣūl al-fiqh* are: *Kitāb fī al-uṣūl* by Abū al-Ḥasan al-Karkhī, *Uṣūl al-jaṣṣāṣ* by Abū Bakr al-Rāzī al-Jaṣṣāṣ and *Uṣūl al-sarakhsī* by Muḥammad al-Sarakhsī.

An advantage of Ḥanafī *fiqh* is that its scholars have accumulated a larger number of *fiqh taqdīrī* than the other Schools of Law. *Fiqh taqdīri* is when scholars put forward hypothetical situations, which have not yet come about and which may even be impossible, in order to test the principles and the methodology, and to prepare potential rulings for future events.[68]

A more detailed discussion on *uṣūl al-fiqh* from the Ḥanafī perspective is the subject of the next chapter.

Ijtihād

From what has been discussed above, we see that the development of traditional Islamic law is grounded in the work of early scholars who founded legal schools based on the interpretation of the Qur'ān and the *Sunna*, and on *ijmāʿ*, *qiyās* and *ʿurf*; that the foundational writings of this early period become the reference works for the schools and that later jurists established the legal methodology of *uṣūl al-fiqh* in order to be able to issue edicts and rulings on cases that do not exist in the foundational texts.

Thus, when a jurist is presented with a new situation which requires a

[66] For an opinion on the usefulness of the Mejelle's application see Ya'akov Meron 'The Mejelle tested by its Application', *Israel Law Review* (vol. 5, 1970), pp. 203-15.

[67] C. Tyser, D. Demetriades and Ismail Effendi, *The Mejelle: Being an English Translation of Majallah el-Ahkam-l-Adliya and a Complete Code of Islamic Civil Law* (Kuala Lumpur: The Other Press, 2001).

[68] Raḥamānī, *Jadīd fiqhī masā'il* (vol. 1), p. 37.

legal ruling, his first recourse is to the legal schools foundational texts. If the answer cannot be found there, then the next step would be to apply the process of *takhrīj*. *Takhrīj*—which literally means 'extraction'—requires the jurist to solve the case by applying *ijtiḥād* according to the methodology of *uṣūl al-fiqh*.[69] *Ijtihād* is the key term in the relationship between theory and practice in Islamic law; defined as the 'greatest possible effort by a qualified jurist to reach a legal decision within the framework of the *sharīᶜa*.'[70] Omar describes it as the process that links the 'immutable and limited texts of the Sharīᶜah on the one hand, and the countless facts, events, and situations on the other.' [71] Also, 'the maximum effort expended by the jurist to master and apply the principles and rules of *uṣūl al-fiqh* (legal theory) for the purpose of discovering God's law.'[72]

The chief educational goal of the Schools of Law was and still is to train and equip jurists with the necessary skills in order to meet the legal requirements of a community.[73] Thus, jurists are obliged to study the textbooks of the *mutūn*, as these contain the dominant doctrine of the School of Law.[74] Once qualified in these, they are required to study certain *furūᶜ* (branch) works; then to conduct a comprehensive review of these works, which can be assisted if the *muftī* takes a teaching post; to issue *fatāwā* according to the dominant view of the School; to master the knowledge of and become adept at utilising *uṣūl al-fiqh*; and to becoming familiar with the social customs and habits of the society within which they are issuing *fatāwā*.[75]

Wael Hallaq arrives at a number of conclusions in his essay 'From *Fatwās* to *Furūᶜ*', two of which are relevant to this study:

> Primary and secondary fatwas incorporated into *furūᶜ* works reflect the growth and change in the doctrine of the School (*madhhab*). This, in turn, mirrors the societal changes to which law was bound to respond. In other

[69] Hallaq, 'From Fatwās to Furū: Growth and Change in the Islamic Substantive Law', p. 51.

[70] Benjamin Jokisch, '*Ijtihād* in Ibn Taymiyya's *fatāwā*', in R. Gleave and E. Kermeli (eds.), *Islamic Law: Theory and Practice* (London: I B Tauris, 1997), p. 119.

[71] Omar, 'Reasoning in Islamic Law: Part Three', p. 23.

[72] Wael Hallaq, 'Was the Gate of Ijtihad Closed?' *International Journal of Middle Eastern Studies* (vol. 16, no. 1, 1984), p. 3.

[73] George Makdisi, *The Rise of Colleges: Institutions of Learning in Islam and the West* (Edinburgh: Edinburgh University Press, 1981), p. 148.

[74] Johansen, *Contingency in Sacred Law*, p. 448.

[75] Hallaq, 'From Fatwās to Furū: Growth and Change in the Islamic Substantive Law', p. 60.

> words, the *fatwā*, reflecting the exigencies of the social order, was *instrumental in the ongoing process of updating and, indeed, amending* the standard legal doctrine as expressed in the *furūᶜ*.
>
> The instrumentality of the fatwa in updating and amending substantive law suggests that the mufti, by definition a *mujtahid*, was charged with the weighty task not only of discovering the law of God but also of verifying that the new law as embodied in the fatwa was consistent with the established doctrine of his school.[76]

From the above, one can see that jurists are obliged to issue *fatāwā* according to the dominant view of the school when there is an existing ruling that is still applicable; this is called *taqlīd*. The relationship between *taqlīd* and *ijtihād* is generally portrayed as dichotomous and in opposition. *Taqlīd* is often translated and described in negative and derogatory terminology, for instance, 'blind imitation' or 'ossified orthodoxy', whereas *ijtihād* is regarded more favourably and is described as 'progressive'. Knut Vikor, however, describes the relationship between the two as dialectical and complimentary, in which the scholar would employ *ijtihād* according to the limits of his or her competence and beyond would adopt *taqlīd*.[77] In some cases, *taqlīd* and *ijtihād* can be seen to work hand-in-hand, for instance, *takhrīj* is the application of *ijtihād* through *taqlīd*, it is the process of 'creation of rules of law by attaching these to the authority of the founders, even if the content of these rules were quite new and adapted to the continuous changes of historical and social reality.'[78] In a similar vein, Hallaq describes *taqlīd* as an 'intellectually independent affirmation of authority and in no way involves "blind" adherence to the legal doctrines of the masters.'[79] Hallaq believes this to be the cornerstone of the legal systems in all complex societies. Furthermore, he posits that *taqlīd* is primarily methodologically focussed rather than being the absolute acceptance of an existing law; and that, rather than imitation, it is the acknowledgment of a higher authority and the manifestation of loyalty to one's school.

The process of *ijtihād* produces conclusions, which are classified as *ẓann,* meaning opinion or conjecture, which is considered different from *ᶜilm* (categorical knowledge). This 'opinion' should not be confused with

76 Ibid., pp. 61-62, our emphasis added.

77 Vikor, *Between God and the Sultan: A History of Islamic Law*, pp. 160-1.

78 Ibid., p. 161.

79 Hallaq. *Sharīᶜa: Theory, Practice, Transformations*, p. 113.

an individual's subjective preference; it is rather an objective view derived from the sources.[80] But the jurist must be extremely careful, must have sincere intentions, be adequately qualified and must extensively exhaust existing rulings before embarking on such an onerous task of interpreting God's Word.

In discussing how jurists apply *ijtihād*, Jasser Auda focuses on the terms *manāṭ*, its applications and their connection with finding the cause (*ʿilla*) for rulings. He defines *manāṭ* as, 'the ratio legis, grounds, effective cause, the prime criterion, or the 'reason' behind the rule;' and, 'Extraction of the grounds (*Takhrīj al-manāṭ*): It is a process of reflection upon the primary script in order to extract as many possibilities as possible for grounds (*ʿilla* or effect cause) for the primary ruling. These possibilities for grounds are the 'attributes' that the subjects or materials mentioned in the primary script, which represent possible candidates for being the *ʿilla* behind the ruling.'[81]

Auda also says, 'Eliminating the alternatives (*Tanqīkh al-manāṭ*): The different attributes that resulted from step number one are examined one by one, in an Exclusive-OR manner ... in order to determine one chosen attribute, after excluding/clearing out all others ... which will be called the *ʿilla* afterwards...' Finally, 'Asserting the realisation of the ratio legis (*Taḥqīq al-manāṭ*): This is the final step in the *qiyās* process, in which the *mujtahid* jurist verifies whether the *ʿilla* applies to the real-life situation under consideration.'[82]

Usually, there is consensus among scholars over one opinion which has become the dominant opinion of the School, and therefore the *fatwā* has to be issued according to it. However, there are three exceptions: i) the ruling/matter is socially dependent and as the society changes so must the *fatwā*, ii) there is undue hardship or difficulty if the *fatwā* is issued according to the dominant opinion, iii) the context in which the ruling was issued is not the same. Obviously, if a new matter arises then the jurists of the time must start the whole process again from *takhrīj al-manāṭ*.

Kevin Reinhart[83] presents this process by which a ruling (*ḥukm*) can change:

80 Weiss, 'Interpretation in Islamic Law: The Theory of *Ijtihād*', pp. 199-212.

81 Auda, *Maqasid al-Shariah as Philosophy of Islamic Law*, p. 116.

82 Ibid, pp. 116-17.

83 Kevin Reinhart, 'When Women Went to Mosques', in M. Masud, D. Messick and D. S. Powers (eds.), *Islamic Legal Interpretation: Muftis and their Fatwas* (Pakistan: Oxford University Press, 2005), p. 120.

Figure 3: The Changing of *Ḥukm* (ruling) due to Changing Context

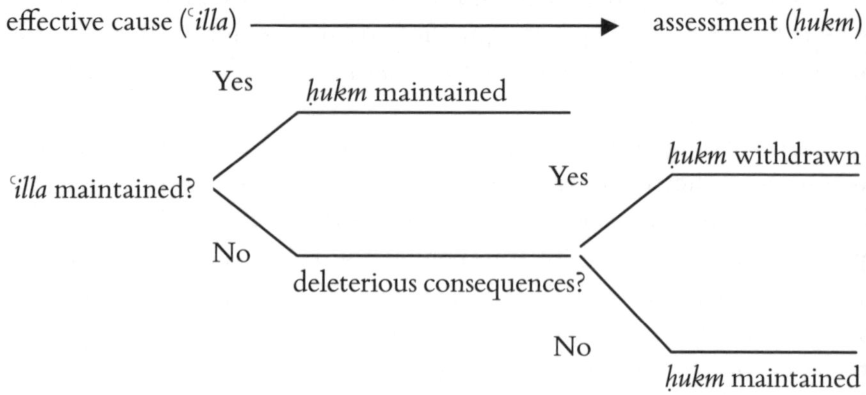

Kevin Reinhart highlights the fact that in some situations the jurists may withdraw the ruling initially established due to potential problems, which may arise in the future. This shows that due to changing circumstances, rulings will change even though the ʿ*illa* still exists. Similarly, if the circumstances change again returning to the earlier situation, then the ruling is maintained. This is the *ijtihād* which most, if not all, traditional scholars refer to. It is a necessity for *muftī*s of every era so that they can deal with all the numerous issues that Muslim communities have to face in a changing world.

As a counter to all the theoretical discussions above, we will give here a practical application of *ijtihād*. *Khamr* (alcohol produced from the fermentation process of grapes) is acknowledged as prohibited (*ḥarām*) from clear and explicit Qur'ānic verses. The first task of the jurist is to determine the possible cause (ʿ*illa*) of the prohibition. There are several possibilities: is it because it is produced from grapes, or is it because it has a certain taste, or is it because it is a liquid drink, or is it because it intoxicates people? Identifying the potential causes is *takhrīj al-manāṭ*. Once the possible causes have been defined, the jurist has to determine which is the actual ʿ*illa* for the impermissibility of *khamr*. It is clear that the consumption of grapes themselves is permissible, as is the consumption of other fruits; being a liquid cannot be the cause as milk, water and fruit juices are permissible; similarly, having a specific taste does not make something impermissible as one is permitted to consume foods which are sweet, sour, bitter, etc. Therefore, it becomes evidently clear that it is its intoxicating nature which makes *khamr* impermissible; this is the process of *tanqīkh al-manāṭ*. Once it has been established that the reason why *khamr* is ruled to be impermissible is because of its intoxicating nature, then any other entity that has that nature will also be impermissible by way of extension. In other words, if this *ʿilla*, which is the cause of *khamr* being impermissible, is found in other edibles, then that other consumable too becomes illegal; this is the process of *taḥqīq al-manāṭ*. To sum up, when the community is faced with a new problem and jurists cannot find a ruling in the existing texts, then jurists must compare and draw parallels between the problem they are dealing with and its equivalent in the sources in order to establish a similarity. The similarity is then regarded as the common denominator, referred to as the *ʿilla* (entities) Once the jurists are convinced that the two, the original and the assimilated, share the same *ʿilla*, then the judgement for the original would pass to the secondary.[84]

Finally, in the Ḥanafī School jurists have recourse to two methods of utilising legal methodology that does not adhere to the legal theory of the Ḥanafī School. The first is when no ruling exists within the Ḥanafī School or when it might prove difficult to act upon a ruling within the Ḥanafī *fiqh*, the School permits referring to one of the other three Schools of Law. 'Due to a general necessity it is permissible to take benefit from the other Schools. However, this is a delicate matter and great care and precaution needs to be taken and these *masā'il* must have the consensus of the ʿUlamā.'[85] And the second, is the concept of *ḥiyal* which is the use of legal strategies to meet the spirit of the law, if not exactly to the letter of the law, in order to prevent excessive difficulty for individuals.

It has repeatedly been asserted that *ijtihād* came to an end and was no longer operative at the close of the third/ninth century. Joseph Schacht explains 'the closing of the gate of *ijtiḥād*' (*insidād bāb al-ijtihād*):

> By the beginning of the fourth century of the hijra (about A.D. 900), however, the point had been reached when the scholars of all schools felt that all essential questions had been thoroughly discussed and finally settled, and a consensus gradually established itself to the effect that from that time onwards no one might be deemed to have the necessary qualifications for independent reasoning in law, and that all future activity would have to be confined to the explanation, application, and at the most, interpretation of the doctrine as it had been laid down once and for all. This 'closing of the door of *ijtihād*', as it was called, amounted to the demand for *taḳlīd*, a term

[84] Hallaq, 'Considerations on the Function and Character of Sunnī Legal Theory', p. 680.
[85] Raḥamānī, *Jadīd fiqhī masā'il*, p. 62.

> which had originally denoted the kind of reference to Companions of the Prophet that had been customary in the ancient schools of law, and which now came to mean the unquestioning acceptance of the doctrines of established schools and authorities. A person entitled to *ijtihād* is called *mujtahid*, and a person bound to practice *taḳlīd, muḳallid*.[86]

Thus, the 'the closing of the gate of *ijtiḥād*' implied that jurists could henceforth only practice *taqlīd* which is to adopt the existing position of a School and could no longer go directly to the sources to derive legal rulings. This seems to suggest a certain element of inflexibility whereby changing times and situations are obliged to 'fit themselves' to the law at the time of its development in the third/ninth century; it also denies the very rights that earlier jurists had to later jurists. But contrary to this view, recent research has shown that *ijtihād* continued beyond the formative period.[87] According to Hallaq, it was used in developing *fiqh* after the formation of the Schools and that even up to fifth/eleventh century there was no use of the phrase *insidād bāb al-ijtihād*. Hallaq also asserts that jurists are capable of exercising *ijtihād* at all times.[88] Others propose that expounding upon the *mutūn* through commentaries (*shurūḥ*) and legal responses (*fatāwā*) is in itself a form of *ijtihād*.[89]

We, therefore, conclude that *ijtihād*, as a method to derive rulings, is valid today just as it was in earlier centuries; that 'the door of *ijtihād*' is not closed and that *taqlīd* is not to be adopted at all times. We believe that one reason for the confusion about the continuing validity of *ijtihād* may result from a misunderstanding of the different levels of *ijtihād*. For example, while no traditional scholar will assert that he is an independent *mujtahid* (i. e., one who is able to set up his own school of law),[90] there should be no problem with a *mujtahid fī'l-madhhab*[91] (i. e., one who is proficient in the law and methodology of his own school). In fact, the existence of the latter is essential for all Muslim societies.

86 Joseph Schacht, *An Introduction to Islamic Law* (Oxford: Oxford University Press, 1982), pp. 70-71.

87 Hallaq, 'Was the Gate of Ijtihad Closed?', pp. 3-41. Wael Hallaq, '*Uṣūl al-fiqh*: Beyond Tradition', pp. 172-202.

88 Hallaq, 'Was the Gate of Ijtihad Closed?', pp. 3-41

89 Johansen, *Contingency in Sacred Law*, pp. 446-47.

90 Hallaq, 'Was the Gate of Ijtihad Closed?', p. 24 and 'Ifta and Ijtihad in Sunni Legal Theory', pp. 33-43.

91 Wael Hallaq, 'Ifta and Ijtihad in Sunni Legal Theory', in Masud, Messick and Powers (eds.), *Islamic Legal Interpretation*), pp. 33-43.

CHAPTER IV

Uṣūl al-Fiqh According to the Ḥanafī School of Law: The Theory[1]

IN THE PREVIOUS CHAPTER, we introduced the foundations on which traditional Schools of Islamic law are based giving the Ḥanafī School as an example. In this present chapter, we will expand on the outlines given in Chapter III, we will add a number of secondary but important concepts and we will do so through translating large sections from traditional Ḥanafī textbooks. In this way, we hope to demonstrate that the traditional approach can continue to be applied today and in any social context as it contains all the material required for the adaptations of legal rulings to new situations. Our aim is to show the scope of this science, but we will not go into extensive detail in each area as the purpose is to show the breadth of the coverage of the traditional approach and not necessarily its depth.

The first textbook we will refer to is Shāshī's *Uṣūl*. The reason to start with Shāshī's *Uṣūl* is because it is an essential textbook of *uṣūl al-fiqh* used across the globe in hundreds of *madāris*. Little is known about Shāshī, to the extent that even his name is disputed. It is reported that out of piety and humility the author did not disclose his name, hence to date there is no agreement regarding the biography of this great author. The opinion of one group of scholars is that he was Abū Ibrāhīm Isḥāq b. Ibrāhīm al-Shāshī al-Samarqandī (d. 325/936), who transmitted *al-Jāmiʿ al-Kabīr* from Abū Sulaymān Jawzjānī via Zayd b. Usāma; that he was born in a city called Shāsh in present-day Iran and died and in Egypt. In *Kashf al-ẓunūn*, *Uṣūl al-shāshī* is referred to as *Kitāb al-khamsīna* (The Book of Fifty) because, it is reported, the author was fifty years old when he wrote it; another view is that it was written in fifty days. *Kashf al-ẓunūn* states that the

[1] We have added 'The Theory' in the title of this chapter as the final chapter will be the 'Applications' of the traditional *uṣūl* described in the present chapter.

author was Nizam al-Dīn al-Shāshī.[2] Therefore, due to the wide acceptance of *Uṣūl al-shāshī*, its educational merit as a teaching tool and its conciseness and accuracy, a significant portion of this chapter will be based on selections from it, with additional notes from the commentary on it by Muḥammad Barakāt-Allāh al-Laknawī al-Farangī entitled *Aḥsan al-ḥāwashī ʿalā uṣūl al-shāshī*. The translations of the extracts are indented and any quotations from *Aḥsan al-ḥāwashī* are within square brackets and preceded by H. Where only square brackets are used, these are our own input in order to clarify the text further.

Uṣūl al-fiqh According to Shāshī

Introduction

Uṣūl al-fiqh is [based on] four: the Book of Almighty God [the Qur'ān]; the *Sunna* of His Messenger; consensus [of opinion] of the *umma* (*ijmāʿ*) [H: of our Messenger]; and analogical reasoning (*qiyās*). Therefore, it is necessary to discuss every one of these in order to understand the method of deducing rulings (*aḥkām*).[3]

The first two of the four are what can be categorically regarded as sources, whereas *ijmāʿ* has value if it is based on either of the two sources and does not go against their established principles. For instance, if the Muslim *umma* were to come to a consensus that the consumption of alcohol is legal, then that would not change the original prohibition on the consumption of alcohol which is derived from the Qur'ān. As for *qiyās*, it is a methodology rather than a source as such. In this introduction the author is stating that there are four means on which Islamic law is based and through which jurists arrive at deducing rulings; the first two are divine and divinely inspired, whereas the latter two involve scholarly agreement and a methodology for interpreting the sources and how rulings are to be arrived at.

The First Discussion Regarding the Book of Almighty God [the Qur'ān]

Section on *khāṣ* (specific) and *ʿāmm* (general):

> *Khāṣ* is a word that is used with a specific known meaning or for a specific known subject, as in our statement of 'Zayd' when specifying an individual,

[2] Jamīl Aḥmad, *Ajmal al-ḥawāshī ʿalā uṣūl al-shāshī* (Karachi: Kutub Khāna Maẓharī, 1999); Muḥammad Barkhusānī, *Tashīl uṣūl al-shāshī* (Karachi: Bayt al-ʿIlm, 2004).

[3] Shāshī, *Uṣūl al-shāshī maʿ aḥsan al-ḥawāshī* (Karachi: Qadīmī Kutub Khāna, no date), p. 5.

'man' when specifying a gender, and 'human' when specifying a species.

ʿĀmm is all those words [H: that indicate a single meaning and includes everything without any specification or limitation], which includes all individuals, either lexically like in our [everyday] statement 'Muslims' and 'polytheists (*mushrikīn*)', or by meaning 'who/whom' and 'that/what' in an [everyday] statement.

The ruling of *khāṣ* from the Book indicates the categorical necessity of acting upon it. An example is in the statement of the Almighty: *they should wait for* thalātha [*three*] qurū [*cycles*] [Q.II.228]. For indeed the word 'three' is specific in defining a known number; hence it is necessary to act upon it.[4]

The above-quoted Qur'ānic verse is regarding the *ʿidda* (waiting) period a divorced woman would serve before remarrying; in this case the number three is purported to be *khāṣ*, therefore it is necessary to act upon it in totality. As it is illegal to issue a divorce when a woman is menstruating, one assumes that divorce is issued during a *ṭuhr* (pure) cycle. Lexically, the word *qurū* has two meanings; either the cycles of menstruation or of purity, but in order for three cycles to be achieved in totality then, *qurū* can only mean 'three cycles of menstruation'. Therefore, one concludes that *qurū* refers to each menstrual cycle in this verse.

If a *khabar wāḥid* [a narration by one or more persons from the first three generations of Muslims] or *qiyās* [i.e. analogy, which apparently] contradicts the Book, and if it is possible to consolidate between them without a change in the ruling of *khāṣ*, then both of them will be acted upon; otherwise, the Book will be acted upon and that which contradicts it will be abandoned.

The *ʿāmm* is of two types: 1) that which has had some [individuals, who make-up a group], specified; 2) that which does not have anything specified. *ʿĀmm* that does not have anything specified is in the same status as *khāṣ* with respect to the necessity of acting upon it without doubt.[5]

As for the *ʿāmm* that has some specificity, its ruling is that it is necessary to act upon the remainder with the possibility that if evidence was established upon the specificity of the remainder [then more would have

[4] Ibid., pp. 5-6.

[5] Ibid., p. 7.

to be specified].[6] It would be permissible due to specificity of *khabar wāḥid* or *qiyās* until [at least] three [individuals] remained, but it would not be permissible after that.[7]

An example of the first type of *ʿāmm* is 'Indeed God is the Knower of all things' in which nothing is specified for omission and therefore none are excluded. An example of the second type of *ʿāmm* is, 'God has permitted trade but made *ribā* illegal;' in this verse all trade is permitted and then one type is specified which is excluded from the ruling whilst the remainder continue to be permissible.

Table 3: The Concept of *Khāṣ* in the Source Texts

Cycles	***Qurū* is Menstrual**	***Qurū* is Pure Cycles**
Ṭuhr 1	Divorce issued half way through	Divorce issued half way through
Ḥayḍ 1	1	
Ṭuhr 2		1.5
Ḥayḍ 2	2	
Ṭuhr 3		2.5 If *ʿidda* complete then less than three
Ḥayḍ 3	3	
Ṭuhr 4	*ʿidda* complete	3.5 If *ʿidda* complete then more than three

Section on *muṭlaq* (absolute) *and muqayyad* (qualified):

Our colleagues are of the opinion that *muṭlaq* with respect to the Book of Almighty God is when it is possible to act upon its absoluteness, then adding

[6] For example, in the case of a group of people made up of men, women, boys and girls. A person walks in and says, 'All those who are minors and of the female gender can leave'; the girls would leave. The remainder would stay dependent on further evidence on the part of the speaker.

[7] Ibid., p. 9.

> to it through the means of *khabar al-wāḥid* and *qiyās* is impermissible. For example, in the statement of the Almighty: *then wash your faces* [Q.v.6]; hence, that which is being ordered is washing exclusively and it cannot be added to by the conditions of intention (*niyya*), order (*tartīb*), continuity (*muwālāh*) or the recitation of *tasmiyya* (reciting God's name before starting something) by a *khabar*. Rather, the *khabar* will be acted upon in a manner that does not change the ruling of the Book. So it is said that non-qualified washing is compulsory due to the ruling of the Book and intention [and all the other modifiers] is *Sunna* due to the ruling of the *khabar*.[8]

Therefore, the ruling of the Book must be applied in as general a state as possible without its ruling being modified by *khabar wāḥid* or *qiyās*.

Section on *mushtarak* (homonym) and *mu'awwal* (interpreted beyond the obvious meaning of the text):

> *Mushtarak* is a word that possesses two or more different meanings. Its example is in our word '*jāria*' which means 'slave-girl' and 'ship'. The ruling of *mushtarak* is that when one meaning, due to some evidence, is intended, and hence is identified, then the potential of intending the second meaning is not valid.[9]
>
> However when one [meaning of a] *mushtarak* is prioritised due to *ghālib al-ra'y* (dominant speculative evidence), it will become *mu'awwal*. The ruling of *mu'awwal* is the need for acting upon it with the possibility of being at fault.[10]

An example is the above discussion on *qurū*, which has two well-known meanings: *ṭuhr* and *ḥayḍ*. Due to the dominant speculative evidence in this example *ḥayḍ* was prioritised and so it became *mu'awwal*. As *mu'awwal* is based on speculation, this also raises the possibility that the Ḥanafī view—that of Abū Ḥanīfa, and other *mujtahids* of the Ḥanafī School—is correct with the possibility of it being mistaken, whereas other Schools' *mujtahids* are mistaken with the possibility of them being correct. This reasoning is based on the view that there is agreement amongst the legal Schools on all explicit issues; while those which require intellectual input are speculative, hence the possibility of being incorrect.

Section on *ḥaqīqa* (literal) and *majāz* (metaphorical):

> Every word that the composer of the language coined for a thing [i.e. its

[8] Ibid., pp. 9-10.
[9] Ibid., p. 12.
[10] Ibid., p. 13.

meaning] is *ḥaqīqa*, and if it [the word] is employed for other than it [was originally coined] then it is *majāz* not *ḥaqīqa*. Hence, in one word and in one instance both the *ḥaqīqa* and *majāz* meaning cannot be intended.[11]

So for this reason we say when sexual intercourse is intended in the Qur'ānic verse of *al-mulāmasa*[12] the potential of intending touching with the hand is dropped.[13]

This verse is discussing those occasions when *wuḍū'* or *ghusl* is required and water is absent; it mentions the word '*lāmastum*', which literally means 'to touch with the hand', but metaphorically means to have sexual intercourse. The Ḥanafī School's view is that it means the latter, and subsequently cannot have the literal meaning in this situation. The reasoning for this is that those who adopt the view that it means 'to touch' exclude certain individuals from this group, for instance, a man's female relations,[14] whereas the Ḥanafī view means the verse can be acted upon in the general sense; which is the superior position as the verse is not being limited by human interpretation and continues to remain relevant.

Ḥaqīqa is of three types: *mutaʿadhira* (unfeasible), *mahjūra* (abandoned) and *mustaʿmala* (applied). In the first two types, the word is referred to the metaphorical [meaning] by consensus [across the Schools]. The example of *mutaʿadhira* is when an individual takes an oath that he will not eat from this tree or from this pot. The eating from the tree or from the pot is *mutaʿadhira* (unfeasible), hence [the meaning] is referred to the fruit of the tree and what is in the pot. So that if he [happened] to eat the actual tree or pot with difficulty then he is not one who has broken his oath.

The example of *mahjūra* is when an individual takes an oath that he will not place his foot in so-and-so's house, then the [actual meaning of the] placing of the foot is *mahjūra* (abandoned) due to the customary [use of the statement].

If the *ḥaqīqa* [word] is *mustaʿmala*, and it does not have a recognised metaphorical meaning, then its *ḥaqīqa* meaning is accepted by consensus. If, however, it does have a recognised metaphorical meaning, then the *ḥaqīqa* meaning is accepted by Abū Ḥanīfa, while according to the two [Abū Yūsuf and Muḥammad] it is superior to act upon the known metaphorical meaning. For example, if an individual takes an oath that he will

[11] Ibid., p. 14.

[12] '*...If you are ill or on a journey or one of you has returned from the toilet or* lāmastum *women and you do not find water...*' [Q.v.43].

[13] Ibid., pp. 14-15.

[14] That is, those female relations that he cannot marry (a mother or sister).

not eat from some particular wheat, then according to him [Abū Ḥanīfa] it will refer to its actual [meaning]; hence he will not break his oath if he eats anything produced from it. However, according to them [Abū Yūsuf and Muḥammad] it will refer to all that which wheat implies by the means of known metaphorical [meaning], so he will break his oath by eating it or bread produced from it.[15]

Section on *ṣarīḥ* (unequivocal) and *kināya* (allusive):

Ṣarīḥ has a plain meaning, like the statement *biʿtu* (I sold) and *ashtaraytu* (I bought) and the like. Its ruling is that it is necessary to bring about its meaning irrespective of which way [it is articulated, whether] by informing, attributing or by calling, and its ruling is independent from intention.

Kināya is that [word] whose meaning is hidden. *Majāz* (metaphorical) has the same status as *kināya*. The ruling for *kināya* is to include in the ruling the presence of intention or the indication of the state in a manner that removes any doubt.

Punishments are not meted out due to *kināya* words, so if someone admits with respect to adultery or stealing [with such words] then the *ḥadd* punishment will not be meted out until *ṣarīḥ* (unequivocal) words are used.[16]

Section on *mutaqābilāt* (antonyms):

We mean by this: *al-ẓāhir* (apparent), *al-naṣ* (explicit), *al-mufassar* (explained) and *al-muḥkam* (firm); with their antonyms: *al-khafī* (hidden), *al-mushkil* (problematic), *al-mujmal* (ambiguous) and *al-mutashābih* (intricate).

Ẓāhir is the name for all those words that the listener can understand just by listening and without contemplation.

Naṣ is the reason for which the text was revealed. For example, in His statement the Almighty says: *And God has permitted trade and made impermissible usury* [Q.II.275]. So this verse was revealed to clarify the difference between trade and usury as a rebuttal to the claim of the non-Muslims that they were the same when they said, *Indeed trade is like usury* [Q.II.275]. Hence, the permissibility of trade and the illegality of usury are known simply by listening [to the statement]. Therefore, that [verse] becomes *naṣ* in the differentiation [between trade and usury] and *ẓāhir* in the permissibility of trade and the impermissibility of usury.

15 Ibid., pp. 16-17.
16 Ibid., pp. 20-21.

The ruling of *ẓāhir* and *naṣ* is the necessity of acting upon them whether they are *ᶜāmm* or *khāṣ* with the possibility that it means something else. This is the same as *majāz* with *ḥaqīqa*.

[An example is] his statement (upon him be peace) to the people of al-ᶜUrayna, 'Drink from their urine and their milk.' [H: it is reported that a group of people came to Medina from al-ᶜUrayna. The atmosphere of Medina did not suit them and they fell ill; they became pale in colour and their stomachs became swollen. So the Messenger of God (peace and salutations be upon him) ordered them to go to the animals of charity and drink from their urine and from their milk. They did this and became better]. [This is] *naṣ* in terms of clarifying the means of curing, and *ẓāhir* in terms of the permissibility of drinking urine. However, his statement, upon him be peace, 'Keep away from urine for indeed the main [reason for the] punishment of the grave is due to it.' [This is] *naṣ* in the necessity of refraining from urine. So the *naṣ* is prioritised over the *ẓāhir*, hence it is not permissible to drink urine in all situations. [H: This is the opinion of Abū Ḥanīfa and the *ḥadīth* is evidence against Abū Yūsuf in making permissible the drinking of urine for medicinal purposes and against Muḥammad [Shaybānī] in the permissibility and its general purity.][17]

In this section the author discusses the various rankings, and their subsequent rulings, of verses of the Qur'ān. Therefore, if a verse clearly speaks about a particular matter so that it is either *zāhir* or *naṣ* then that is its ruling, and therefore one cannot deduce the ruling from another generic verse, which requires interpretation, or rather more accurately, may be open to misinterpretation.

Mufassar (explained) is that [word] whose meaning becomes apparent due to the clarification of the speaker, so that the possibility of *ta'wīl* (interpretation) and *takhṣīṣ* (specificity) no longer remains. For example, in the statement of the Almighty: *So the angels prostrated, all of them, together* [Q.xv.30]. Hence the noun 'angels' is *ẓāhir* in generality [H: referring to all angels]; but it does possess the possibility of specifying, so the [possibility of] specificity is eliminated by His saying '*all of them*'. There then remains the possibility of separation in prostration, so the [possibility of such an] interpretation is eliminated by His saying '*together*'.

Muḥkam (firm) is superior in strength [of reliability] to the *mufassar* in the sense that it is not permissible to oppose it in any state. Its example in

17 Ibid., pp. 21-22.

the Book is: *Indeed God is Knower of all things*, and *Indeed God does not oppress mankind in any way* [Q.II.231 and Q.X.44, respectively].

The ruling of *mufassar* and *muḥkam* is that it is necessary to act upon them without doubt.[18]

Those source texts which have the ruling of *mufassar* or *muḥkam* cannot be opposed as they tend not be socially focussed, context dependent or require dispensations due to the potential difficulty of acting upon them—as a result they can be termed the immutable from the source texts.

It becomes quite clear that before rulings are passed, the verses or, more accurately, all the material dealing with a subject which are to be found in the source texts have to be assessed and given a value, namely *muḥkam*, *mufassar*, *naṣ* and *ẓāhir*. These are then ranked in terms of applicability in that order. Once this value is attached, the ruling can be passed.

Then for these four there are four others, which oppose them; hence the antonym of *ẓāhir* is *khafī*, and the antonym of *naṣ* is *mushkil*, and the antonym of *mufassar* is *mujmal* and the antonym of *muḥkam* is *mutashābih*.

Khafī is that [word] whose meaning is hidden due to an impediment, not due to the language. For example the statement of the Almighty: *The thief, male and female, so cut off their hands* [Q.V.38]. Hence it is *ẓāhir* with respect to the thief and *khafī* with respect to the pickpocket and the grave robber. The ruling of *khafī* is the necessity of researching until the 'hiddeness' is removed from it.[19]

What is clearly understood from the text is that when someone steals his hand is to be cut off, but this is not clear with respect to a pickpocket and grave robber as they are, strictly speaking, not called thieves; therefore it is difficult to infer from this verse as to whether the ruling applies to the other two also. The definition of thieving requires serious contemplation before it becomes applicable: the item has to be regarded as valuable; it is permissible by the Sharīʿa to take benefit from it; the item is safe-guarded (i.e. protected) and it is at least equivalent to ten dirhams. In conclusion, a pickpocket will have his hand cut off, but a grave robber will not as the owner (the dead person) is not guarding his item(s).

Mushkil is [a word which has a meaning] even more hidden than *khafī*. It is as though after its [i.e. the word's] reality became hidden to the listener it

[18] Ibid., pp. 23-24.

[19] Ibid., p. 24.

became so much like those that resemble it and are similar to it, to such an extent that it cannot be understood except with research and subsequent contemplation, in order to differentiate it from those which are similar to it. Its example in rulings is when an individual swears that he will not eat condiment, then this is *ẓāhir* with respect to vinegar and treacle [of grapes], but it is *mushkil* with respect to meat, eggs and cheese until the meaning of condiment is researched and investigated as to whether it is applicable to meat, eggs and cheese or not.

Above *mushkil* [in terms of obscurity] is *mujmal* and it is that which has several possibilities [in terms of meaning]; and its state is one whereby the meaning cannot be understood without the speaker clarifying it. Its example in the Sharīʿa is the statement of the Almighty: *made usury* (ribā) *impermissible* [Q.II.275]. [Lexically] *ribā* can be understood to mean a general increase, but that is not what is intended [by the Qur'ānic verse]. Rather a transaction between identical items of measure that brings about an increase, in which the increase has nothing in exchange [for it], is what is meant. The word [*ribā*, on its own] does not point towards this [meaning]; hence its [Qur'ānic] meaning cannot be understood [even] with contemplation.

Then above *mujmal* in obscurity is *mutashābih*. An example of *mutashābih* is the individual letters at the beginning of the chapters [of the Qur'ān].

The ruling of *mujmal* and *mutashābih* is the belief in the reality of their meaning [i.e. that they have a meaning] until the clarification is arrived at. [H: The belief that what is intended by it is fact even though we will not know before the Day of Judgement. As for after the Day of Judgement, then it will be made apparent to everyone if God the Almighty so chooses. This is in regards to the *umma*, as for the Prophet (may God bless him and grant him peace) these were know.][20]

Section on those occasions when the *ḥaqīqa* meaning of a word is abandoned:

Those items by which the *ḥaqīqa* (literal) meaning is abandoned are five: One of them is the evidence of *ʿurf* (societal custom or culture). That is because the occurrence of rulings is based on statements, and the evidence of the word is based upon the meaning intended by the speaker. Hence, if there is a meaning known amongst the people, then this known meaning is evidential

[20] Ibid., pp. 24-25.

that that is what was intended, which is *ẓāhir*; so the ruling is given according to it. For example, if an individual takes an oath that he will not buy a *ra's* (head), then it [i.e. the oath] is applicable to that which the people recognise [as *ra's*]. Hence, his oath will not be broken due to a sparrow's or a pigeon's head [H: as in his community 'head' refers to a roasted lamb, sheep, goat or cow head].

This also makes it apparent that by the abandoning of the *ḥaqīqa* it is not necessary to turn to *majāz*, but rather it is permissible to establish *ḥaqīqa qāṣira* (partial literalism), and its example is the qualifying of the *ʿāmm* with something. [In other words it is similar to that *ʿāmm* which has some particulars specified from it.]

The second [occasion] when the *ḥaqīqa* is sometimes abandoned is due to the statement itself. Its example is when an individual [who has slaves] says, 'Everyone that I own, they are free.' Then the *mukātabūn*[21] will not be freed nor one who is [already] partially freed except if he intends to include them. This is because the word 'owned' is *muṭlaq* and it includes ownership from every possibility and angle [i.e. in all its completeness and totality] and a *mukātab* is not owned from every angle [i.e. the slave is not wholly owned by the master, only partially].

The third [occasion] when the *ḥaqīqa* is sometimes abandoned is due to the indication of the context of the statement. [Shaybānī] said in *al-Siyar al-kabīr* that when a Muslim says to an enemy, 'Come down,' then he is protected.[22] If he [the Muslim] says, 'Come down if you are a man,' then if he comes down, he will not be protected. If the enemy says, 'Clemency, clemency,' and the Muslim replies, 'Clemency, clemency,' then he is protected.

The fourth [occasion] when the *ḥaqīqa* is sometimes abandoned is due an indication on the part of the speaker. For example in the statement of the Almighty: *So whomsoever decides* [to believe] *should believe and whomsoever decides* [to disbelieve] *should disbelieve* [Q.XVIII.29]. This is so because Almighty God is *al-Ḥākim* (the All-Wise) and disbelief is *qabīḥ* (repugnant) and [it is inappropriate for] *al-Ḥākim* to order it [i.e. disbelief]. Hence, the indication of the words upon an order is abandoned due to the wisdom of the One who has ordered.

[21] A slave who is contracted to pay for their own manumission from their owner, i.e. buy their own freedom.

[22] He has received immunity and is under protection from being attacked.

> The fifth [occasion] when the *ḥaqīqa* is sometimes abandoned is due to the indication of the context, in that the place [in which the statement has occurred] does not accept the *ḥaqīqa* words. Its example is in the contraction of marriage of a free woman by using words[23] of *bayᶜ*, *hiba*, *tamlīq*, and *ṣadaqa*.[24]

This last point refers to the marriage vows where an individual chooses to use words of sale, gift, ownership and donation rather than the usual terms of accepting or offering marriage.

Section on *mutaᶜallaqāt al-nuṣūṣ* (textual indications):

> We mean by this [i.e. textual indications]: *ᶜibārat al-naṣ* (explicit meaning of the text), *ishārat al-naṣ* (alluded meaning), *dalālat al-naṣ* (inferred meaning) and *iqtiḍā'at al-naṣ* (required meaning).
>
> So as for *ᶜibarat al-naṣ* it is that for which purpose the statement has been made and it is what is intended [by the statement]. As for *ishārat al-naṣ* it is that which is established by the text without increasing [upon the words]. It is not apparent from every angle nor is the statement made for that reason. Its example is in the statement of the Almighty: *for the emigrated* fuqarā' (*poor*), *those who were exiled from their homes* [Q.LIX.8]. So it [i.e. statement] was made to identify those who possessed the right to the war booty, so this becomes [*ᶜibarat*] *al-naṣ*, and their poverty is established due to the text so this is *ishārat* [*al-naṣ*], in that the non-Muslim overpowering and taking the wealth of the Muslim is a means to establish ownership for the non-Muslim. This is [because] had the wealth remained in their ownership [the emigrating Muslims], then their poverty would not have been established.
>
> As for *dalālat al-naṣ* it is that in which the meaning is known in terms of *ᶜilla* (effective cause) for the ruling that is based upon it, linguistically not by *ijtihād* (legal reasoning) or by *istinbāṭ* (rational deduction). For example in the statement of the Almighty: *Do not say 'uff'* [express anger or displeasure] *to them* [parents] *and do not reproach them* [Q.XVII.23]. So a knowledgeable person, due to the placing of the words, will understand immediately on hearing [the verse] the impermissibility of expressing anger and displeasure [and the need] not to bring difficulty upon them. The ruling of this type is the general

[23] His statement, 'I bought you'; her statement, 'I gift myself to you'; his statement, 'I own you'; her statement, 'I give myself in charity to you', respectively. The *ḥaqīqa* words cannot be acted upon as a free woman cannot be bought, nor can she give herself away as a gift or charity.

[24] Ibid., pp. 25-28.

> [applicability] for which the text has been revealed due to the general nature of its effective cause. Therefore, due to this meaning, we say it is impermissible to strike, to swear at, to make one's parent one's servants, to imprison due to a [unpaid] debt and to kill due to *qiṣāṣ* (the law of equal retaliation).[25]

This is a useful example which can be utilised to illustrate the difference between the three interpretive methodologies; for the traditional approach—as opposed to the literal and liberal approaches—the *ʿilla* is derived from the source, in this instance the verse of the Qur'ān. The *ʿilla* is that one should cause no harm, of any form, to parents or put one's parents through difficulty. The verse actually prohibits the use of the word '*uff*', similar to the groans some children make when parents make a request. However, if the word *uff* means 'I love you' in a certain language then not only would it become permissible, it would actually be *mustaḥab* (praiseworthy) in direct literal contradiction of the source.

The literal interpretive model would have to accept that it is not permissible to say *uff* in all cases as it would be in direct violation of this verse and its prohibition. The liberal/modern model would be influenced from beyond the source; hence if it is acceptable within society to be disrespectful to parents this would be interpreted in another way, and if respect was the order of the day then this verse would justify the status quo.

> Then that which is required [due to *iqtiḍā'at al-naṣ*] is an increase upon the text whereby without it the meaning of the text would not be fulfilled. It is as though the text requires it in order to bring out its meaning. For example, in the Sharīʿa, there is the statement [i.e. a man's statement to his wife], '*Anti ṭāliq* (You are divorced).' Its meaning is a description of a woman, but a description requires the *maṣdar* (verbal noun), therefore it is as though the *maṣdar* is present by the means of the requirement.[26]

Section on understanding the methodology of what is intended by the texts:

> One must be aware that there are a number of methods for determining what is intended by the text. One of them is that if a word has a *ḥaqīqa* meaning and a *majāz* meaning, then the *ḥaqīqa* meaning is preferred.
>
> Another is if [a word has the potential for two meanings and] one of the two meanings requires specification in the text and the other not, then the one that does not require specification will be adopted.

[25] Ibid., pp. 29-30.

[26] Ibid., pp. 31-32.

Another is that if a text is recited in two ways or [a narration] is narrated in two ways, then the method to act upon both is preferable.[27]

Section on the discussion of *ḥurūf*[28] (conjunctions and prepositions):

Wāw (and) is [used] for general linking [of entities].

Fā' (then) is [used] for a dependent conjunction [of entities][29]. It is for this [reason] that it is used in *ajziya* (results) because it follows a condition. [H: An example is, 'If you enter the house, *fa* (then) you are divorced.' Hence the divorce occurs immediately upon entering.]

Thumma (thereupon) is [used] for delay[30]. According to Abū Ḥanīfa it gives the benefit of delay in wording and ruling, whilst according to the two [Abū Yūsuf and Shaybānī] it gives the benefit of delay in the ruling [not in the wording]. Its clarification is that if a man says to [his new bride, one who is] *ghayr madkhūl bihā*,[31] 'If you enter the house, *thumma* (thereupon) you are divorced, *thumma* you are divorced, *thumma* you are divorced.'[32] So according to him [Abū Ḥanīfa], the first [*thumma* you are divorced] is associated with entering, the second occurs immediately and the third is futile; and according to the two all are associated with entering and therefore with entering the order becomes apparent, hence only one occurs.[33]

For Abū Ḥanīfa, the first declaration of divorce is the result of the condition, and then it is regarded as a barrier before the next declaration of divorce takes place. As she is a *ghayr madkhūl bihā* (a new bride in an as yet unconsummated marriage) then with the second declaration she becomes divorced *bā'ina* (irrevocably) and will serve no *ᶜidda* period. Since she is divorced *bā'ina*, the third

27 Ibid., pp. 49-52.

28 *Ḥurūf* literally means 'letters of the alphabet'. This is why Shāshī refers to the letters *wāw* and *fā'* which can be used as conjunctions in Arabic. We have intentionally not given translations for all the possible meaning of the different *ḥurūf* as their meanings are usually based on the context and hence it would be misleading to give a single meaning or translation. The translations included between brackets are just examples.

29 That is, what appears after a *fā'* is connected to the first entity but follows in terms of time and order.

30 There is a delay between the first entity before *thumma*, and the entity after it.

31 That is, when the marriage has not yet been consummated. According to Islamic Law, there are different terms for consummated and unconsummated divorces.

32 An Islamic divorce requires a husband to make the above statement three times for an irrevocable divorce.

33 Ibid., pp. 52-57.

declaration is futile and not required in this case. The result is that she is divorced immediately. According to Abū Yūsuf and Shaybānī all three declarations are a result of the condition and therefore one will take place when she enters, and the remaining two will be futile. In summary, all agree on the verdict but follow different processes in reaching it.

Bal (rather) is [used] for the rectification of a mistake with the replacement of the first by the second.

Lākin (however) is [used] for supplementing after a negation; hence its ruling is to establish that which is after it. As for the negation of that which is before it, its evidence asserts it. The conjoining by this word in order to join a sentence is correct. So if the sentence is linked, then the negation is associated with the assertion that is after it, otherwise it is a new sentence.

Aw (or) is [used] for encompassing one of two mentioned [entities].

Ḥattā (until) is [used] for the extreme limit like *ilā*. If that which is before it is acceptable to extensibility [in time] and that which is after it possesses the ability to reach the extreme limit of this extension, then *ḥattā* will be used in its right[way.][34]

Ilā (up to) is [used] for the end of the extreme. So in some situations it renders the meaning of the extension of the ruling, and in other situations it renders the end of the meaning.[35]

The word *ʿalā* (upon) is [used] for incumbent [upon], and its origin is to render the meaning of superiority and enhancement.

The word *fī* (in) is [used] as a preposition of time and place.

The letter *bā* (with) is [used] for joining [words] in a sentence.[36]

Section regarding the types of *bayān* (explanation):

Bayān is of seven types: *bayān al-taqrīr* (explanation of confirmation), *bayān al-tafsīr* (explanation of exposition), *bayān al-taghyīr* (explanation of modification), *bayān al-ḍarūra* (explanation due to necessity)[37], *bayān al-ḥāl*

[34] For example, 'Fast *ḥattā* (until) night.'

[35] For example, does 'Wash your arms *ilā* the elbows,' mean that the elbows are included or excluded?

[36] Ibid., pp. 57-66.

[37] From this explanation further knowledge can be obtained by deduction.

(explanation due to state)[38], *bayān al-ʿaṭf*, (explanation due to addition)[39] and *bayān al-tabdīl* (explanation of change)[40]. As for the first, it is when the meaning is apparent yet it can possibly mean something else [too], so the [speaker] explains that the [intended] meaning is the apparent [one]; hence the ruling of the apparent is confirmed by his explanation.

As for *bayān al-tafsīr* it is when the word is of unclear meaning so he explains it by his exposition.

As for *bayān al-taghyīr* it is when he modifies, by his explanation, the [apparent] meaning of his statement.

As for *bayān al-ḍarūra*, its example is in the Almighty's statement, *And will inherit from him his parents, for his mother is a third* [Q.IV.11]. It is necessary to divide [the inheritance] between the parents; so He explains the portion of the mother and hence this becomes an explanation [by necessity] of the father's portion.[41]

As for *bayān al-ḥāl* its example is when the lawgiver [in this case the Prophet Muḥammad] witnesses a certain action and he does not forbid it,[42] then his silence is of the same order as an explanation.

As for *bayān al-ʿaṭf* it is similar to the conjoining of a measure of volume or weight upon an undefined phrase, [therefore] that is an explanation for the undefined phrase.

As for *bayān al-tabdīl* it is abrogation and that is permissible only for the Lawgiver and it is not permissible for mankind [to conduct].[43]

[38] This is the silence of an individual at an opportune moment for comment, which is regarded as tacit approval.

[39] This statement is usually a number followed by an item of measure linked by a *wāw* (the general letter of conjunction).

[40] This is abrogation, with respect to the texts, by God in the case of the Qur'ān and by the Prophet in the case of *ḥadīth*.

[41] Putting it another way, the mother's portion is mentioned; therefore it is necessary that the father receive the remainder, as he is the only other individual entitled to a share in this situation.

[42] I.e. tacit approval.

[43] Ibid., pp. 67-73.

Second Discussion Regarding the Sunna[44] *of the Messenger of God (may God bless him and grant him peace) and these are more than the grains of sand.*

Section on the types of *khabar* or *ḥadīth*[45]:

The *khabar* of the Messenger of God (may God bless him and grant him peace) is of the same rank of the Qur'ān in the right of necessity of belief in it and acting upon it. This is because whomsoever obeys him then indeed he is obeying God. That which has preceded in the discussion of *khāṣ, ʿāmm, mushtarak, and mujmal* in the Book is similarly applied with respect to the *Sunna*. [The difference being] that doubt may exist with respect to *khabar* in confirming that it was [actually said] by the Messenger (may God bless him and grant him peace) and in linking it to him. It is for this reason that *khabar* is of three types: 1) the first type is verified from the Messenger of God (may God bless him and grant him peace) and confirmed from him without any doubt and that is called *mutawātir*; 2) the second type is that in which there is a small element of doubt and that is called *mashhūr*; 3) and the third type which contains the possibility [that it is from the Messenger] and [yet there is an element of] doubt [regarding its authenticity] and that is *aḥad*.

Mutawātir is that which has been narrated by a large number of people from a large number of people; their agreement upon falsehood is not possible due to their large number and this is how it has reached you. Its examples are the text of the Qur'ān, the number of *rakaʿāt* [of the ritual prayer] and the fixed amounts for *zakāt*.[46]

Mashhūr is that which at the beginning was *aḥad*, then it became widespread[47] in the second and third generation.[48] The *umma* accepted it, so it became like *mutawātir* until it reached you; for example, the *ḥadīth* of wiping on the *khuff* and stoning with respect to *zinā*.

Mutawātir leads to *al-ʿilm al-qatʿī* (definitive knowledge) and its rejection

44 H: Lexically it means a path and custom, technically it means non-compulsory acts of worship. In this context it means that which emanated from the Holy Prophet (may God bless him and grant him peace), other than the Qur'ān, from his statements, which is called *al-ḥadīth*, or actions or tacit approvals.

45 *Ḥadīth* and *khabar* are not exactly synonymous but are sometimes used interchangeably.

46 One of the pillars of Islam, *zakāt* is a fixed tax on wealth.

47 *Mashhūr* literally means famous.

48 The generation of the *tābiʿīn*.

> is disbelief. *Mashhūr* leads to *al-ʿilm al-tamānīna*[49] and its rejection is *bidʿa* (an illegal innovation), and there is no difference of opinion amongst the *ʿulamā'* in the necessity of acting upon them both.
>
> There is a discussion with respect to *aḥad*. So we say *khabar wāḥid* is that which one individual narrates from another, or one from a large number, or a large number from one. The number [of narrators] is not taken into consideration when it has not reached [the number of] *mashhūr*. It is necessary to act upon it with respect to the rulings of the Sharīʿa with the condition that the narrator is Muslim, just, of [good] memory, of [good] intellect and links to you that [*khabar*] from the Messenger of God (may God bless him and grant him peace) with these condition[s].
>
> Narrators are of two types. Firstly, [those] recognised for knowledge and *ijtihād*, like the four Caliphs and ʿAbd Allāh b. Masʿūd, ʿAbd Allāh b. ʿAbbās, ʿAbd Allāh b. ʿUmar, Zayd b. Thābit, Muʿādh b. Jabal and those similar to them [like Ubayy b. Kaʿb, Abū Mūsa al-Ashʿarī, ʿAbd al-Raḥmān b. ʿAwf and ʿĀ'isha] (may God be pleased with them all). Therefore, when their narration is [verified to be] correct, it reaches you from the Messenger of God (may God bless him and grant him peace), [then] to act upon their narrations is superior to acting upon *qiyās*.
>
> [As for] the second type of narrators [it consists of] those individuals who are recognised for their memory and uprightness, but not *ijtihād* and *fatwā*, like Abū Hurayra and Anas b. Mālik [and ʿUqba b. ʿĀmir]. Therefore, when a narration of this kind is [verified to be] correct [and it] reaches you, then if the *khabar wāḥid* conforms with *qiyās* then the necessity of acting upon it is clear. If it contradicts it [i.e. *qiyās*], then it is superior to act upon *qiyās*.[50]

This discussion highlights when the source text, specifically the *khabar wāḥid*, is prioritised over *qiyās* and vice versa; the reason for the difference is due, as the author mentions, to the juristic aptitude of the individual.

> Taking into consideration the different types of the narrators, we say that the condition of acting upon a *khabar wāḥid* is that it does not contradict the Book or the *Sunna mashhūra* or the *ẓāhir* (obvious meaning). He said (upon him be peace), 'The *aḥādīth*[51] will multiply for you after me, so if a

[49] *ʿIlm tamānīna* is knowledge which a person feels is sound, however it does not lead him to absolute certainty *ʿilm qaṭʿī*.

[50] Ibid., pp. 73-75.

[51] Plural of *ḥadīth* when referring to the different sayings of the Prophet.

narration is narrated to you from me, compare it to the Book of God; so accept that which correlates to it and reject what contradicts it.[52]

Aḥsan al-ḥāwashī ʿala uṣūl al-shāshī asserts that the *ḥadīth* which is quoted at the end of the section is in *Ṣaḥīḥ al-Bukhārī* whereas Barkhusānī[53] disagrees and states that this *ḥadīth* is not found there. Upon research, I agree with Barkhusānī and it could be argued that this *ḥadīth* itself goes against the Qur'ān: *O those of you who believe, obey God and His Messenger*...[Q.VIII.20]. This verse is as applicable now as it was at the time of revelation, obviously in terms of following the Qur'ān and *ḥadīth*. Therefore, the *aḥādīth*—not just as *mutawātir* and *mashhūr* but also as *khabar wāḥid*—are a source for the Law independent from the Qur'ān.

We say: when the *khabar wāḥid* opposes the *ẓāhir* (obvious meaning) then it will not be acted on. Among the types that contradict the *ẓāhir* is that *khabar* which did not become *mashhūr* in that period in which *balwā* (tribulation) became widespread during the first and second generation,[54] because they [the Companions] could not be accused of being lax in following the *Sunna*. Therefore, if the *khabar* did not become *mashhūr* when there was severity of need and at the time of *ʿumūm al-balwā* (widespread tribulation), then that is a sign of its incorrectness.[55]

A number of reasons have been put forward by specialists in *ḥadīth* collection (*muḥaddithūn*) for not acting on *khabar wahid*: either they found that the narrator acted against the *khabar wāḥid* he himself had previously narrated, or that the action the narrator was purporting had been abrogated, or the narrator had previously forgotten about this *khabar*. The *khabar* will therefore not be acted upon because either the narrator who intentionally acts against his own narration is a *fāsiq* (transgressor) and his narration is rejected as he is untrustworthy, or acting upon an abrogated *khabar* is impermissible, or the narration of a narrator who is prone to forgetfulness is unacceptable. The author then states that when the *khabar wāḥid* contains such a ruling, at a time when the majority of the people are in need due to widespread

[52] Ibid., pp. 75-76.

[53] Barkhusānī, *Tashīl uṣūl al-shāshī*, p. 151.

[54] In the first two generations of the Muslim community there was significant political unrest after the assassination of Caliph ʿUthmān in particular and the resultant battles. In this great turmoil any lesser known *ḥadīth* which could be applied due to the situation would have been practiced and hence become *mashhūr*, but this did not happen.

[55] Shāshī, *Uṣūl al-shāshī*, p. 77.

tribulation, yet the *khabar wāḥid* does not reach the rank of *mashhūr*, and that when this is within the era of the Companions and the Successors, then this is a sure sign that the narration is incorrect.[56]

> *Khabar wāḥid* is considered as evidence in four places: [1] with regards to the right of God exclusively which carries no punishment; [2] with regards to the right of the person exclusively in which there is an accusation against another; [3] a person's right exclusively where there is no accusation; [4] a person's right exclusively where there is an accusation [against another] from one point and not from another. As for the first, the *khabar wāḥid* will be accepted because the Messenger of God (may God bless him and grant him peace) accepted the testimony of a Bedouin with regards to the new moon of Ramaḍān. As for the second, it is conditioned by number and by uprightness; the example [of its application] is in *munāẓaʿāt* (disputes with respect to wealth). As for the third, the *khabar wāḥid* will be accepted whether [the individual] is upright or a transgressor; the example [of its application] is in *muʿāmalāt* (general dealings). As for the fourth, it is, according to Abū Ḥanīfa, conditioned by either number or uprightness and the example [of its application] is in *ʿazl* (dismissal of an agent) and *ḥijr* (curtailing the one given permission).[57]

Shāshī details that when a *khabar wāḥid* is taken in evidence with respect to Islamic law, he is not therefore discussing the individual *khabar wāḥid* but how this type of *khabar* is utilised by the Sharīʿa. Its definition is when it does not reach the rank of *mashhūr* or *mutawātir*; putting it another way, if it is neither *mashhūr* nor *mutawātir* then it is *khabar wāḥid*. For instance, the testimony by two witnesses or the testimony of four witnesses is regarded as *khabar wāḥid* according to Islamic Law except obviously when there is another higher order text.[58]

Third Discussion Regarding Ijmāʿ *(Consensus)*

> In *furūʿ al-dīn* (the branches of the religion), the consensus of this *umma* (*ijmāʿ*), after the passing of the Messenger of God (may God bless him and grant him peace), is considered as an honour for this *umma*. [H: It is taken

56 Aḥmad, *Ajmal al-ḥawāshī ʿalā uṣūl al-shāshī*, pp. 343-44.

57 Shāshī, *Uṣūl al-shāshī*, p. 78.

58 Aḥmad, *Ajmal al-ḥawāshī ʿalā uṣūl al-shāshī*, pp. 346-47.

in evidence with respect to the principles of the religion like *tawḥīd* (the Oneness of God), the Attributes of God, and prophethood, as these are established by the *qawāṭiᶜ al-naqliyya* (definitive transmissions) and hence are in no need for affirmation]. *Ijmāᶜ* is of four types: 1) *Ijmāᶜ* of [all] the Companions (may God be pleased with them) upon *ḥukm al-ḥāditha* (the ruling regarding an incident) is [considered to be] evidence. 2) Their [Companions'] consensus that is brought about by the suggestion of some, and the silence of the remainder on [its] rejection. [H: This is when some expound on a ruling of a recently occurred situation and the remainder do not state anything after the ruling has reached them and a significant amount of time has passed for contemplation and research into the matter. 3) The consensus of those who came after them [the Companions] when they could not find a *qawl al-Salaf* (an injunction/ruling from the previous generation [namely that of the Companions]). 4) The consensus [by later generations (*muta'akhkhirūn*)] on a single *qawl al-salaf.*

As for the first type, it is of the rank of a verse from the Book of Almighty God. [The second type, which is] if their consensus is brought about by the suggestion of some and the silence of the remainder on [its] rejection is in the rank of *mutawātir*. Then [the third type which is] the consensus of those [who came] after them [the Companions] is in the rank of *mashhūr* from the *akhbār*[59]. [And finally the fourth type, which is] the consensus of the *al-muta'akhkhirūn* upon a *qawl al-salaf* is in the rank of *ṣaḥīḥ*[60] from the *āḥād*. [The consensus] which is considered in this section [the fourth type] is the consensus of scholars of *ra'y* (opinion) and *ijtihād*, therefore it does not include the statement[s] of the *ᶜawām* (laypersons), *mutakallimūn* (theologians) and those *muḥaddithūn* (*ḥadīth* scholars) who have no insight into *uṣūl al-fiqh*. [61]

It is clear from the above text that, according to Shāshī, the consensus of the Companions mirrors, on the level of *ijmāᶜ*, the rank of the Qur'ān, whilst the remaining three types of consensus mirror the three different type of *ḥadīth*. The last type is also considered to be the consensus of jurists of the present day. Finally, an acceptable consensus cannot be based on the opinions either

59 Plural of *khabar*.

60 *Saḥīḥ* are the highest level of *ḥadīth* due to the accuracy of their *isnād*.

61 Shāshī, *Uṣūl al-shāshī*, pp. 78-79.

of laypersons, or scholars with expertise in theology or *ḥadīth,* as they do not possess the required legal training.

Fourth Discussion Regarding Qiyās (*Analogical Reasoning*)

Qiyās is one of the proofs of the Sharīʿa. [When dealing] with new matters, it is necessary to act upon it in the absence of that which is above it in terms of means of providing evidence. *Akhbār* and *āthār* (narrations of the Prophet and statements of the Companions) exist in [support] of that. May God bless him and grant him peace asked Muʿādh b. Jabal when he was about to send him to Yemen, 'By what will you judge, O Muʿādh?' He replied, 'By the Book of Almighty God.' He asked, 'And if you do not find [the ruling]?' He replied, 'By the *Sunna* of the Messenger of God, may God bless him and grant him peace.' He asked, 'And if you do not find [the ruling]?' He replied, 'Then I will strive (*ajtahidu*) with my own reason.' The Messenger of God (may God bless him and grant him peace) patted him on the chest and said, 'All praise be to God who has made consistent the messenger of the Messenger of God upon that which He loves and that which pleases Him.'

And it is narrated that a woman of the *Khathʿamiyya* tribe approached the Messenger of God (may God bless him and grant him peace) and asked, 'My father has become extremely old and he must perform *ḥajj* yet he struggles to ride a mount so is it permissible for me to perform *ḥajj* on his behalf?' Upon him be peace replied, 'What would you say if your father was in debt and you paid [his debt] for him, would it be permissible for you?' So she replied, 'Of course.' Upon him be peace replied, 'Then the debt due to God is more worthy [to be paid].'

The Messenger of God (may God bless him and grant him peace) drew an analogy between the *ḥajj* as an obligation for an extremely old man with the rights [of the Sharīʿa] over wealth and he indicated a recorded *ʿilla* [in the paying of a debt] in the permissibility of fulfilling it [the *ḥajj* on behalf of one's father].

The conditions for the correctness of *qiyās* are five: 1) it is not in contradiction of the texts; 2) it is not responsible for changing one of the rulings [already accepted] from the rulings of the text; 3) it is not a ruling [which has been derived from the *aṣl* to the *farʿ* and] whose meaning cannot be comprehended; 4) that the effective cause is due to a legal ruling, not a lexical matter; 5) the *farʿ* does not already have a text [regarding it].

The example of *qiyās* contradicting the text is in what was narrated about al-Ḥasan b. Ziyād being asked about *qahqahā* (laughing out loud) in *ṣalāt*. He replied, 'It invalidates ritual purity (*wuḍū'*).' The questioner [further] asked, 'If a man slanders a chaste woman in *ṣalāt* [then] this does not invalidate *wuḍū'*, even though slandering a chaste woman is more severe in terms of sin, so how can it [*wuḍū'*] be invalidated by *qahqahā* when that is less severe?' This is *qiyās* in contradiction to a text of a *ḥadīth*… .

The example of the second…is that it is said that *niyya* (intention) [should] be a condition in *wuḍū'* due to *qiyās* upon *tayammum* (dry ablution). This would make necessary a change of the Qur'ānic verse of *wuḍū'*[62] [which would change it] from absolute (*muṭlaq*) to qualified (*muqayyad*).

The example of the third is…with respect to the permissibility of one who makes *wuḍū'* with *nabidh al-tamar*;[63] [another person might think that] it must be permissible with other *nabidh* by *qiyās* upon *nabidh* of dates [but this is not the case].

The example of the fourth is…of the *sāriq* (a thief) who steals because he takes the wealth of another in secret [without the knowledge of the owner or others], and the grave robber is included in this definition so he becomes a thief by *qiyās*. [However], this is *qiyās* in linguistics [when it should be based on *ʿilla* as has been demonstrated previously] with the admission that this noun is not used for him in the language.

The example of the fifth…is it is said that it is impermissible to free a non-Muslim slave due to *kaffārat al-yamīn* (expiation of an oath) and *ẓihār* (expiation of *ẓihār* divorce) because of *qiyās* upon *kaffārat al-qatl* (expiation for murder).[64]

The verses in the Qur'ān do not specify what kind of slave for *kaffārat al-ẓihār* (*As to those of you who commit* ẓihār *with their wives then they revoke that which they said so free a slave before you touch* [Q.LVIII.2]) and *kaffārat al-yamīn* (*So its expiation is the feeding of ten poor people from that which you feed your families or clothe them or free a slave* [Q.V.89]). Basing it on *kaffārat al-qatl* which stipulates

62 '*So wash your faces and your arms until the elbows and wipe your heads and* [*wash*] *your feet until the ankles*' (Q.V.6).

63 This is when dates are left to soak in water for several hours; the liquid that remains after removing the dates is called *nabidh al-tamar*.

64 Ibid., pp. 83-87.

a Muslim slave (*...so free a Muslim slave...* [Q.IV.92]) is incorrect as the first two are *muṭlaq* (absolute) and the latter is *muqayyad* (qualified).

Qiyās al-Sharīʿa (Sharīʿa Analogical Reasoning):

Qiyās al-sharīʿa is the arranging of the ruling for [something where there is] no evidence in the texts upon a clear meaning; it [this meaning] is the *ʿilla* (evidential cause) for the ruling which is has its evidence in the texts. This meaning is recognised as an evidential cause from the Book, the *Sunna*, the consensus, *ijtihād* and *istinbāṭ* (rational deduction).

An example of a known evidential cause from the Book is *kathrat al-ṭawāf* (regular coming and going, i.e. regular visitors), therefore it is regarded as an evidential cause in order to remove difficulty in requesting permission [to enter], in His statement the Almighty said, *There is no sin upon you nor them, some of them are* ṭawwāfūn (regular visitors) *upon you and some of you upon them* [Q.XXIV.58]. Also, the Messenger of God (may God bless him and grant him peace) removed the difficulty [of making] water left by a cat after drinking impure due to this evidential cause. For he said (may God bless him and grant him peace), 'The cat is not impure for indeed it is from the *ṭawwāfūn* and *al-ṭawwāfāt*[65].' So our colleagues reasoned analogically that everything that resides in a house like a mouse and snake to be like a cat by the evidential cause of coming and going [and therefore the water they have left over from where they drink would also not be regarded as impure].[66]

I have not detailed the examples from the other sources, namely the *Sunna*, consensus and analogical reasoning, as the above is sufficient to highlight the methodology.

Then, after this, we say that *qiyās* is of two types: first of the two is a ruling that is arrived at on the basis of the [same] *nawʿ* (type) of ruling which is established in the *aṣl* [hence, the type is the same in both *aṣl* and *farʿ*]. The second is that which is from the [same] *jins* (species) [therefore, the species is the same in both *aṣl* and *farʿ*].

The example of similarity in *nawʿ* is that we say that being a minor is an effective cause for the guardianship[67] in *nikāḥ* (marriage) in the case of

[65] *Ṭawwāfāt* is the feminine of *ṭawwāfūn*.

[66] Ibid., p. 88.

[67] I.e. a minor cannot contract a marriage on his or her own, they require a parent/guardian.

minor boys, so the guardianship of *nikāḥ* in minor girls is established due to the presence of the above effective cause.

The example of similarity in *jins* is that which is said concerning excessive coming and going (*ṭawāf*) as an effective cause for removing the difficulty of asking permission [to enter] for one's slaves, and disregarded the difficulty [of considering] water left behind to be impure due to this effective cause; therefore, this difficulty is from the *jins* of that difficulty, not from its *nawᶜ*.[68]

The first case highlights when the *nawᶜ* is the same; if the ruling applies to one 'type' of minor, then it applies to all minors. In the second case, the *jins* is the same, that is, 'excessive coming and going', however the *nawᶜ* is different. The first is due to the difficulty of continuously asking permission to enter and the second is to the difficulty of verifying water left behind.

	(*ᶜIlla*) *Nawᶜ*	*Jins*	*Ḥukm* from *aṣl to farᶜ*
Case 1	(minor) male	n/a	guardianship (*aṣl*)
	(minor) female	n/a	guardianship (*farᶜ*)

In this case the *nawᶜ*, which is the causative effect, is found to be the same hence the ruling of guardianship transfers from the minor male to minor female.

	Nawᶜ	*Jins*	*ᶜIlla-ḥukm* transfers
Case 2	seeking permission	difficulty	coming and going (*aṣl*)
	the basic purity of water	difficulty	coming and going (*farᶜ*)

In Case 2 slaves are excused from seeking permission from their masters due to the difficulty it would cause as they regularly come in and out of the house and move freely from room to room; therefore the *ᶜilla* is free movement or 'coming and going'. This is also found in creatures which generally inhabit houses with humans; in a normal situation the water they leave behind after drinking would be regarded as impure, however exceptionally

[68] Ibid., pp. 89-90.

it is permissible to use it due to the difficulty it would cause to people in having to dispose of it if they were not permitted to do so. This would be especially difficult in areas where water is scarce. In conclusion, the same *ʿilla* is found in their situation and because the *jins* is the same therefore the water left behind will be regarded as pure.

Section on Rulings:

> The ruling is associated with its *sabab* (way) and it is established by its *ʿilla*, and it is brought about by its condition (*sharṭ*). So the *sabab* is a way by which something is reached, like a path, because the *sabab* is the reaching of a destination by the process of walking and [similarly] a rope is a *sabab* for obtaining water by casting [into a well]. Therefore, based on this, everything that is a way to a ruling by a means is called its *sabab sharʿī* and the means is the *ʿilla*. The examples of *sabab* are the opening of the doors of the stable and cage and the untying of the ropes of the slaves, these are *sabab* (ways) of losing animals, birds and slaves.
>
> When the *sabab* and *ʿilla* come together the ruling is linked to the *ʿilla*, not the *sabab*, except if the linking to the *ʿilla* is difficult, then it is linked to the *sabab*. Regarding this our scholars say that if an individual hands a knife to a child and the child kills himself then [the individual] is not responsible. [However] if it was to drop from the child's hand and he was to injure himself then he will be responsible. [Likewise] if he was to mount a child upon an animal and he rode it and [the animal was to] sway right and left so he falls and dies [then the individual] is not responsible. [Another example is] if an individual directs [another] individual to somebody else's wealth and he steals it, or to another person and he kills him, or to a caravan so he attacks it then there is no compensation to pay for directing.[69]

In terms of an individual passing a knife to a person who subsequently kills himself, the view is that the former individual is not responsible for the latter's actions. This is understood by considering the passing of the knife as the *sabab* and the *ʿilla* is the recipient's subsequent actions. As has been stated the ruling is linked to the *ʿilla* and not the *sabab*, which is why the first individual is not responsible. However, in the second situation, where an individual passes the knife to a person who subsequently drops it and injures

[69] Ibid. pp. 96-97.

himself because of it, the *sabab* is the same as before, whereas the *ʿilla* is the involuntary dropping of the knife. It is not possible to link the ruling here to the *ʿilla* as it was an unintentional action; hence it will be associated with the *sabab*, which holds the first individual responsible.[70]

> This is contrary to when a trustee directs a thief to the trust [which is entrusted to him] so he steals it, or a *muḥrim*[71] indicates to another the birds of the *Ḥaram* so he kills it [one or more]. Therefore, the necessity for the trustee to pay compensation is due to forsaking the protection, which was necessary upon him, not the indication; and upon the *muḥrim* by the consideration that indicating is prohibited in his *iḥrām* like using perfume and wearing sewn garments, so he is responsible due to committing a prohibited act and not due to indication.[72]

Aḥkām Sharʿiyya (Sharīʿa Rulings):

> The Sharīʿa rulings are based upon their *sabab* that is because the [actual] necessity [i.e. the *ʿilla*] is not apparent to us, therefore it is necessary for signs [to exist in order] for the individual to identify the necessity of the ruling. Furthermore, due to this consideration the rulings are associated with the *sabab*. Hence, the *sabab* of the necessity of *ṣalāt* is the time [for *ṣalāt*]; [a person] performs *ṣalāt* not before the time enters, but rather after the time enters.[73]

Therefore, with all ritual matters which are not or cannot be rationally understood as to the reason for their performance or omission, then the ruling is based upon the *sabab*; in the case of the *ṣalāt* it is the decreed five times a day.

Shāshī's Terminology for the Different Gradation of Rulings:[74]

> *Farḍ* lexically means to estimate, to hypothesise, to assume, to fix; and the *shay'* is that which is fixed and in which there is no possibility for increasing or decreasing. In the Sharīʿa, it is that which is established by a definitive

[70] Aḥmad, *Ajmal al-ḥawāshī ʿalā uṣūl al-shāshī*, p. 411.

[71] A *muḥrim* is someone who is about to perform the rites of *ʿumra* or *ḥajj* at the holy mosque in Mecca, the *Ḥaram*. A *muḥrim* is prohibited from killing anything while in a state of *iḥrām*.

[72] Shāshī, *Uṣūl al-shāshī*, p. 97.

[73] Ibid., p. 99.

[74] This is a list of the different gradations of rulings according to Shāshī. For a more comprehensive list, please see the section Terminology of the Different Gradation of Rulings below.

evidence (*dalīl qaṭʿī*) in which there is no doubt and its ruling is that it is necessary to act upon it and to believe in it.

Wujūb [lexically] is 'to fall', i.e. that which descends upon a servant without his choice. It is [derived] from *wajaba* and [lexically, it] is 'disruptive', so it is called *wājib* because of it being disruptive between *farḍ* and *nafl* [for *nafl* see below]. So it becomes *farḍ* with respect to acting [upon it] to such an extent that it is not permissible to leave it, and *nafl* with respect to believing [in it]. Therefore it is not necessary upon us to bring a definitive belief [upon it]. In the Sharīʿa, it is that which is established by an evidence in which there is doubt, like a Qur'ānic verse which has been interpreted and a *ṣaḥīḥ* from narrations and its ruling is according to what we have mentioned.

Sunna is a name for the pleasing path which the Sharīʿa has chosen whether it is from the Messenger of God (may God bless him and grant him peace) or from the Companions. Upon him be peace said, 'Take hold of my *Sunna* and the *sunna* of the *khulafā'* (caliphs) after me, hold tightly to it with your [very] molars.' [H: Ibn Māja quotes this through three changes in a long *ḥadīth* from al-ʿIrbāḍ b. Sāriyya as *marfūʿ*, as does Tirmidhī]. Its ruling is that an individual should seek to revive it and he is blameworthy for leaving it, except if he leaves it due to a reason.

Nafl is a name for extra and bonus—war-booty is referred to as *nafl* because it is a bonus upon that which was intended in *jihād*. In the Sharīʿa, it is a name for that which is additional to the *farḍ* and *wājib*. Its ruling is that an individual is rewarded for performing it, but not punished by abandoning it. *Nafl* and-*taṭawwuʿ* (voluntary as opposed to obligatory actions) are one of the same.

As for *rukhṣa*, it is a name for *yusr* (ease) and *suhūla* (convenience). In the Sharīʿa, [it is] to make something that is difficult easy due to a reason [which is] facing the one expected to carry it out [so that they may] be excused. Its types are different due to the different *sabab* and they are the reasons for people to be excused [from a difficult matter]; the result is one of two types. The first is *rukhṣat al-fiʿl* (concession in action) with it [the initial action] remaining illegal, like forgiveness with respect to [punishable] crimes. This is like the verbal expressing of words of disbelief with contentment [of faith] in the heart under duress and force, or swearing at the Prophet (may God bless him and grant him peace), or destroying the wealth of a Muslim, or killing someone under duress and force. Its ruling is if he remains patient until he is killed, then he would be rewarded [in the Hereafter] due to his refraining from the illegal exonerating himself from disobeying the Prophet, upon him be peace. The second type is changing the attributes of the act so that it becomes permissible as it is. Almighty God has said, *So whomsoever is compelled due to starvation without inclining to sin, then indeed God is All-forgiving and All-merciful* [Q.v.3]. This is similar to compulsion in eating non-*ḥalāl* meat and drinking alcohol [in a time of dire necessity where one's life is under threat]. Its ruling is that refraining from acting thus would lead [to the person] to become a sinner by refraining from [consuming] the permissible, for it would become like suicide.[75]

In the first type of concession the act remains illegal; the difference is that on the Day of Judgement the person will not be punished for it due to the situation the person was in when the act was committed. However, in the second case the act actually changes from being illegal to legal to such an extent that if the person were to avoid it they would be regarded as a sinner as they are avoiding a permissible substance which could save their life.

The Role of the Mujtahid

It is necessary for the *mujtahid* to seek the *ḥukm al-ḥāditha* (ruling regarding an incident) from the Book of Almighty God, then from *Sunna* of the Messenger of God (may God bless him and grant him peace) by explicit text or its indications by the above mentioned [methodology]. For indeed there is no way to act upon pure speculative reason with the possibility of acting upon source texts.[76]

[In the case of contradictory evidence], if the contradiction is between two verses of the Qur'ān,[77] then he will incline towards [the clarification found in] the *Sunna*. If it is between two *Sunna* [i.e. *khabar*], he will incline towards the statement of the Companions (may God be pleased with them) and correct *qiyās*. Then when two applications of *qiyās* are contradictory, the *mujtahid* will *yataḥarrā* (he will strive in contemplation and thought),

[75] Ibid., pp. 103-05.

[76] Ibid., p. 81.

[77] The Qur'ān was revealed over a period of approximately twenty-three years, hence circumstances were changing and the Qur'ān spoke about those situations. So later verses abrogated earlier verses. Similarly some verses may appear to be contradictory but are clarified by the examples found in the *Sunna*.

> then act upon one of the two [applications] because he has no further religious means of obtaining evidence after *qiyās*.[78]

Here end the extracts from *Uṣūl al-shāshī*.

Istiḥsān: Reasoning Based on Equity and Fairness

There is another type of *qiyās* which is not detailed in *Uṣūl al-shāshī*. It is referred to as reasoning based on equity and fairness and is widely employed by the Ḥanafī jurists as well as jurists from other Schools in different ways;[79] it is called *istiḥsān* and is also referred to by some as concealed or subtle *qiyās*.[80] Shāshī does not include it because the four subjects he discusses—of the Qur'ān, *Sunna*, *Ijmā*ᶜ and *qiyās*—are accepted as the sources for the Law by most scholars and because there is some difference of opinion with respect to *istiḥsān* as will become apparent. For *istiḥsān* is not necessarily based on the letter of the law but rather on the spirit of the law.[81] Shaybānī, as cited by Libson, asserts:

> *Istiḥsān* is the renunciation of *qiyās* and the adoption of what is more fitting for people. Some say, *istiḥsān* seeks to introduce more lenience in laws in connection with difficulties encountered by the individual and the general public. Some say, it is to give wide latitude and to solicit comfort.'[82]

Shaybānī's definition is also the position of this present work and is confirmed by this traditional model as we will determine from Mullah Jewan's interpretation.

In order to put forward the traditional understanding of *istiḥsān* a section from *Nūr al-Anwār* by Aḥmad b. Abu Saᶜīd (more commonly known as Mullah Jewan) is presented. The original text is *al-Manār* by ᶜAbd Allāh b. Aḥmad al-Nasafī and *Nūr al-Anwār* is a commentary on it. As with Shāshī's text, these works are widely accepted by the School and extensively used as teaching tools. Hence *al-Manār* is the original text (**in bold**) with the commentary (in regular text). The super-commentary of the text is called *Qamr*

[78] Ibid., pp. 82-83.

[79] Mohammad Hashim Kamali, *Equity and Fairness in Islam* (Cambridge: The Islamic Texts Society, 2005) is a work dedicated to the subject of *istiḥsān*.

[80] Hence, 'standard' *qiyās* is sometimes referred to as manifest or apparent *qiyās*.

[81] John Makdisi, 'Legal Logic and Equity in Islamic Law', *American Journal of Comparative Law* (vol. 33, 1985), pp. 67-69.

[82] Gideon Libson, 'On the Development of Custom as a Source of Law in Islamic Law', *Islamic Law and Society* (vol. 4, no. 2, 1997), p. 151.

al-Aqmār by Muhammad Saʿīd and it will be used when clarification is required within square brackets and preceded by H:

It [*istiḥsān*] is evidence which opposes manifest *qiyās*, I refer to its discussion by his statement **and *istiḥsān* occurs due to *āthār* (text referring to *khabar*), *ijmāʿ* (consensus), *ḍarūra* (necessity) and subtle *qiyās*** i.e. manifest *qiyās* wants to bring about a certain thing and text, consensus, necessity, subtle analogical reasoning wants to bring about that which opposes it. Hence acting upon *qiyās* is abandoned and *istiḥsān* is turned to instead. So he clarifies [by] an example of each type and he says **like *salam*** [H: Transaction in which the product is transferred from seller to buyer with deferred payment] is an example of *istiḥsān* due to text because *qiyās* objects to its permissibility as it is a *bayʿ al-maʿdūm* (a transaction which is lacking, i.e. there is nothing in exchange for the product at the time of sale), however, we regard it as permissible due to text, which is his saying (may God bless him and grant him peace), 'Whomsoever trades by means of *salam* from amongst you should carry it out [in products] of known volumes and known weights to known times.' [Both Bukhārī and Muslim record this *ḥadīth*.] ***Istiṣnāʿa*** is an example of *istiḥsān* due to *ijmāʿ* and that applies to ordering a person, for instance, that he prepares for him *khuff* in such and such manner and he describes its quality and its proportions but does not mention the deadline [for completion]. This is because, *qiyās* objects to its permissibility as it is a *bayʿ al-maʿdūm* however we abandon [*qiyās*]. *Istiḥsān*-wise it is permissible due to *ijmāʿ* [H: It is an accepted practice from the time of the Prophet (may God bless him and grant him peace) to this time now without any objection] because of the practice of the people in this; if a deadline is given then it is *salam*. **The purifying of utensils** is an example of *istiḥsān* due to necessity. *Qiyās* wants to bring about its impurity when they become impure because it is not possible to squeeze it in order to remove impurity from it [as that is the general process of cleansing]. However we [regard] *istiḥsān* [applicable] in its purification because of the necessary difficulty caused by this and the distress in its impurity. **The purity of the water left over from birds of prey** is an example of *istiḥsān* due to subtle *qiyās*, for indeed apparent *qiyās* wants to bring about its impurity due to the fact that its meat is impermissible[83] and [the same would apply to] water left over from them [i.e. the birds of prey] as does to the water left over from animals of prey, however

[83] Islam prohibits the consumption of the flesh of birds and animals of prey.

> [adopting] *istiḥsān* in [accepting] its purity due to subtle *qiyās*, which is that they eat with their beaks and that is a bone which is pure from a live or dead [animal] contrary to animals of prey because they eat with their tongues so their impure saliva mixes with the water.[84]

Therefore, in all these situations the spirit of the law and seeking ease for the people is sought. In trade the purpose is to exchange money for items or items for items so even though some practices would be impermissible the were made permissible by the Prophet as these were practices of the people, which the Muslims were also involved in. The practice of achieving or maintaining purity is a necessary requirement, even in those situations where it is not possible due to the unnecessary difficulty it would cause; the difficulty is removed by the methodology of *istiḥsān*. Therefore, as has been indicated throughout this work, societal practices and the removal of unnecessary difficulty via the means of *istiḥsān* (and *ʿurf* in some cases) can bring about changes in the way Islamic Law is practiced.

> **We prioritise *istiḥsān* that which is subtle *qiyās*, over *qiyās*, when its effect is strong**. [This is] because [the ruling] is based upon the strength of the effect and its weakness not upon its apparentness or its concealment for indeed the world is apparent and the Hereafter is concealed however it is given priority over the world because of the strength of its effect due to its everlasting nature and serenity. [There are] many examples among them is the [example of] leftover water of birds of prey, which has been mentioned [earlier]. For indeed in *istiḥsān* there is strong effect and for that reason it is prioritised over [H: apparent] *qiyās* like I have explained. In this is an indication towards the fact that acting upon *istiḥsān* is not outside of the four evidences but it is a strong type of *qiyās*. So there can be no justified accusation against Abū Ḥanīfa that he used other than the four evidences.[85]

There is an acknowledgement at the end of the translated text above of an objection to *istiḥsān*. The objection is whether in following *istiḥsān*, when the other four sources of the Law exist, one would be following one's desires in order to leave the truth and seek ease in a religious matter through unregulated illegal means? Imām Sarakhsī replies in his *Uṣūl*:

> It [*istiḥsān*] according to the *fuqahāʾ* is of two types: [firstly] acting upon

[84] Mullah Jewan, *Nūr al-anwār* (*sharḥ* of *al-manār*) *maʿa qamr al-aqmār* (Karachi: Saeed Company, no date), pp. 243-44.

[85] Ibid., p. 244.

> *ijtihād* and the *ghālib al-ra'y* (dominant rational view) in determining that which the Sharīʿa has entrusted upon our views like the mentioned benefits in His statement, *A benefit* bi'l-maʿrūf (with equity, fairness, fitting) *is a right on those who do good* [Q.II.236]. It is necessary that it is [referring to] via the means of ease and difficulty and the condition is that it be by *maʿrūf*. Therefore we acknowledge that the meaning of recognising its *istiḥsān* is by the dominant rational view. Similarly, His statement, *And upon the father their food and their clothes* bi'l-maʿrūf [Q.II.233]. [In conclusion,] none from the jurists would oppose this type of *istiḥsān*. The second type is that evidence that opposes the apparent *qiyās*, which the initial thought rushes towards before [serious] fruitful contemplation. Once [serious] fruitful contemplation has taken place, with respect to the *ḥukm al-ḥāditha* (ruling of the issue), and its like from the *uṣūl* it becomes apparent that the evidence that opposes it [i.e. *qiyās*] is stronger, therefore acting upon it is correct.[86]

Therefore, *istiḥsān* is of two types: what the intellect informs the jurist as to what is fitting in matters for the people, and a more detailed rational understanding of a matter rather than the application of apparent simplistic logic. He further explains the difference between the terminology of *qiyās* and *istiḥsān*:

> The use of the terminology of *qiyās* and *istiḥsān* by our *fuqahā'* is to clarify between two opposing [pieces of] evidence. If one of them is specified by *istiḥsān* then has to be acted upon.
>
> The acting upon *istiḥsān* is due to the stronger of two evidences not *ittibāʿa al-hawā* (the following of whims) or *shahwat al-nafs* (desires of the lower self) in anything.
>
> We recognise that the correct procedure is to abandon *qiyās* altogether in that situation where *istiḥsān* is taken [as evidence]. This clarifies that acting upon *istiḥsān* does not take place with the existence of opposition [from *qiyās*] but rather the weakness [in this case *qiyās*] is abandoned by the strong [in this case of *istiḥsān*]. He says in the chapter of theft: If a group of individuals enter a house and they gather the contents on to the back of one of them and he leaves with it and they also leave with him, then according to *qiyās* only the one who carried the wealth has his hand cut off, yet according to *istiḥsān* all of them will have their hands cut off.[87]

[86] Aḥmad al-Sarakhsī, *Uṣūl al-sarakhsī* (Beirut: Dār al-Kutub al-ʿIlmiyya, 2005), vol. 2, p. 200.

[87] Ibid., p. 201.

He continues:

> So we have recognised that *qiyās* is abandoned altogether in that situation where it is possible to act upon *istiḥsān*. They are only referred to as opposing evidences with respect to the original situation for both of them not because between the two of them there exists opposition in one situation. The proof that this is what is intended is what he says in the chapter of divorce: If a man says to his wife, 'When you [next] menstruate then you are divorced.'[88] To which she replies, 'I have menstruated,' and her husband does not believe her, hence she cannot be proved to be correct due to *qiyās* because of the condition of it having to be apparent [i.e. *qiyās* can only be applied to the apparent]. Menstruation, which is [here] a condition for divorce, is not like her entering of a house and her speaking to Zayd [which on the other hand can be observed and verified]. [Now] according to *istiḥsān* she is divorced because menstruation is something which is in her, he cannot establish its existence except from her. Hence he has no choice but to accept her statement regarding it, [this is] like love and hatred [i.e. a man does not know if his wife loves or hates him except if she says so].[89]

In conclusion, *istiḥsān* must be in harmony with the spirit of the Law and obviously cannot be in conflict with the immutable sources. The matter in discussion must be rational and acceptable to individuals of sound reason, which includes matters pertaining to transactions and the like, but not ritual matters, as they are generally not within the scope of reason. It must have general application rather than be specific to a small number of individuals and there must be a need or requirement for the removal of a hardship. Hence, this completes the discussion on *uṣūl al-fiqh* according to the Ḥanafī School, which the founding jurists and those that followed them adopted in order to derive rulings; this was subsequently referred to as *ẓāhir al-riwāya*, the agreed Law of the School. Having said that, there are three distinct concepts which cause a jurist or *muftī* to issue a ruling that could and should be different from the *ẓāhir al-riwāya*; the first is *ʿurf* or *ʿāda* (custom or habit),[90] the second is the context[91] (*qarā'in al-aḥwāl*) and the third is *ḍarūra* (necessities), all are dependent upon the society in which the

[88] The reason behind such a statement is because the couple need to identify if the woman is pregnant or not as there would be a number of legal obligations for the father if there is a child.

[89] Ibid., p. 202.

[90] *ʿUrf* and *ʿāda* are virtually synonymous.

[91] Context (*qarā'in al-aḥwāl*) will be discussed in detail in the next chapter on Political-legal Jurisdictions.

muftī is serving and will be discussed in detail in order to bring about an accurate understanding. It could be presented that the first (*ʿurf*) is a modification of the rulings, not the methodology and principles, in order to 'best fit' the law within a society, and the second—context—is more drastic as, on a number of occasions, it converts the illegal to the legal, while *ḍarūra* to a certain extent exists within the Qur'ān, *ḥadīth* and *ijmāʿ*.

ʿUrf: Societal Customs

An area which is recognised as essential when reaching a conclusion in a *mas'ala* (transmitted legal opinion) is taking into consideration the traits, habits, customs, culture and use of language amongst the people of the time.[92] One must not confuse it as a source, even though sometimes contemporary scholars regard it as such, but rather as a means or a context, which is adapted and recognised when passing rulings. Had it been a source then it could challenge the Qur'ān and *Sunna*; for instance, if gambling were widespread within a population then would this *ʿurf* make it permissible? This would not be acceptable, hence *ʿurf* cannot be considered as a source.

ʿUrf has been incorporated into Islamic law through a variety of ways: some due to *Sunna* and *ijmāʿ*; some through the utilisation of *istiḥsān*, secondary sources like *fatāwā*, and legal strategies (*ḥiyal*).[93] Therefore, those rulings that are based on *ʿurf* or *ʿāda* will change due to the changing *ʿurf* as this is the context they are based on. This has already been highlighted above when analysing the use of language by taking into account the context, dialect and habits in conjunction with what the individuals who use it mean by it. For example, the Qur'ān is clear in its ruling in the following verse, '*Do not say "uff"* [express anger or displeasure] *to them* [parents] *and do not reproach them*.' In this verse, Almighty God is clearly commanding the individual not to use the word '*uff*' to his parents, but if this word meant 'I love you' in a language other than Arabic, then the ruling would be that it is permissible to use '*uff*', rather, it would be praiseworthy to use those words to one's parents. Hence the ruling is based upon the meaning of those particular words to a certain people and it can quite easily be envisaged that they be praiseworthy and permissible in one land and not in another, and also praiseworthy and permissible in one era and not in another.

92 Umar Abd Allah, *Islam and the Cultural Imperative* (A Nawawi Foundation Paper, 2004).

93 Libson, 'On the Development of Custom as a Source of Law in Islamic Law', pp. 131-55.

However, how far can *ʿurf* be utilised? What if taking usury becomes widely accepted in a Muslim society? Or that the consumption of alcohol? In answer to this the jurists state, 'If *naṣṣ* is found which opposes it [*ʿurf*] then it is inappropriate for it [*ʿurf*] to abrogate or qualify it [the *naṣ*], if not then it will be considered in many places.'[94] The *naṣṣ* referred to are absolute unequivocal verses of the Qur'ān that carry the ruling of *mufassar* and *muḥkam*, and *mutawātir ḥadīth* which contain the essentials of Islam and cannot be abrogated or qualified by *ʿurf*.

A traditional scholar who has written about *ʿurf* is Ibn ʿĀbidīn, whose poem on *uṣūl*—*ʿUqūd rasm al-muftī*—is translated in full in the Appendix. Ibn ʿĀbidīn wrote a commentary on *ʿUqūd rasm al-muftī* entitled *Sharḥ ʿuqūd rasm al-muftī* and in it he says:

> *al-ʿurf fī al-sharʿa lahū iʿtibār* — *ladha ʿalayh al-ḥukm qad yudār*
>
> Custom in Law is considered — And so upon it a ruling can be established.
>
> He [Ghazālī] says in *al-Mustaṣfā* that *ʿurf* and *ʿāda* are those [things] which exist in the hearts brought about by the intellect, and which good, natural disposition accept. In *Sharḥ al-taḥrīr* [it is stated that] *ʿāda* is that matter which occurs repetitively without any intelligible input. In *al-Ashbāh wa'l-naẓā'ir* the sixth legal maxim 'Habit (*ʿāda muḥkama*) is taken into consideration when passing judgement.' Its origin is his statement (may God bless him and grant him peace), 'That which the Muslims consider to be good then it is good with God.'[95] Take note that the consideration of *ʿāda* and *ʿurf* was resorted to in many situations until they [the *fuqahā'*] made it an *aṣl*. So they say that the *ḥaqīqa* is abandoned due to use and *ʿāda* (habit).[96]

More and more it became apparent to the religious scholars that context played a huge part with respect to the rulings, both in the past and in the present, to such an extent that it was duly recognised as an *aṣl* or a 'source'. Hence, *ʿurf* has become of significant value with respect to Islamic law.

> In Bīrī's commentary on *al-Mabsūṭ* [it is quoted], 'That which is established by *ʿurf* is like that which is established by [source] text.' Then know many of the rulings of *mujtahid ṣāḥib al-madhhab* [i.e. Imām Abū Ḥanīfa] were based on that which was in his *ʿurf* and his era, so they [the rulings] will have changed with the changing of the eras due to *fasād ahl al-zamān* (the corruption of the people of later times) or due to the *ʿumūm al-ḍarūra*

94 Ibn ʿĀbidīn, *Radd al-muḥtār ʿalā durr al-mukhtār*, vol. 4, p. 16.

95 This *ḥadīth* to my knowledge is found as *mawqūf*, i.e. it is a statement of ʿAbd Allāh b. Masʿūd which Imām Aḥmad has collated in his *Musnad*.

96 Ibn ʿĀbidīn, *Sharḥ ʿuqūd rasm al-muftī*, p. 37.

(generalised applicability of necessity) [the example of which] we have mentioned earlier in the *fatāwā* of later scholars regarding the permissibility of taking a wage for teaching the Qur'ān.[97]

A point worth emphasising is Ibn ʿĀbidīn's assertion that the ruling on many issues has changed since the time of Abū Ḥanīfa due to two reasons: 1) corruption of societies, and 2) the general application of necessity. In terms of the first reason, he was comparing the society he lived in to the period at the time of the Prophet Muḥammad, and possibly the caliphates of Abū Bakr and ʿUmar. Muslims have always considered the time of the Prophet as the most perfect and that all other ages after his are corrupt to varying degrees and that this is based on sayings of the Prophet himself. As for the second reason—the general application of necessity—see the discussion below on *ḍarūra*.

> So with respect to all of these [issues] whose ruling changes due to the changing times, either because of ***ḍarūra*** **(necessity) or** ***ʿurf*** **(custom/culture) or** ***qarā'in al-aḥwāl*** **(context/circumstance). These [rulings] are not outside the** ***madhhab*** **because if the** ***Ṣāḥib al-Madhhab*** **[Abū Ḥanīfa] lived in this era he would also say the same and had this change occurred in his time then he would not object to it. This is what has encouraged the** ***mujtahidūn fī 'l-madhhab*** **and the People of Correct Opinion[98] from the latter scholars in going against the texts from the** ***Ṣāḥib al-Madhhab*** **in the Books of** ***Ẓāhir al-riwāya*** **as these were established on the basis of what occurred in his era.**[99]

There are two very important points here: firstly, that there are three situations that bring about a change in a ruling: necessity, custom/culture and context. Ibn ʿĀbidīn gives the example of divorce in different countries and how in some places the custom can make it applicable while in other places it is not applicable. Secondly, and this is a crucial point, though later scholars may issue *fatāwā* contrary to the *Ẓāhir al-riwāya* these will still not be contrary to the Ḥanafī School of Law. The reason why there is no contradiction is because the principles remain the same, and among the principles is the necessity of taking into consideration changing times and context when issuing rulings. Furthermore, to apply rulings exclusively from the *Ẓāhir al-riwāya* to issues based on *ʿurf* in a different era will, in fact, be contrary to the Ḥanafī School as

[97] Ibid.

[98] That is, the scholars who uphold traditional Islam.

[99] Ibn ʿĀbidīn, *Sharḥ ʿuqūd rasm al-muftī*, p. 38, emphasis added.

this would be 'blind imitation', which is not permissible for jurists except in the matter of canonical rites.

> So if you say that ʿ*urf* changes time after time and if another ʿ*urf* comes about which has not occurred in the preceding era is it permissible for the *muftī* to oppose the [previous] texts and follow the recently occurred ʿ*urf*? Then I would reply, 'Yes,' for indeed the later scholars, those who opposed the texts in earlier issues, did not oppose them except due to the occurrence of a new ʿ*urf* after the era of the Imām so it is [correct] for the *muftī* to follow the recently occurred ʿ*urf* and those rulings which the *mujtahid* established upon ʿ*urf* of his era. Hence the changing of his ʿ*urf* to another ʿ*urf* which should be followed. However, this can only if the *muftī* is an individual who has correct opinion, good rational view and is knowledgeable of the *qawāʿid al-Sharīʿa* (principles of the Sharīʿa) so that he can differentiate between that type of ʿ*urf* which is permissible to establish rulings on and that which is not. For indeed the *mutaqaddimūn* (earlier scholars) made *ijtihād* a criteria for a *muftī* and they are no longer present in our era. Therefore, the minimum criteria is the recognition of *masā'il* (issues [i.e. legal opinions]) with their conditions and qualifications; many of which are not detailed in full or clearly explained and as a result are left to the understanding of the student *muftī*. Likewise it is necessary [for him] to understand the ʿ*urf* of his era and the state of his fellows, and to facilitate understanding from an able teacher. It is stated at the end of *Muniyya al-muftī*, 'If a man were to memorise all the books of our scholars it would [still] be necessary to study [with a teacher] for *fatwā* until he is guided to it because on many issues one has to respond according to the ʿ*ādāt*[100] of the people of [one's] time on those issues which do not oppose the Sharīʿa.[101]

The *ijtihād* which Ibn ʿĀbidīn refers to is when the founder of the School works on *qawāʿid al-Sharīʿa* (principles of the Sharīʿa) which are the first principles; this is work that only the founders of Schools could and did do. For those who came after, they would firstly have to understand the rationale and principles utilised by the School's founders and then from that, issue *fatāwā* based on that understanding, while taking into consideration the customs of their own era.

[It is stated] in *al-Qunniyya* that it is not correct for the *muftī* or *qāḍī* to pass

100 ʿ*Ādāt* is the plural of ʿ*āda* (habit).

101 Ibid., pp. 38-39.

> judgement according to *Ẓāhir al-madhhab* and abandon *ʿurf*...It is quoted in *al-Ashbāh* from *al-Bazzāziyya* that a *muftī* should give *fatwā* according to his understanding of *maṣlaḥa* (what is good and provides ease for the majority).
>
> We say acting upon *ʿurf* [is permissible] when it does not oppose the Sharīʿa like tax and *ribā* and similar matters. It is necessary for the *muftī, qāḍi* and even the *mujtahid* to be fully aware of the conditions of the people for it is said that, 'Whoever [referring to scholars] is ignorant [of the state] of the people, he is an ignoramus.'[102]

Ibn ʿĀbidīn details the two types of *ʿurf* and when they should be considered:

> Then take note that *ʿurf* is of two types, *ʿāmm* (general) and *khāṣ* (particular). A general ruling can be established by *ʿāmm* and it can act to specify a *qiyās* or text.[103] This is contrary to *khāṣ* through which only a specific ruling is established that which does not oppose *qiyās* or text.
>
> *Al-ʿurf al-ʿāmm* is not considered when it is necessary to abandon that which is evidenced from texts; it is only considered when it is necessary to specify the text. *Al-ʿurf al-khāṣ* is not considered in both places. It is only considered in the rights of its people[104] when it does not make it necessary to abandon text nor will it specify it even if it opposes *Ẓāhir al-riwāya*. It is used in those recognised words used in oaths and in the habits/customs during transactions like buying and selling and renting. Hence these words and transactions will accord in every city with the habit of its residents.[105]

This understanding of *ʿurf* which Ibn ʿĀbidīn purports could be developed further to include politics, citizenship and international affairs as they are not contrary to the Sharīʿa and are the *ʿurf* of most, if not all, societies/states at the moment.

Ḍarūra: Sharīʿa-compliant Necessities

As has been highlighted above, impermissible matters may become permissible out of necessity (*ḍarūra*). However, the jurist's definition of 'necessity' is specific

[102] Ibid., p. 39.

[103] Specifically *ḥadīth*. For instance, if an act is forbidden due to text, then according to that *ʿurf* which is *ʿāmm* we would specify the prohibition of that act alone and not other acts which may be similar in type.

[104] It is that which affects a specific group of people for instance market traders, stock market workers, solicitors, etc.

[105] Ibid., p. 40.

and may be somewhat different from how society employs it. From the perspective of the jurists, the principle of necessity can be applied in two cases: firstly, when individuals find themselves in a difficult situation, for instance, a Muslim required to eat pork rather than starve to death, or a seafarer throwing another's goods into the sea if their boat is about to sink. This application of *ḍarūra* has strict parameters and limits. Secondly, cases dealing with economic, social and arguably political situations. Here the application requires more subtlety.[106] Shāṭibī discusses all of these:

> *Ḍarūriyyāt*[107] (essentials): Its meaning is that they are essential in establishing [human] well-being in religion and in worldly [matters], such that if they were absent then the [humanity's] well-being in the world would cease. In fact, there would be corruption, disorder and loss of life; and in other [situations] it would be loss of safety and sanctity and there would be grave loss [in the breakdown of social order].[108]
>
> *Ḍarūriyyāt* are five [in number]:[109] they are the preservation and safeguarding of religion (*dīn*), life (*nafs*), progeny (*nasl*) property (*māl*) and intellect (*ᶜaql*).[110]

In these cases, if acting upon the impermissible were not made permissible then Muslims would suffer a great loss, which is not the purpose of the Sharīᶜa. For instance, if due to thirst or hunger there is a possibility of death, then it is permissible—in the absence of legal alternatives—to drink alcohol or consume pork -because it would not be possible to sustain life without them. In fact, not only is it permissible, it becomes compulsory. Similar indispensable necessities are also termed *ḍarūriyyāt*:

[106] Bernard Lewis, 'Legal and Historical Reflections on the Position of Muslim Populations under Non-Muslim Rule', *Journal Institute of Muslim Minority Affairs* (vol. 13, no. 1, 1992), p. 3.

[107] *Ḍarūriyyāt* is from the same root as *ḍarūra* and is here being used in a more limited sense than *ḍarūra*.

[108] Shāṭibī, *Muwāfaqāt*, vol. 2, p. 7.

[109] Abou El-Fadl, in *Islam and the Challenge of Democracy*, p. 10, defines the safeguarding of religion as 'the protection of religious belief; the protection of life should mean the taking of life must be for a just cause and the result a just process; the protection of the intellect should mean the right to free thinking, expression and belief; the protection of honor should mean the protecting of the dignity of the human being; and the protection of property should mean the right to compensation for the taking of property.' Abdul Bari, in *Race, Religion & Muslim Identity in Britain*, pp. 112-3, adds human dignity to *ḍarūriyyāt* and states that the list of issues which come under *ḥājiyyāt* and *taḥsīniyyāt* is endless.

[110] Shāṭibī, *Muwāfaqāt*, vol. 2, p. 8.

Ḥājiyyāt (complementary): Its meaning is that there is a need for them [for the sake of] easing and for the removal of a straitening affliction for the majority [of people] who [would suffer] distress and associated difficulties in the absence of what is needed.

Taḥsīniyyāt (improvements/perfecting): Its meaning is the adopting what is associated with the best in habits, customs and practices.[111]

Three examples can be put forward to explain the levels of *ḍarūra* which the Sharīʿa recognises:

1. Clothing: If a person covers their body with cheap, ordinary material then it will be sufficient for an individual; this is *ḍarūra*. If, however, the individual chooses to wear clothes according to the climate and season, as otherwise the individual would go through unnecessary difficulty and hardship, then this is *ḥāja*. Finally, by wearing beautiful clothes of quality which are legally sanctioned[112] in order to appear well-dressed, then this is referred to as *taḥsīn*.

2. Food: Eating unappealing food which lacks flavour but which provides sufficient nourishment to keep a person alive would fulfil the criterion for the first level. In order to reach the complementary level, a meal would consist of food that is well-prepared, appetising and sufficient to completely satisfy the appetite of the individual. The manner in which the food is served, the different courses and the etiquette with which the diner prepares and consumes the food would be part of the *taḥsīn*.

3. Shelter: A roof over one's head, whether it is a tent, shed or cave would meet the requirements of *ḍarūra*. To have access to running water, electricity, energy, furniture and fittings and a sewage system with the ability to provide security in the form of locks would reach the stage of *ḥāja*. For the house to be well-furnished and decorated with good quality appliances would mean that it is at the level of *taḥsīn*.

Therefore, when it is said that 'due to *ḍarūra* many illegal issues become legal' this is referring to those situations which have been described above, in which the need is essential for man's survival, and which then become legal due to an unusual situation. Likewise, *ḥāja* includes all those matters which had they not become permissible would have caused significant difficulty and therefore they are regarded as permissible. This interpretation or level of *ḥāja*

111 Ibid., p. 9.

112 An example of clothes that are not legally sanctioned is the wearing of silk clothes for men; this is not permitted by Islamic Law.

is sometimes subsumed into necessity (*al-ḍarūra*). However, when *ḥāja* only causes slight difficulty it cannot be regarded as *al-ḍarūra*. Neither secondary *ḥāja* nor *taḥsīn* can be regarded as permissible at any time if they contradict the Qur'ān and *ḥādīth*.

The criteria to adopt in deciding whether it is justified to permit the impermissible are: firstly, the legal evidence which prohibits them must be existent, explicit and require obedience; secondly, one of the five *maqāṣid* of the Sharīʿa must be affected with certainty or at least high probability; thirdly, all permissible means must be exhausted; fourthly, a similar or greater harm will not result by acting on the impermissible; and finally, the impermissible act may be performed but only to the extent that is required to fulfill the necessity.[113]

Ḥiyal or Makhārij: Legal Devices or Stratagems

As we have seen above, *istiḥsān*, *ʿurf* and *ḍarūra* are taken into consideration when passing legal rulings. In addition to these, there is a final means of finding a legal way for resolving a difficult situation and this is *ḥiyal* or *makhārij* (legal devices or stratagems). This is used mostly in the Ḥanafī School.[114] *Ḥiyal* are the 'relaxation of strict interpretation of the Law' and are therefore similar to dispensations (*rukhaṣ*). The application of *ḥiyal* is legitimised by examples of the dispensations granted by God in texts and their aim is to take an individual out of a sinful situation to a position of correctness (*al-khurūj min al-ithm ilā'l-ḥaqq*). For instance, 'God mitigated the prohibition of proposing marriage to a woman observing her waiting period by permitting indirect statements that allude to a proposal in marriage.'[115] In fact, *ḥiyal* are another means by which the spirit of the Law is achieved, rather than the strict application of the letter of the Law; hence to a certain extent, even though it is not openly acknowledged, the *maqāṣid al-Sharīʿa* concept is being applied. There are rules as to when *ḥiyal* can and cannot be utilised.[116]

113 Mansour Mutairi, *Necessity in Islamic Law* (PhD thesis, Edinburgh University, 1997), p. 185.

114 The Ḥanafīs are the only School of law which has a systematic use of *ḥiyal* and which has developed it into 'a special field of jurisprudence called *makhārij* i.e "exits" to escape from the unlawful to the lawful.' (Horii, 'Reconsideration of Legal Devices (*Ḥiyal*) in Islamic Jurisprudence: The Ḥanafīs and their "Exits" (*Makhārij*)', p. 313).

115 Satoe Horii, 'Reconsideration of Legal Devices (*Ḥiyal*) in Islamic Jurisprudence: The Ḥanafīs and their "Exits" (*Makhārij*)' *Islamic Law and Society* (vol. 9, no. 3, 2002), p. 321.

116 Ibn ʿĀbidīn, *Radd al-muḥtār ʿalā durr al-mukhtār*, vol. 5, p. 173.

Four treatises have been written on this subject:[117] the first by Abū Yūsuf is no longer extant, the second is a study by Shaybānī[118] and the third and fourth are commentaries on it by Sarakhsī[119] and Khaṣṣāf.[120] A proper definition of *ḥiyal* is not put forward by any of these jurists. However, Khaṣṣāf states that the practice is to be found in a *ḥadīth* in which the Prophet instructed a person to sell dates and then with the revenue purchase fewer higher quality dates, as that would not fall under the ruling of usury (*ribā*) A key area where this methodology was applied is in the interpretation of oaths:

> 'When a man who is oppressed by others [a *maẓlūm*] is required to take an oath, his oath [is interpreted] according to what he intended thereby [i.e. according to his *niyya,* intention]. However, when he is in a position to oppress [*ẓālim*], his oath [is interpreted] according to the purpose of the person who made him take the oath.'[121]

In summary, *ḥiyal* were employed in order to safeguard the higher objectives of the Law and are legitimate as they are in accordance with the spirit of the law; this is the reason why jurists have made efforts to incorporate these procedures within the legal system. However, as we have seen above with Shāshī, not all jurists approve of *ḥiyal* as they have the potential of being abused.

Terminology of the Different Gradation of Rulings

When a new matter arises, or the context of a ruling changes, or there is a change in societal customs, or when a necessity prevails then it is the jurist's responsibility to issue a new ruling according to the methodology detailed above. Furthermore, in the discussion of issuing *fatāwā*, especially related to the two chapters which follow, it is appropriate to bring about an understanding of the different grades of rulings a *muftī* can proclaim ranging from impermissible to praiseworthy and everything in between; and an understanding of the rationale adopted by jurists when issuing these rulings; this was introduced in the preceding chapter. These technical definitions are based on those presented

117 Horii, 'Reconsideration of Legal Devices (*Ḥiyal*) in Islamic Jurisprudence: The Ḥanafīs and their "Exits" (*Makhārij*)', p. 317.

118 *Kitāb al-makhārij fī al-ḥiyal.*

119 Included in the margins of Shaybānī's *Kitāb al-makhārij fī al-ḥiyal.*

120 *Kitāb al-ḥiyal wa'l-makhārij.*

121 Horii, 'Reconsideration of Legal Devices (*Ḥiyal*) in Islamic Jurisprudence: The Ḥanafīs and their "Exits" (*Makhārij*)', p. 319.

by ʿAbd al-Fattāḥ Abū Ghudda in the introduction to his book *Fatḥ bāb al-ʿināya bī sharḥ kitāb al-niqāya,* cited by Sulaymān;[122] we have chosen to translate his definitions below due to their depth, detail, accuracy and wide acceptance.

Farḍ (compulsory): *Farḍ* is that ruling which is established upon definitive evidence [i.e. Qur'ānic verse or a *mutawātir ṣaḥīḥ ḥadīth*] in which there is no doubt whatsoever, like the compulsory nature of the five daily prayers, *zakāt*, fasting and *Ḥajj* which are all established by the Qur'ān and *ḥadīth*. That act whose ruling is *farḍ* is compulsory on every *mukallaf* (entrusted individual)[123] in that he must believe in it and he must act upon it. The individual who rejects its compulsory nature is regarded as a non-Muslim. The individual who believes in its compulsory nature but does not act upon it is regarded as a *fāsiq* (transgressor) and [in a state that applies Sharīʿa Law] he may be liable to severe punishment.

Sharṭ (condition) and *rukn* (essential part): Sometimes *farḍ* is referred to as *sharṭ* or *rukn*. These terms are applied when the *farḍ* is either not incorporated in the intended action—it is then referred to as *sharṭ*, or when it is incorporated in the intended action—it is then referred to as *rukn*. For example: the state of purity (*wuḍū'*) is *farḍ* for *ṣalāt*, however it is not a part of *ṣalāt* therefore it is called a *sharṭ*. *Rukūʿ* and *sajda* are *farḍ* for *ṣalāt*, they are part of *ṣalāt* hence they are called *rukn*.

Then *farḍ* is of two types: *farḍ ʿayn* and *farḍ kifāya*. *Farḍ ʿayn* is a ruling which is compulsory on every *mukallaf* or entrusted individual and no other person can fulfil it for them like the canonical prayers and the fasting of Ramaḍān. *Farḍ kifāya* is a ruling which is compulsory on every entrusted individual, but when a group of individuals fulfil it, it is no longer required from the rest. As *farḍ kifāya* is compulsory, if no one fulfils it at all then everyone is considered sinful. There are many examples of *farḍ kifāya*, some which are only religious in nature, some which are worldly in nature, and some which are a combination of the two. The ones that are only religious in nature are: memorising the Qur'ān; the washing of the corpse, praying the funeral prayers and burying the corpse. The ones that are only worldly in nature are farming and the like. Those which are a combination of the two are enjoining good and forbidding evil.

122 Sulaymān, *al-Mu'taṣar al-ḍarūrī*, pp. 9-14.

123 *Mukallaf* is one who is commissioned or entrusted, i.e. an adult Muslim who is sane and who is not excused due to a religious reason. Minors and persons incapable of independent mental judgements fall outside this category.

Wājib (necessary): *Wājib* is that which is established by speculative evidence. Now speculative evidence is weaker in authority than definitive evidence because there is either doubt in verifying the evidence or the evidence making it compulsory is doubtful. For instance, *ṣalāt al-witr* (odd-number of *rakaʿāt* prayer which conclude prayers at the end of the day) is *wājib* not *farḍ* because its evidence is in *kabar wāḥid* and not in *mutawātir ḥadīth*. Hence, this evidence is not as strong as definitive evidence, therefore that which is established due to it is not regarded as *farḍ* but rather *wājib*. Its ruling is that it is necessary for every entrusted individual, but belief in it is not compulsory [like *farḍ*], because it was established by speculative evidence and the necessity of belief is only established by definitive evidence. Therefore, the one who rejects *wājib* cannot be regarded as a non-Muslim unless he abandons it in contempt. The one who abandons it due to *ta'wīl* (interpretation) will not be regarded as a *fāsiq* or deviant. However the one who abandons it without *ta'wīl* and not in contempt will be regarded as a *fāsiq*, because he leaves a form of obedience incumbent upon him. [In a state that applies Sharīʿa Law,] he would be liable for severe punishment due to his abandoning; however this punishment will be a grade less than the one who abandons the *farḍ*.

Similar to *farḍ*, *wājib* is of two types: *wājib ʿayn* and *wājib kifāya*. *Wājib ʿayn* is a ruling that is necessary for every entrusted person and no other person can fulfil it for them; for example, *witr* prayers, *ṣadaqat al-fiṭr*, and *ʿīd* prayers. *Wājib kifāya* is a ruling which is compulsory on every entrusted individual, but when a group of individuals fulfil it, it is no longer required from the rest. However, only the ones who performed the act will obtain the reward. Like *farḍ kifāya*, *wājib kifāya* is compulsory, if no one fulfils it at all then everyone is considered sinful. For example, if an individual says *salām*[124] to a large group of people, then replying has become necessary upon everybody present. However, if one individual replies[125] to the *salām*, then the rest are absolved from the responsibility, however, only the one who replied gains the reward for it.

Sunna (example): are the rulings which are established from our Prophet Muḥammad (may God bless him and grant him peace). *Sunna* is of two types: *Sunna mu'akkada* are those actions which the Prophet performed on a

124 *Al-salām ʿalaykum wa-raḥmatuLlāhi wa-barakātu*, or any of its shorter versions.

125 *Wa ʿalaykum al-salām wa-raḥmatuLlāhi wa-barakātu*, or any of its shorter versions.

regular basis and which he encouraged others also to perform. For instance, to use the *miswāk* at the beginning of *wuḍū'*, to bathe on Friday, to perform *ṣalāt* in congregation and to perform twenty *rakaʿāt* in *tarāwīḥ*. The ruling for *Sunna mu'akkada* is that the one who performs it will be rewarded and the one who abandons it will not be sinful. However it is *makrū tanzīhī*, which means that the one who abandons *Sunna mu'akkada* is closer to *ḥalāl* than *ḥarām*. It is the intention of the Sharīʿa that abandoning it should be avoided, and its performance is likened to the completion of the religion and to abandon it without a valid religious reason is deviation.

Sunna ghayr mu'akkada is also referred to as *mandūb* and *mustaḥab*. These are the actions the Prophet (may God bless him and grant him peace) performed occasionally and which he encouraged others to do likewise now and then; for example, facing the *qibla* when performing *wuḍū'*, to refrain from talking and other activities in order to listen to the *adhān*, and giving preference to the right hand side in most things. Its ruling is that the one who performs the act is entitled to reward and the one who abandons it is not liable to punishment but he is avoiding great goodness, reward and benefit.

Similar to *farḍ* and *wājib*, there is a *Sunna ʿayn* and *Sunna kifāya*. *Sunna ʿayn* is a ruling that is necessary for every entrusted person and no other person can fulfil it for them; for example, *Sunna* of *ṣalāt*, bathing for Friday *ṣalāt*, bathing for *ʿīd* and invocations after *ṣalāt*. *Sunna kifāya* is a ruling which is compulsory on every entrusted individual, but when a group of individuals fulfil it, it is no longer required from the rest. However, only the ones who performed the act will obtain the reward. Like *farḍ kifāya* and *wājib kifāya*, if *Sunna kifāya* is abandoned and no one fulfils it then everyone is considered sinful. An example is to perform *iʿtikāf* (religious seclusion) in the mosque during the last ten days of Ramaḍān.

Ḥarām (forbidden): An entity whose illegality is established by definitive evidence [i.e. Qur'ānic verse or a *mutawātir ṣaḥīḥ ḥadīth*] is regarded as *ḥarām*; for example, to usurp somebody's property, to oppress people, to steal, to drink alcohol, to partake in usury, etc. Its ruling is that the one who partakes in these acts is liable for severe punishment and the one who avoids it is entitled for reward.

Makrūh taḥrīmī is that which the Sharīʿa has forbidden but it is based on speculative evidence as in a *khabar wāḥid*. For example, delaying *ʿaṣr* prayer until close to sunset or performing *ṣalāt* when one needs to relieve oneself. It is close to *ḥarām* and is far from *ḥalāl*. Its ruling is that the perpetrator will be punished but a lesser degree than the punishment for acts which are *ḥarām*, and the one who desists from such actions will be rewarded.

On many occasions, our *fuqahā'* [i.e of the Ḥanafī School] give *ḥarām* as *makrūh taḥrīmī*. In fact, according to Imām Muḥammad [Shaybānī] everything which is *makrūh taḥrīmī* is [in reality] *ḥarām*; it is only called *makrūh* and not *ḥarām* because no definitive evidence could be found for its illegality. Therefore, if definitive evidence is found regarding its illegality, it will then be called *ḥarām*. But, if definitive evidence is found regarding its legality then it will be called *ḥalāl*. Otherwise, Shaybānī says, when it is permissible due to speculative evidence, 'There is nothing wrong with it,' or when it is impermissible due to speculative evidence, 'I dislike it.' This is the methodology of the four *Mujtahidūn A'imma* (the founders of the Four Sunni Schools of Law) and others from the early *fuqahā'* (*fuqahā al-salaf*). This is only cautiousness on their part so that the statement of Almighty God cannot be levelled against them, *And do not say that which your tongues put forward falsely, 'This is* ḥalāl (legal) *and this is* ḥarām (illegal)' *so as to fabricate lies against God* [Q.XVI.116]. The ruling for *makrūh taḥrīmī* is that the individual who commits it will be punished but not to the level of a *ḥarām* action; and the one who abandons it will be rewarded by Almighty God.

When the word *karāha* or *makrūh* is used generally in the Ḥanafī School then it is usually referring to *makrūh taḥrīmī*.

Makrūh al-tanzīhī is that act which the Law disapproves of however no punishment is mentioned for the perpetrator, like using excessive water whilst performing *wuḍū'*, to not bathe on Friday and to not utilise *miswāk* before *wuḍū'* or not recite *tasmiyya* before beginning anything. Such acts are closer to *ḥalāl* with respect to *ḥarām*. The ruling is that the person who avoids acts qualified as *makrūh tanzīhī* is rewarded and the one who does not is not liable for punishment.

Mubāḥ (permissible): It is that entity which the Sharīʿa has not qualified as being either reward-worthy or punishable; for example, sitting, standing, buying and selling, etc. Its ruling is that there is no reward or punishment for the individual who partakes in these acts, mankind has a choice as to whether the act is performed or not. Having said that, if an individual carries out a *mubāḥ* act with a good intention then he is entitled to be rewarded, in this way the *mubāḥ* act becomes *mustaḥab* like,

> sleeping for part of the day in order to have strength to stand in worship at night or wearing good quality clothes in order to show the favours which Almighty God has bestowed [upon an individual].

A firm understanding of the various gradations of rulings is essential for jurists when interpreting new situations and issues. We will see this in the next two chapters which investigate the application of the Sharīᶜa to the British context.

But before we move from this theoretical section of our work to the application of the theory, we would like to conclude by saying that Islamic Law, as we have seen through the Ḥanafī School of Law, has a wealth of principles and methodologies available to the jurist to search and interpret God's rulings on any issue, within any era, for any people. In other words, knowledge of traditional *uṣūl al-fiqh* allows a *muftī* of any era and/or location to issue rulings to Muslims. The traditional approach is directly linked via an unbroken chain of scholars (*isnād*) to the Prophet (may God bless him and grant him peace) whose link to God is undisputed by Muslims; hence the traditional approach speaks with authority and accuracy, and has the added dimension that it has been accepted by scholars and laypersons from the time of the foundation of the Schools of Law till today.

Qawāᶜid Fiqhiyya: Legal Maxims of Fiqh

Our final discussion of *uṣūl* is *qawāᶜid fiqhiyya* or legal maxims. These maxims are the Law in concentrated form, that is, reduced to 'legal sayings' or 'aphorisms'. *Fuqahā'* over the years accumulated a number maxims from the sources and works of *fiqh* as a means for the scholar and the student alike to effortlessly attain an understanding of legal rules by the memorisation of simple phrases without having to wade through a mass of literature. Thus these maxims are a synthesis of the Law and are referred to in resolving legal matters. For instance, 'There is no reward except by intention;' from this maxim we may deduce that any act, even if it is worthy of merit, cannot earn reward for the perpetrator of that act unless the individual in question had the intention to perform it. Hence, from this one maxim many rulings can be derived.

We will include here a number of legal maxims relevant to our study in order to illustrate their nature, breadth and general applicability. The maxims are taken from various texts gathered together by Muḥammad

al-Mujaddidī in his '*al-Qawāᶜid al-fiqhiyya*'.[126] These are the abbreviations for the texts in Mujaddidī's collection:
[UK] for *Uṣūl imām al-karkhī* (d. 340/951)
[SK] for *Sharḥ al-siyar al-kabīr* of Imām Abū Bakr al-Sarakhsī (d. 428/1036)
[TD] for *Ta'sīs al-naẓr* of Imām al-Dabūsī (d. 430/1038)
[HM] for *Hidāya* of Imām Abū'l Ḥasan ᶜAlī al-Marghīnānī (d. 593/1197)
[MU] for *Manāra al-uṣūl* of Imām Ḥāfiẓ al-Dīn al-Nasafī (d. 710/1310)
[SN] for *Ashbāh wa'l-naẓā'ir* of Imām Ibn Nujaym (d. 1005/1596)
[DM] for *Durr al-Mukhtār* of Imām al-Ḥaṣkafī (d. 1088/1677)
[MTh] for *Muslim al-thubūt* of Imām Muḥib Allāh al-Bahārī (d. 1119/1707)
[RM] for *Radd al-muḥtār ᶜalā durr al-mukhtār* of Imām Ibn ᶜĀbidīn (d. 1252/1836)
[MJ] for *Majallah* a compilation of the Civil Code of the Ottoman caliphate based on the Sharīᶜa (1301-1350/1883-1931).

1. A ruling based on *ijtihād* cannot be negated by another [ruling based on *ijtihād*] and nor can it oppose text. [SK/SN]

Abū Bakr [al-Ṣiddīq] (may God be pleased with him) made a judgement and ᶜUmar (may God be pleased with him) opposed him on it but this did not invalidate Abū Bakr's ruling.

2. Cautiousness should be used with respect to the rights of God not with respect to the rights of humans. [UK]

Hence, if there is a possibility that the *ṣalāt* is invalid then one should act so as not to transgress the right of God and should repeat the *ṣalāt*.

3. When two matters of one type come together and their purposes are the same then the one [less dominant] is to be integrated into the dominant one. [SN]

For instance, if a woman is in a state of major impurity and then starts to menstruate, at the end of her menstrual cycle one ritual bathing of purification will suffice for all.

4. When *ishāra* (indication) and *ᶜibāra* (actual) come together then the *ishāra* takes precedence. [HM]
5. When [there is conflicting evidences whether a thing is] permissible or impermissible, it should be considered impermissible. [SN]
6. When the *aṣl* is null and void then the *farᶜ* is null and void. [MJ]

[126] Muḥammad Mujaddidī, *Majmūᶜat qawaᶜid al-fiqh* (Karachi: Mīr Muhammad Kutub Khāna, 1960), pp. 49-144.

7. When a judgement is passed which opposes the *ijmāʿ* then it is not legally valid. [SN]

That which opposes the Four Imāms is opposing *ijmāʿ* even if there is opposition amongst them.

8. The usage of the people is evidence and it is necessary to act upon it. [MJ]

According to *Uṣūl imām al-bazdawī* the *ḥaqīqa* is abandoned due to usage and custom. The meaning of usage is the transferring of a word from its original, coined meaning to a *majāz* meaning.

9. The origin in anything is permissibility. [RM]
10. Shaybānī says that the eating of an already dead animal and the drinking of alcohol is not impermissible [in itself] but because of the prohibition [in the Qur'ān]. So originally they were legal and then became illegal because of the prohibition.
11. Matters are according to their objectives. [SN]
12. *ʿĀda* is considered when it is dominant. [MJ/SN]

If a person trades in a society where there are number of monetary systems then the transaction will be according to the dominant monetary system. For instance, if a person in England says that he will buy a car for five thousand, then it would mean five thousand GBP not five thousand Euros or five thousand US dollars.

13. Particularisation by *ʿurf* is like particularisation by text. [MJ]
14. The qualifying of *muṭlaq* is not permissible except by [further] evidence. [SK]
15. That which is established by necessity is limited to its requirements. [SK/SN]

If necessity brings about a change in a particular ruling then that ruling cannot be transferred to other matters. Also, as soon as the necessity is removed either due to time, condition or situation then the ruling is lifted.

16. That which is established by *ʿurf* is like that which is established by text. [SK]
17. The answer of a question is based upon that which is common amongst people in their location. [UK]

If an individual takes an oath that he will not nourish himself, he will break his oath by drinking milk if he is in Arab countries but not in non-Arab countries; nourishment is understood according to what is common amongst the people of a location.

18. *Ḥāja* (need) is equivalent to *ḍarūra* (necessity) general or specific. [SN]
19. *Ḥudūd* is averted when there is doubt. [SN]

Ḥudūd is corporeal punishments which are solely legislated by revelation. All the conditions have to be met before these punishments are carried out and these punishments are specific and cannot be meted out for any other crime.

20. It is permissible to establish [rulings] in two places based on one reality (fact). [TD]
21. *Khabar wāḥid* quoted against the *uṣūl* is not accepted. [TD]

This is a good example where literalism cannot overrule a rationally developed system.

22. Two narrations when they contradict one another, then both are abandoned. Hence, one should turn towards another evidence (*sharḥ wiqāya*).

If two texts oppose one another and one of them cannot be prioritised over the other, both will be abandoned. Then, it will be necessary upon the *mujtahid* to turn towards *qiyās*, hence that which correlates with *qiyās* will be taken and that which does not will be abandoned.

23. Extending on [the rulings of] the Qur'ān is rejected; it can only occur by a [another] verse or *mashhūr ḥadīth*. [MU]

For example, it is not correct to consider the conditions of continuity, order and intention found in *khabar wāḥid* about *wuḍū'* as *farḍ* when the Qur'ānic verse on *wuḍū'* (Q.v.6) does not specify them; they can only be regarded as *Sunna*. However, it is correct with respect to the wiping of *khuff* as an extension on the verse of *wuḍū'* due to a *mashhūr ḥadīth*.

24. Harm must be removed. [SN]
25. A greater harm is removed by a lesser harm. [SN]
26. Necessity permits the [usage of the] impermissible. [SN]

It is permissible to eat dead animal not slaughtered according to the Law in severe starvation and to pronounce words of disbelief under duress and compulsion.

27. That which is permitted due to necessity is limited to its requirement. [SN]

Hence, a person should eat enough of a dead animal not slaughtered according to the Law to keep him alive and not to the extent of satisfying his hunger.

28. In the general use of a word, *ʿurf* will be taken into consideration. [SK]

29. The breaking of a bone from a dead person is like the breaking of a bone from a living person. [SK]
30. Every *ṣalāt* which is completed with *makrūh taḥrīmī* makes its repetition necessary. [DM]

For example, if an individual leaves out the recitation of the *Fātiḥa* in the *ṣalāt* and then does not perform *sajdat al-sahwa* (prostration of forgetfulness) then the individual would be required to repeat the *ṣalāt*.

31. Every loan that brings about [financial] benefit is *ribā harām* (illegal usury). [SN]
32. Priority is not given to the number of the narrators but rather the *fiqh* of the narrator. [MU]
33. There is no obedience of the created in the disobedience of the Creator. [SK]

It is necessary to obey the leaders of one's community in those matters in which are beneficial to people with respect to their faith; and in those matters in which they do not know whether obedience will benefit them or not. This is because the necessity of obedience is established by definitive text and it cannot be rejected by opinion. However, if they are commanded to act in a matter which they fear would bring about their own destruction and it is the majority view of the people, then obedience is not required due to the Prophet's statement, 'There is no obedience of the created in the disobedience of the Creator.' This *ḥadīth* is recorded by al-Ḥakīm and Aḥmad.

34. Do not cause harm to yourself or to another. [SN/MJ]

A *ḥadīth*, which Mālik records in his *Muwaṭṭā*; Ḥākim in his *Mustadrak* and is also recorded by Bayhaqī, Dāruqutnī and Ibn Māja.

35. *Dalāla* (indication) is not considered when it opposes the *ṣarīḥ* (explicit). [MJ]
36. It is not possible to rule on an entity on the basis of a partial *ʿilla*. [SK]
37. It is not permissible to abandon *wājib* for *mustaḥab*. [SK]
38. It is not permissible to oppose *ijmāʿ*. [SK]
39. The *fatwā* of disbelief will not be passed on a Muslim if at all possible. [DM]

The verdict of *kufr* (disbelief/apostasy)—rejecting those matters from the religion which are necessary to accept—based on the interpretation of *kufr* in the books of *fatāwā* will not be passed on a Muslim except when scholars agree upon it.

40. The changing of the ruling due to the changing of the era will not be rejected. [MJ]

For example, locking the door of the mosque outside of prayer times is permissible in our time due to the fear of stealing.

41. That which is established by firm belief cannot be removed except by firm belief. [SN]
42. That established ruling which is contrary to *qiyās* (i.e. irrational or non-logical) does not permit another ruling to be established on it via *qiyās*. [MJ]

In other words, you cannot establish a ruling by reasoning when the original ruling was not obtained through logical means.

43. That which is illegal to take, is illegal to give. [SN]
44. That which is illegal to commit, is illegal to seek. [SN]
45. That which is obtained by ill-gotten means should be returned. [SK/RM]

One should return it, however if it proves almost impossible to return it then one should give it in charity without the intention of seeking reward.

46. That which the Muslims see as good, then it is good in the sight of God. [SK]

This is the statement of the Companion ʿAbd Allāh b. Masʿūd (may God be pleased with him) quoted in Aḥmad, Bazār and Tabrānī.

47. The wealth of the Muslims cannot be retained permanently as war booty by Muslims. [SK]

ʿAlī b. Abī Ṭālib (may God be pleased with him) did not take from the wealth of Muslims in the Battles of *al-Siffin* or *al-Jamal* except for a short while during the battle and until he and his army were safe from further attack. Then, what he took was returned to those who were still alive or became the inheritance of those who had been killed.

48. It is obligatory upon the Muslim that he removes the means of destruction from himself. [SK]

Meaning that a Muslim should seek whatever means to remove harm to himself as his life is of paramount importance.

49. Hardship brings about ease. [SN]

A ruling may be a hardship in the short term but is better in the long term. For example, a divorce in the case of a couple who are not able to reconcile their differences.

50. General statements are qualified by the context. [SK]

51. That which is conditioned is non-existent before the condition [exists]. [SK]

An act that is dependent on a condition does not exist until the condition itself exists.

52. Text is stronger that *ʿurf*. [DM]

In the case where text exists. This is referring to absolute unequivocal verses of Qur'ān and *mutawātir ḥadīth*.

53. Averting harm is superior to giving benefit. [MJ]
54. *Wājib al-kifāya* is necessary upon everybody and it is dropped by the action of some. [MTh]
55. The specific harm will be acted upon in order to remove the general harm. [SN/MJ]
56. Certainty is not removed by doubt. [SN]
57. Harm is not to be removed by harm. [SN]
58. The lesser of the two harms is the one to choose. [MJ]
59. The mentioning of part which is not separate from a whole is like mentioning the whole. [SN/MJ]

For example, 'I don't want your hand anywhere near me,' would include in that the person's foot or arm, etc., as the human body is not in separate parts, hence mentioning one part is like mentioning the whole.

60. It is not permitted for the *mujtahid* to strive in order to arrive at the meaning of a point of law or religion when there is a definitive text. [MJ]
61. A person who does an act, even if he does not act intentionally, is responsible. [MJ]

The above legal maxims and their like can be used when seeking for *ḥukm al-ḥāditha* when one finds the source texts to be silent or in order to avoid searching through voluminous texts, especially in cases which involve the transfer of a ruling due to a similar *ʿilla*. In fact, one finds the jurist employing these maxims regularly as will be demonstrated in developments taking place in Britain in order to determine traditional Islam's position on these new matters.

CHAPTER V

Traditional *Uṣūl* and Political-legal Jurisdictions (*Diyār*)

EARLIER IN THIS WORK, we touched upon the negative image that Islam occasionally has in the West and the rejection of some Muslims living in Western countries of Western societies. Lewis, when analysing Islam's relationship with the West, claims that there is an inherent hostility between the two due to the dichotomy between *dār al-Islām* and *dār al-ḥarb*.[1] This interpretation has been refuted by other scholars.[2] In this chapter, we will discuss the concept of *diyār* (pl. of *dār*)—political-legal jurisdictions—and we will attempt to illustrate how traditional jurists have divided different territories according to their relationship with Islam and to majority-status and minority-status Muslims. The purpose is to determine where and to what extent Islamic Law can be applied, and to lay some foundations for relations between Muslims and non-Muslims in this new century.

Historical Development of Religious and Political Jurisdictions within Muslim Lands

At the birth of Islam, religious and political power was united in the person of the Prophet Muḥammad. For Sunni Islam, this religious-political leadership passed to the first four Caliphs during what is considered the 'golden period'. In these two phases, Muslim society became a polity defined by religious alliances whose 'religious and political values and religious and

[1] Lewis, *The Crisis of Islam: Holy War and Unholy Terror*, p. 27.

[2] See, for example, Shadid and van Koningsveld, *Religious Freedom and the Position of Islam in Western Europe*, pp. 63-64; Heiko Henkel, 'Rethinking the *dār al-harb*: Social Change and Changing Perceptions of the West in Turkish Islam', *Journal of Ethnic and Migration Studies* (vol. 30. no. 5, 2004), pp. 961-77.

political offices were inseparable.'[3]

But this situation was not to last and there are even *aḥādīth* from the Prophet that predict the separation of religious and political authority: Tirmidhī and Abū Dā'ūd include 'The caliphate after me is thirty years, after which it will become an unjust (*ʿaḍūḍ*) kingdom;'[4] and, 'The caliphate of the Prophet will last thirty years then God will give the kingdom to whom He wishes.'[5] Thus for Muslim societies, the notion in which political and religious authority lay with one person, and in which the former was subservient to the latter, lasted only for a short period of time and was rarely witnessed subsequently.

With the death of Caliph ʿAlī and for a period of about a hundred years, Muslim lands had one supreme leader serving as the head of state with the title of caliph. This title was retained more because of its prestige as the holders were no longer religious leaders but secular sultans or kings mostly responsible for public order, defending the population and for the administration of the state. During the Abbasid dynasty, the Muslim empire split into two, and then further divisions took place as the Abbasids lost Spain to the Umayyads, Tunisia to the Aghlabids, and Egypt and Syria to the Fatimids. A superficial unity did remain in that the caliph was mentioned in the Friday sermon and his name appeared on the currency.[6] Within a few centuries, three dynasties simultaneously claimed the leadership of the Islamic *umma* and the position of caliph; the Umayyads in Spain, the Fatimids in North Africa and in the southern part of the Arabian Peninsula and the Abbasids in the northern and eastern Arab lands. With the passing of time more dynasties founded separate political entities administered by princes or sultans who were 'ordinary' rulers to whom the Muslim subjects paid taxes in exchange for protection by the rulers' armies.[7] These leaders could wage war, make peace, establish treaties, and administer their regions

[3] Ira Lapidus, 'The Separation of State and Religion in the Development of Early Islamic Society', *International Journal of Middle East Studies* (vol. 6, no. 4, 1975), pp. 363-64.

[4] Yusuf, *Imām Abū Ḥanīfa's Al-Fiqh Al-Akbar Explained*, p. 140.

[5] Abū Dā'ūd, *Sunan*, vol.2, p. 290.

[6] Piscatori, *Islam in a World of Nation-States*, p. 63.

[7] Patricia Crone, *Medieval Islamic Political Thought* (Edinburgh: Edinburgh University Press, 2004), p. 243.

with nominal allegiance to the caliph.[8] Thus, apart from the first hundred years, the totality of Muslims have never pledged their allegiance to one supreme leader.

The split of the political from the religious in the function of the head of state was mirrored in Muslim societies by a separation of the religious and political spheres. Scholars and religious institutes became responsible for religious issues. As a result, Islamic Schools of Law developed and thrived independently of the state and regulated the communal and religious life of Muslims 'by serving as judges, administrators, teachers, and religious advisers to Muslims.'[9] The Schools of Law dealt with a range of issues to assist the populace in how to live a proper Muslim life covering family law, commercial life, charitable funds, legal services and the settling of disputes.[10] Religious scholars no longer regarded the caliph's statements as a source of law and, on a number of occasions, they even opposed the caliph-sultan; the caliphate and traditional Islam represented by the Schools of Law became disentangling and developing separately.[11] The outcome as Lapidus states was that, 'eventually, Muslims everywhere came to be identified as subjects of a regime on the one hand, and adherents of one or another religious body.'[12]

This criticism of the caliphs by religious scholars was lead by the very founders of the Sunni Schools of Law. Mālik b. Anas, founder of the Mālikī School, and Shāfiʿī, founder of the Shāfiʿī School, were both persecuted for the legal positions they took; while Abū Ḥanīfa, the founder of the Ḥanafī School, was actually put to death by the Abbasid Caliph Manṣūr.[13] Caliph Ma'mūn imposed the *miḥna* (the Inquisition) in which all, including the religious scholars, had to accept that the Qur'ān was created. As this was contrary to the accepted traditional view advocated by a number of scholars, this was a period of great hardship for them. Aḥmad b. Ḥanbal, the founder of the Ḥanbalī School of Law, became a symbol of opposition to the *miḥna* and as

[8] Muhammad Hamidullah, *The Muslim Conduct of State* (Lahore: Muhammad Ashraf Publishers, 1990), p. 88.

[9] Lapidus, 'The Separation of State and Religion in the Development of Early Islamic Society', p. 364, and 'State and Religion in Islamic Societies' (*Past and Present*, no. 151, 1996), p. 11.

[10] Lapidus, 'The Separation of State and Religion in the Development of Early Islamic Society', p. 364.

[11] Ibid., p. 369.

[12] Ibid., p. 384.

[13] El-Affendi, *Who Needs an Islamic State?*, pp. 72-73.

a result personally suffered greatly.[14] But it was not just the religious leaders who were persecuted, but Muslim populations on occasion had to resort to taking refuge from the caliph even in non-Muslim political domains, for instance during the caliphate of al-Hajjāj b. Yūsuf many Muslims fled Iraq for India where they had to adopt the clothes of the Hindus and limit the public display of their Islamic identity.[15]

In summary, this distinction made the *ʿulamāʾ* the true leaders of the Muslim community, with their various institutes independent within the caliphal order.[16] The *miḥna* (Inquisition) was the turning point, which crystallised this separation of paths. As a result, the caliph was a symbol of Muslim unity but did not hold any religious authority, while the religious scholars led the faithful in matters of religion. 'Henceforth the caliphate would evolve, contrary to the Muslim ideal, as a largely military and imperial institution legitimated in neo-Byzantium and neo-Sassanian terms, while the religious elites would develop a more complete authority over the communal, personal, religious and doctrinal aspects of Islam.'[17] In the eleventh century, religious scholars like Bāqillānī, Māwardī and Ibn Taymiyya developed the idea of the state as a secular institution required to uphold Islam, and that the real leaders of the community of Muslims were the religious scholars who continued the legacy of the Prophet in daily life.[18]

In conclusion, throughout the history of Islam there have been two types of Muslim community: one whose membership requires the belief in one God and in the Prophet Muḥammad, hence exclusively Muslims, which was and is a global concept not bound by territorial boundaries—this is what is called the *umma*; and the other, which is made up of subjects of a Muslim sovereign state, a state which may include a non-Muslim minority—examples of this are different Muslim empires, sultanates and kingdoms. More recently, especially since the middle of the nineteenth century, a third type of community has come into being: Muslims living in majority-Muslim states that have adopted the foreign concept and applications of the nation-states. And finally, since the beginning of the twentieth century, there are now communities of Muslims living as minorities in the West.

[14] Ibid.

[15] Hamidullah, *The Muslim Conduct of State*, p. 123.

[16] Lapidus, 'State and Religion in Islamic Societies', p. 12.

[17] Ibid.

[18] Ibid., p. 19.

Nationalism and Nation-states

We have referred above to the *umma* and the Muslim sovereign state. The latter can be translated as *dār*. Literally, *dār* is a house, abode, domain, territory, area or land.[19] *Dār*, and its plural *diyār*, will also be used in this study to mean a political-legal jurisdiction.

As the *ijmāᶜ* of the Muslim community globally now accepts the principle of a 'country',[20] if not of a nationality, it seems appropriate to translate *dār* as 'country' or 'state'. We appreciate that the nation-state is a European concept which entered the Muslim world in the nineteenth century when rulers of Muslim areas adopted secular political-legal systems borrowed from Europe;[21] we also appreciate that a significant number of Muslims to this day do not accept the concept of nationality.[22] However, even if one does not agree with the idea of the nation-state, one has to accept that this is the status quo in most Muslim countries today and we have to work within it in developing Islamic political-legal law in the twenty-first century.

A change in political ideas was already taking place in Muslim lands at the beginning of the twentieth century. Kohn[23] observed, 'A few years back[24] religion was the determining factor in the East. Nationalism is not ousting religion, but more or less rapidly it is taking a place beside it, frequently fortifying it, beginning to transform and impair it. National symbols are acquiring

[19] For a viewpoint of the concept of an Islamic state since the time of the Prophet, see Asma Afsaruddin, 'The "Islamic State": Genealogy, facts and Myths', *Journal Of Church and State* (vol. 48, 2006), pp. 153-73 and Sherman Jackson, 'Shariᶜah, Democracy, and the Modern Nation-State: Some Reflections on Islam, Popular Rule, and Pluralism', *Fordham International Law Journal* (vol. 27, 2003), pp. 88-107.

[20] Pakistan was founded on the basis of religion, i.e. as an Islamic country for Muslims. The state issues national identity cards and passports that are accepted and used by all, scholar and layperson alike, which suggests, therefore a tacit approval. This is not restricted to Pakistan alone but virtually to all the Islamic countries in the world.

[21] Nathan Brown, 'Shariᶜa and State in the Modern Muslim Middle East', *International Journal of Middle East Studies* (vol. 29, no. 3, 1997), p. 360.

[22] Abdullah al-Ahsan, *Ummah or Nation?: Identity Crisis in Contemporary Muslim Society* (Leicester: The Islamic Foundation, 1992), p. 30; Dilwar Hussain, 'British Muslim Identity', in M. Seddon, D. Hussain and N. Malik (eds.), *British Muslims between Assimilation and Segregation* (Leicester: The Islamic Foundation, 2004), p. 92.

[23] Hans Kohn, *A History of Nationalism in the East* (New York: Harcourt, 1929) and *Nationalism and Imperialism in the East* (New York: Howard Fertig, 1969).

[24] This book was first published in 1926 in Germany.

religious authority and sacramental inviolability. The truth which men will defend with their lives is no longer exclusively religious, on occasions even it is no longer religious at all, but in increasing measure national.'[25] He added, 'Only twenty-five[26] years ago the Turks, the Arabians and the Egyptians described themselves first and foremost as Mohammedans. They were not yet conscious of ethical designations, or only accorded them secondary consideration. Today the Mohammedan is primarily a member of his nation or a citizen of his state, and afterwards a Mohammedan.'[27]

Jackson asserts that this western influence brought about three major changes: firstly, the underlying theory of nation-state granted the government complete authority in terms of interpreting and applying the Law, hence traditional jurists were marginalised; secondly, the concept of citizenship and equality before the Law removed Islamic legal pluralism which resulted in the four Schools of Law having to give way to 'the law of the land'; and finally, due to colonisation much of the colonising powers' legal codes replaced the Sharīᶜa, with the exception of family and personal law.[28] This was a reversal of the situation that had existed in the Muslim world for centuries where the religious scholars were the ones to decide the law and the state, including the caliph, was subservient to the legal system.

The question that arises is where was the opposition within the Muslim world to this change, in terms of serious debate, turmoil and even political resistance? Brown[29] argues this was due to the secular states courts not affecting the Islamic institutions and courts. He notes, 'The reform was to negotiate the relationship between the two systems, generally by separating them to a greater extent and by enlarging the jurisdiction of the state courts.'[30] Therefore, most civil and criminal cases went to the European-style courts, whilst personal status cases were assigned to the Sharīᶜa-based courts.

We therefore repeat that whether we accept the application of the nation-state to the Muslim world or not, we have no alternative but to utilise the

[25] Kohn, *Nationalism and Imperialism in the East*, p. 19.

[26] Based on the 1926 edition.

[27] Ibid., p. 24.

[28] Sherman Jackson, 'Jihad and the Modern World', *The Journal of Islamic Law and Culture* (vol. 7, no. 1, 2002), p. 4.

[29] Brown, 'Shariᶜa and State in the Modern Muslim Middle East', pp. 359-76.

[30] Ibid., p. 366.

concept as it is the reality on the ground. Muslim lands today are separate entities based on citizenship and the citizens are a territorial-based community irrespective of faith, ethnicity and other social identifiers who have shared goals and interests with other territorial communities that are both Muslim and non- Muslim (as in the relations between North African countries and the EU), and Muslims cannot travel from one 'Muslim' country to another without the appropriate passport, visa and associated paperwork. In addition, the caliphate no longer exists.[31]

Identity of Muslims: Global and Local

The Global Muslim Community: al-Umma.

Identity is paramount for human beings; it gives a sense of belonging and stability. It is about the relationship to one's past which makes the present understood in order to be able to move forward to the future.[32] Faith as an identifier is essential to many as nationality and other identifiers do not provide answers to philosophical and moral questions. However, when one accepts a certain belief system, there is usually an obligation to also accept and apply its creed and its laws. In the case of Islam, aside from the tenets and practices of the faith, there is a comprehensive legal system covering areas such as finance and politics amongst many others.

One of the key goals, arguably the most important, of Islam is to bring about equality for men and women in their relationship with their Creator;[33] hence, differences like race, ethnicity, tribe, clan, class and nationality are not a measure of primary identification but of secondary identification as one's relationship with God is the determining factor. The Prophet Muḥammad declared in his Farewell Sermon, 'There is no superiority for an Arab over a non-Arab, or for a non-Arab over an Arab, or for the white man over the black man, or for the black man over the white man, except in God-consciousness.' The Qur'ān describes the Muslims as one *umma* (see for example Q.xxi.92 and Q.xxiii.52), a community and a brotherhood that unites along articles of faith. This was observed in the Medina of the Prophet Muḥammad which

[31] With the end of the Ottoman empire, the caliphate was abolished by the first president of the Turkish Republic Mustafa Kemal Ataturk (on 3 March 1924).

[32] Abdul Bari, *Race, Religion & Muslim Identity in Britain*, p. 9.

[33] Hussain, 'British Muslim Identity', pp. 91-92.

challenged the primary identifier of that era, namely the tribe.[34] It must be said that this notion of *umma* did not come to eradicate tribes, clans or other forms of differentiation which exists amongst people, but rather it came as a unifying force in order to bring a variety of diverse peoples together. The current secular concept utilises the nation-state as its source of unity, whilst in the Muslim *umma* faith is the source of unity and race, ethnicity and nationality come second.[35]

As was mentioned above, after the period of the four Rightly-guided Caliphs and arguably the Umayyad period too, Muslims have lived under different sultans, leaders and kings, therefore there has not been a single leader or single state. But despite this, Muslims still regarded themselves as one *umma*-community, and were free to travel across all Muslim lands, and had equal rights within Muslim lands irrespective of birth place.

We discussed earlier that over the past century a significant minority of Muslims have become established in Western countries. This concept of the *umma* and the Muslims' sense of being part of a global Muslim identity has brought about accusation against Muslims living in Britain and other Westerns countries of divided allegiances and of Muslims being an 'enemy within.'[36] Modood and Ahmad recognise that Muslims give religion priority over national origins in a number of political issues, some recent significant ones are: the Rushdie affair in 1988–89, in which British Muslims united with the Muslim world in condemning the author in opposition to the position of the British state; the first Gulf War in 1991, in which British troops invaded a sovereign Muslim state; the issues around Muslim faith schools, which some view as isolationist; the fallout following the 'September 11' attacks, and the resulting wars in Afghanistan and Iraq.[37]

Furthermore, there is a view that the concept of the *umma* could challenge the Western secular concepts of national sovereignty and law with the possibility of bringing the *umma* into conflict with the ideas of individual rights and democracy.[38] This has raised questions about Muslims' allegiance to the nation-state and how this can be hindered because of their compliance

[34] Al-Ahsan, *Ummah or Nation?: Identity Crisis in Contemporary Muslim Society*, p. 3.

[35] Kettani, *Muslim Minorities in the World Today*, pp. 254-55; Abdul Bari, *Race, Religion & Muslim Identity in Britain*, pp. 84-85.

[36] Baxter, 'From Migrants to Citizens: Muslims in Britain 1950s-1990s', p. 187.

[37] Modood and Ahmad, 'British Muslim Perspectives on Multiculturalism', p. 187.

[38] Ansari, *The Infidel Within* (London: Hurst and Company, 2004),p. 7.

to the Sharīʿa Law.[39] Seán McLoughlin[40] asserts that the tendency for Muslims to unite across the globe on political and social issues could be due to lack of representation locally, therefore a global identification relieves the sense of exclusion. Also, many of the issues discussed are not necessarily religious by nature but arguably secular and nationalistic, protesting against political power and dominance.[41]

Exploring nationalism in the Muslim world, one finds that Muslim states' primary aim is to serve national interests, and that they tend to ignore the collective interests of the Muslim *umma*.[42] An example of this was observed in 1978 when the Egyptian government signed the Camp David agreement in order to regain the Sinai Peninsula and to secure its borders with Israel, and disregarded the frustration and anger of the Muslim world as represented by the Organisation of Islamic Conference.[43] It is clear from this example that a Muslim state may prioritise its strategic needs over the needs or demands of the Muslim *umma* and may enter into allegiances with a foreign and even non-Muslim state.

This has a profound significance for Muslims as the Qur'ān stipulates:

> *Indeed those who have believed and have migrated and have striven with their wealth and selves in the Path of God and those who shelter and assist [them]: these [all] are the protectors of each other. [As for] those who believe and have not migrated [to you] then it is not incumbent upon you to protect them until they migrate. [However]* ***if they request help from you with respect to matters of religion then it is necessary upon you to assist except if it is [regarding] a*** **qawm** ***(people) with whom you have a covenant.*** *For God is All-Seer of what you do.* (Q.VIII.72, emphasis added.)

This verse was revealed regarding the Islamic state of Medina following the migration of Muslims from Mecca. However, principles can be derived from it which are applicable today. The verse brings about an understanding that

39 Hellyer, 'Minorities, Muslims and Shariʿa: Some Reflections on Islamic Law and Muslims without Political Power', , p 86.

40 Seán McLoughlin, 'In the Name of the Umma', in W.A.R. Shadid and P.S. van Koningsveld (eds.), *Political Participation and Identities of Muslims in Non-Muslim States* (Kampen: Kok Pharos Publishing House, 1996), pp. 206-28.

41 Ansari, *The Infidel Within*, p. 13.

42 Mir Husain, *Global Islamic Politics*, (New York: Harper Collins, 1995), p. 20.

43 K. Valakatzi, *Clash of Civilisations: Islam and the West* (University of Bradford: MA Dissertation, 1999).

it is not the responsibility of a Muslim state, which has an agreement with a non-Muslim state, to protect or take care of the Muslim citizens living in the non-Muslim state. In general, Muslim states must offer and give assistance to a Muslim community in a non-Muslim country which is being persecuted because of their faith. However, if there is an agreement or treaty then the assistance cannot be offered, as it would be in direct violation of the existing treaty.

The Local Territorial Community: Qawm

The Qur'ān differentiates thus between the territorial community and the religious community: *And from the* qawm *of Mūsā an* umma *who guides with truth and through it act justly. And we divided them into twelve tribal* umam[44], *and we revealed to Mūsā when his* qawm *asked for water that, 'Strike, with your staff the stone.' From hence (the stone) gushed out twelve springs every group of people knew their drinking place.* (Q.VII.159-160)

The *qawm* referred to in these verses were all the individuals within the geographical location in which Moses preached, while the ones who accepted his message and followed him were regarded as an *umma*. Each of the twelve tribes were referred to as an *umma* as they had three identifiers: geographical because they were part of the *qawm*, religious as they were of one faith and tribal as they were of one tribe.

Hussain Madani,[45] when opposing the idea of the partitioning of India into a secular state and a Hindu state, draws upon this premise and argues that the two identifiers utilised are *millat* and *qawm*, whereby the first means religion or Sharīʿa or *the way of life*, and the second refers to men exclusively or a group of men and women whether Muslims or non-Muslims. He argues that *umma* is a synonym of *millat*.[46] In his *Muttaḥida qawmiyyat aur Islām*, after acknowledging the pan-Islamic relationship which exists between Muslims, Madani raises and answers a pertinent question, 'Can Muslims join in co-operation with non-Muslims in order to form a nation? Furthermore, can they, based on this *ittiḥād qawmiyyat* [generally translated as 'composite nationalism'] establish economical, political, commercial, agricultural, industrial links? Is there a

[44] *Umam* is the plural of *umma*.

[45] Hussain Madani, *Composite Nationalism and Islam*; translation of *Muttaḥida qawmiyat aur Islām* (New Delhi: Ajay Kumar Jain, 2005).

[46] Ibid., p. 87.

need for it in India?'[47] He continues, 'There is no doubt that Islam consists of principles that underlie the rectitude of doctrinal, practical and moral matters. Not only is it a means for reforming the individual but also for the regulation of the particular collective [household] and the general collective [civilised politics]. It sheds light on all necessities of life, and it provides all forms of regulation. However, we must consider whether Islam, being based on principles which regulate the individual and collective life, and pertaining to the relationship between the Creator and humans and between humans themselves, permits [Muslims] to join with non-Muslims as a nationality due to shared residence, race, colour and language and then due to this relationship an enemy can be defeated? [Does it allow this community] to achieve common political, economical, commercial, agricultural and military goals? [Does Islam permit] this extensive interaction as long as there is no threat to its basic principles? To the extent that we have studied the [foundational] religious texts it seems clear to us that depending on the situation, [this interaction] is at times obligatory, at other times recommended, sometimes permissible, disliked and in some cases illegal.'[48] Therefore, he concludes by stating that the answer depends on the context and there will be occasions where this composite nationalism will be permissible, recommended and, at times, necessary.

On the other hand ʿUthmānī[49] holds that *qawmiyya muttaḥida*[50] is objectionable whether Muslims are in a political majority or minority; that is, if the ruling power is in the hands of the Muslims then they would be required to apply Islamic Law, and if Muslims were in a political minority then the non-Muslim government would impose its own values to the detriment of the Islamic ones and with an eventual destruction of the Muslim minority's identity and rituals and this is forbidden by Islamic Law. However this is based on a misunderstanding of *qawmiyya al-muttaḥida/ittiḥād qawmiyyat*. ʿUthmānī views composite nationalism to be 'the *ikhtilāṭ tām* [complete mixing] between people of different walks of life, Muslims and non-Muslims, to such an extent that there is no distinct difference in terms of culture, community or way of life. All of them are united in one *dīn* (religion); either through the creation of a new religion by the composite of all the different religions or that the

[47] Ibid., p. 334

[48] Ibid., pp. 334-35.

[49] Ẓafar ʿUthmānī, *Aʿlā al-sunan* (Karachi: Idārat al-Qur'ān wa'l-ʿUlūm al-Islāmiyya, 1996), vol. 2, pp. 688-713.

[50] *Qawmiyya al-muttaḥida* is the Arabic equivalent of the Urdu *ittiḥād qawmiyyat*.

religion has no trace except in one's inner self [i.e. belief only] and outwardly they become like one people.'[51]

One can clearly see that ʿUthmānī is referring to assimilation whereas Madani did not talk of a 'melting-pot' which would result in a single faith or the eradication of the Muslim identity as all traditional scholars, including Madani, would refute assimilation. ʿUthmānī has misunderstood Madani's concept of *qawmiyya muttaḥida/ittiḥād qawmiyyat* which is the integration of Muslims by adopting citizenship of a state in which Muslims would be a political minority.

In fact, Madani's concept is not new. According to Salam, scholars in Egypt started to use the term of *waṭan* (country) as early as the eighteenth century, obviously influenced by Western Europe's concept of nation-state. They clearly distinguished it from the *umma* because of the territorial nature of the notion of *waṭan*. Furthermore, in establishing the notion of nationalism the concept of citizenship emerged which had a negative impact on the religious criterion, i.e. the *umma*.[52] When Muslims are in a political minority, the secularism of the nation-state was and is regarded as acceptable by some scholars. The type of secularism, which is problematic, is one that is regarded as being in opposition to God, and is described as procedural or 'hard' secularism. Whereas the type of secularism that is acceptable is termed programmatic or 'soft' secularism, in which the state is secular but recognises the religious voice and allows it public space for debate in order to influence policy.[53] In other words, the secular state 'is always open to being persuaded by confessional or ideological argument on particular issues, but is not committed to privileging permanently any one confessional group', and therefore allows and facilitates 'public engagement between varieties of both religious and non-religious argument.'[54] Bearing in mind the trans-national nature of Islam, this 'soft' or programmatic secularism facilitates the Muslim to hold

[51] Uthmānī, *Aʿlā al-sunan*, vol. 2, pp. 688-713.p. 688.

[52] Nawaf Salam, 'The Emergence of Citizenship in Islamdom', *Arab Law Quarterly* (vol. 12, 1997), pp. 141-42.

[53] Rowan Williams, 'Rome Lecture: 'Secularisation, Faith and Freedom', http://www.archbishopofcanterbury.org/654, 2006; Barry Kosmin, *Secularism & Secularity: Contemporary International Perspectives* (Hartford, CT: Institute for the Study of Secularism in Society and Culture (ISSSC), 2007).

[54] Rowan Williams, 'Rome Lecture: 'Secularisation, Faith and Freedom', http://www.archbishopofcanterbury.org/654.

both identities, national and pan-Islamic, with relatively minimal contradiction as 'the critical presence of communities of religious commitment means that it is always possible to challenge accounts of political reasoning that take no account of solidarities beyond those of the state.'[55]

In summary, even though the nation-state is alien to Islam, the concept has been accepted, wholeheartedly in some cases and begrudgingly in others, across the Muslim world. But Muslims today also find themselves in nation-states within the 'non-Muslim' West. This gives rise to a number of questions; for example: if Britain is based on secular principles is it permissible for a Muslim to live there? Can Muslims show allegiance to a non-Muslim or, more generally, to a non-religious, leadership? Are Western countries the 'abode of war' (*dār al-ḥarb*)? If so, what form of relationship should a Muslim maintain with the state and the indigenous population? We will now discuss these and other questions through the positions of three interpretive models with a special emphasis on the traditional approach.

Interpretations of Political-legal Jurisdictions (diyār)

The Literal Approach

In terms of political-legal jurisdictions (*diyār*), the literalist approach divides the world into two halves: *dār al-ḥarb* and *dār al-Islām*.[56] Thus, there two types of state in the world, 'enemy state' (*dār al-ḥarb*)[57] and 'Muslim state' (*dār al-Islām*)[58]. This is based on the embryonic stage of political Islam when the Prophet had established the fledgling Muslim community in Medina; all parties then were either friend or foe. With the growth of Islam as an empire, most empires surrounding it viewed it through enemy eyes, therefore the dichotomy of the domain of Peace (*dār al-Islām*) and the domain of War (*dār al-ḥarb*) was a reality. In other words, the status quo between empires was a 'state of war'; empires were continuously on a state of alert and either on the offensive or defensive. Today, the relationship between nations is of a 'state of peace'. If the dichotomous model propagated by the literalist approach is accepted, its permanent application in the twenty-first century would be extremely difficult, if not impossible. Life for Muslims in so-called 'enemy

[55] Ibid.

[56] Ibn Baz and Uthaymeen, *Muslim Minorities*; Khan, *The Fiqh of Minorities*.

[57] Literally, the 'abode of war'.

[58] Literally, the 'abode of Islam'.

states' would be impossible; they would not be able to retain an Islamic identity and would be obliged to migrate to a Muslim country. The literalist approach gives little attention or thought to the potential consequences of the application of *dār al-ḥarb* and to the mass migration and other issues which would be brought about by this model. This 'utopian' model lacks pragmatism and realism. According to the literalist interpretive model all non-Muslim countries are *dār al-ḥarb*.

The Liberal Approach

Most scholars of the liberal/modernist approach believe that the dichotomous *dār al-ḥarb* and *dār al-Islām* is no longer relevant.[59] As opposed to the literalists, the liberals view of political-legal jurisdictions is non-confrontational and is based more on 'time' than 'place'. They advocate the concepts of *dār al-ijāba* (abode of response),[60] the states under Muslim rule, and *dār al-daʿwa* (abode of those being called),[61] those territories invited to become Muslim and which potentially could come under Muslim rule.[62] The terms *dār al-ijāba* and *dār al-daʿwa* have also been applied to populations rather than to territories; hence the use of *ummat al-ijāba* (the nation that responds) and *ummat al-daʿwa* (the nation being called).[63] More radically, the whole world is called *dār al-Islām*.[64]

Therefore, Muslims are not obliged to migrate but rather remain, albeit for the purpose of inviting others to Islam. Alwani[65] compares the situation of the Muslim minorities in the West to the situation of the Prophet's Companions who immigrated to Abyssinia a few years before the mass migration of the Muslims from Mecca to Medina in 622 CE. He concludes that, just as the Muslims were allowed to stay in Abyssinia and not follow the Prophet to Medina because they were treated well by the Negus, so the Muslims in the West are allowed to stay because they are also treated well. However, this seems more akin to a philosophical division of the world rather than a political or legal one; it does not take into consideration or discuss the exemptions from

59 Ramadan, *To be a European Muslim*, p. 141.

60 Literally, 'the abode of response', i.e., the abode of those who have accepted the call to Islam.

61 Literally, 'the abode of the call', i.e., the abode of those who are being called to Islam.

62 Ramadan, *To be a European Muslim*, p. 149. See also, Alwani, *Towards a Fiqh for Minorities*, p. xii and p. 29.

63 Attia, *Towards Realization of the Higher Intents of Islamic Law*, pp. 141-42.

64 Alwani, *Towards a Fiqh for Minorities*, p. 117.

65 Ibid., pp. 30-32.

religious obligations that Muslim minorities are granted as a result of not living in a Muslim-majority territory. For example, an Islamic government would be required to fulfil the following obligations which would not be expected of a Muslim community living as a minority: validation of the community, namely the maintenance of a moral order based on divine law; validation of public worship, for instance the collecting and distribution of *zakāt*; *tanfīdh al-aḥkām* (execution of the law); execution of the *ḥudūd*; *jihād*; commanding right and forbidding wrong; *ḥifẓ al-dīn* (preservation of the religion); the collection and distribution of three taxes, *jizya* (poll tax), *kharāj* (land tax) and *ʿushr*[66] sometimes referred to as *sadaqa* (tithe). These responsibilities are referred to as *ḥuqūq Allāh*, the 'rights of God'; but, practically speaking, this refers to governments as trustees and administrators of God's Law. Whilst governments are obliged to uphold the 'rights of God', they can only become involved in *ḥuqūq al-ʿibād*, the 'rights of mankind', at the request of the parties involved.[67] It goes without saying that there are other non-Sharīʿa responsibilities that the government must acknowledge and complete, for instance the building of roads, bridges and the maintenance of mosques.[68] Muslim minorities are exempt from the obligations that are imposed on a Muslim-majority state and this has to be taken into consideration when discussing their rights and responsibilities.

The position of liberals/modernists on Western countries is that they are at best *dār al-Islām* and at worst *dār al-daʿwa*.

The Traditional Approach

In order to elucidate the position of the traditional approach, we will base ourselves on Shaybānī's *al-Siyar al-kabir*, quoted in Sarakhsī's *Mabsūṭ*, for the different *siyar* and *diyār* recognised by the traditional model. The term *siyar* was first coined by Abū Ḥanīfa and it concerns the relationship of a ruler with other rulers or political bodies at times of peace and war and has been translated as 'international law' by Hamidullah.[69]

In most of the academic literature on political Islam, one finds that 'according

[66] Johansen, *Contingency in Sacred Law*, pp. 129-52.

[67] Ibid., pp. 189-218.

[68] Crone, *Medieval Islamic Political Thought*, pp. 286-314.

[69] Hamidullah, *The Muslim Conduct of State*, p. 10.

to classical scholarship' the world is divided into: *dār al-ḥarb* and *dār al-Islām*.[70] However, one also finds scholars who consider this an oversimplification or too general an inference. For example, Affendi speaks of 'a mistranslation' and 'an omission'.[71] First and foremost, according to the traditional approach there is not just one monolithic land mass referred to as *dār al-ḥarb* and another monolithic land mass referred to as *dār al-Islām*.[72] The view that *dār al-Islām* is not a single land mass is clear from Ibn ʿĀbidīn's explanation of the manner in which inheritance can be applied and suspended in different territorial states, '...the fourth [reason] is due to the *ikhtilāf al-dārayn* [the existence of two different *dār*]. The difference is due to the different power, i.e. army, and because of different kings. [For instance] one of the two kings is in India and he has a state and an army and another [king] is in Turkey and he has another state and army and the [treaty of] protection is terminated between them so that it is no longer illegal for one [from one state] to kill the other, then these two become *dārān* (two separate states). Hence, between the two [states the transfer of] inheritance ceases because it [i.e. the transfer] is based upon protection and friendship. However, if there is assistance and co-operation between the two against mutual enemies then this is [regarded as] one *dār* and [the transfer] of inheritance will subsist.'[73]

In this section a *dār* is defined by what modern terminology would refer to as a 'country' or a 'sovereign state' which has a leader and an independent force that protects the state. At the time this text was written, India and Turkey were Muslim states therefore the potential, however remote or hypothetical, of being mutual enemies existed. Likewise even though being separate states with their own leaders, governments and armies, they could form a coalition and would then be regarded as one state.

[70] See, Abdur-Rahman Doi, 'Duties and Responsibilities of Muslims in non-Muslim States: A Point of View', *Journal Institute of Muslim Minority Affairs* (vol. 8, no. 1, 1987), pp. 42-61; Khalid Masud, 'Being Muslim in an Non-Muslim Polity: Three Alternate Models', *Journal Institute of Muslim Minority Affairs* (vol. 10, no. 1, 1989), pp. 118-28; Bernard Lewis, 'Legal and Historical Reflections on the Position of Muslim Populations under Non-Muslim Rule', *Journal Institute of Muslim Minority Affairs* (vol. 13, no. 1, 1992), pp. 1-16; Samuel Huntington, *The Clash of the Civilizations and the Remaking of the World Order* (New York: Simon & Schuster, 1996); Sherman Jackson, 'Jihad and the Modern World', *The Journal of Islamic Law and Culture* (vol. 7, no. 1, 2002), pp. 1-26; Hyder Gulam, 'Islam, Law and War', *University of New England Law Journal* (vol. 3, 2006), pp. 187-209.

[71] El-Affendi, *Who Needs an Islamic State?*, pp. 112-13.

[72] Aḥmad al-Sarakhsī, *Kitāb al-mabsūṭ* (Beirut: Dār Iḥyā' al-Turāth al-ʿArabī, 2002), vol. 10, p. 85.

[73] Ibn ʿĀbidīn, *Radd al-muḥtār ʿalā durr al-mukhtār*, vol. 5, p. 542

As this example illustrates, international law as it is to be found in classical texts is quite complex. In fact, throughout the Ḥanafī foundational texts of *siyar* we find no less than six different political definitions of a territory: *dār al-Islām*[74] (Muslim state), *dār al-ḥarb*[75] (enemy state), *dār al-shirk*[76] (a non-monotheistic state), *dār al-kufr*[77] (non-Muslim state),[78] *dār al-ṣulḥ* (peace-treaty state) *and dār al-muwādaʿa*[79] (also peace-treaty state). Other variants put forward more recently are: *dār al-amān* (peaceful state) and *dār al-hudna* (truce state); these are more or less the same as *dār al-ṣulḥ*. Whenever we use *dār al-ṣulḥ* below, it will include these definitions.

When Islam, as a military and political force, started to expand after it had established itself in Mecca, all states which confronted it became *dār al-ḥarb*. Jurists then were concerned exclusively with Christendom, Byzantium being the dominant empire in the region, and paid little attention to political affiliation with smaller colonies of Muslims in India, Africa, China and in other parts of Asia.[80] This further substantiates the claim that different types of *diyār* existed: the Christians were part of *dār al-ḥarb* due to the mutual animosity between them and the Muslims, and the colonies were neutral and were thus, at worst, part of *dār al-kufr* (or *dār al-shirk*) and, at best, *dār al-muwādaʿa*. Furthermore, when Muslims travelled to non-Muslim lands they would do so under the protection of the host-ruler for a short period in order to trade and would return forthwith. Hence, the traditional books of *fiqh* are full of rulings with respect to traders travelling to non-Muslim lands, but completely devoid of rulings for Muslims taking up residence in these lands, interacting as citizens and engaging with the wider non-Muslim society. The reason is that this concept was alien to early Islam.[81] There is one exception worthy of mention and that is the Muslims referred to as *Mudejars* who lived in Spain after the re-conquest by the

74 Sarakhsī, *Kitāb al-mabsūṭ*, vol. 10, p. 21.

75 Ibid.

76 Ibid., vol. 14, p. 56.

77 Ibid., vol. 10, p. 111.

78 Classical texts understand *dār al-shirk* to be for those who accept God as Islam understands Him but associate partners with Him, and *dār al-kufr* to be for those who do not accept God as Islam understands Him. Some scholars argue that certain sects within Christianity are *mushrik* as they accept God but ascribe His qualities to Jesus.

79 Sarakhsī, *Kitāb al-mabsūṭ*, vol. 10, p. 83.

80 Lewis, 'Legal and Historical Reflections on the Position of Muslim Populations under Non-Muslim Rule', p.7.

81 Ibid., p. 6; Raḥamānī, *Jadīd fiqhī masā'il*, vol. 4, p. 70.

Christians. Mālikī jurists (the Mālikī School of Law was the predominant one in al-Andalus) regarded the re-conquered territories as *dār al-ḥarb*.[82]

Traditional scholars have usually used *dār al-muwāda'a* when Muslims were recognised within the political and legal framework as co-citizens and fully integrated within the wider society. However, when government policy was to disregard key Islamic personal and family laws and to deny Muslims the possibility of living according to their religious commitments, then this would lead the jurists to declare the country *dār al-ḥarb*. This latter ruling meant that Muslims had to take into consideration the possibility of migrating to a more congenial country; if migration proved difficult or near impossible then the community should isolate itself, as much as possible, from the wider hostile society.

Looking at the list of *diyār* highlighted above, the natural and most fitting antithesis for *dār al-Islām* is *dār al-kufr*[83] rather than *dār al-ḥarb*. Hence, the following figure would represent the traditional view:

Figure 4: The Relationship between the Political-legal Jurisdictions

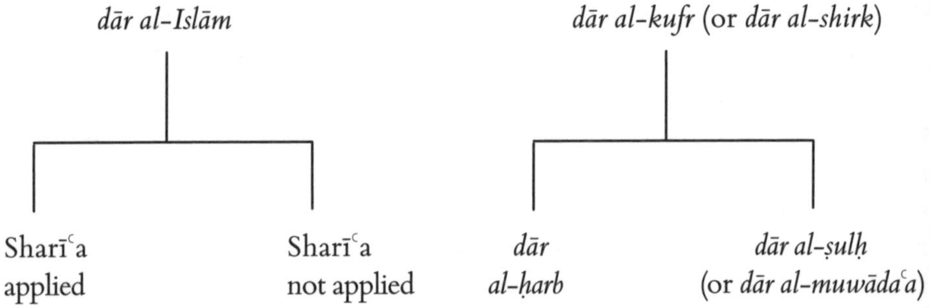

Dār al-Islām states possess the ability to apply Islamic Law and are legally bound to do so, which would make all—citizens, politicians and law-makers alike—sinful at varying degrees if they do not apply the Law. It is the responsibility of the government to provide *amān* (state security, civil order) to all its

[82] See Kathryn Miller, 'Muslim Minorities and the Obligation to Emigrate to Islamic Territory: Two *Fatwās* from Fifteenth-Century Granada',, pp. 256-88; Delfina Serrano, 'Legal Practice in an Andalusī-Maghribī Source from the Twelfth Century CE: The *Madhāhib al-ḥukkām fī nawāzil al-aḥkām*', *Islamic Law and Society* (vol. 7, no. 2, 2000), pp. 187-234; Maribel Fierro, 'Islamic Law in al-Andalus', *Islam Law and Society* (vol. 7, no. 2, 2000), pp. 119-21.

[83] Some may argue that to call non-Muslim states *dār al-kufr* is derogatory. This is what early jurists used and our intention here is to emphasis the category and not the choice of language. We have chosen to translate *dār al-kufr* as 'non-Muslim state' rather than the emotive 'infidel state'.

citizens, Muslim and non-Muslim, but if it does not it will still be considered *dār al-Islām* and the government will be considered in dereliction of duty and sinful. As for *dār al-kufr* even though *amān* may exist, it is not sufficient for it to become *dār al-Islām*, as it is not *mukallaf* (required by God, therefore responsible) to apply Islamic Law. Hence, *amān* is not the deciding factor in determining the status of a state and the ruling that jurists pass on it. *Dār al-Islām* is gained through the potential or actual application of Islamic Law. But what then of the Muslim-majority state which does not allow any manifestations of Islam? If, for example, it does not allow mosques to be built, prohibits Muslim women from wearing *ḥijāb*, or forbids ritual slaughter. And, what of the Muslim-minority state which allows Muslims to adjudicate by their own laws? In the first case, the state would no longer be *dār al-Islām* as the 'Muslim' politicians and leaders would no longer be regarded as Muslims. Hence, the state would be *dār al-kufr* initially, but if it is actively hostile towards the essentials of Islam, it would then become *dār al-ḥarb*. The second situation, where the non-Muslim state allows the Muslims to judge for themselves on religious issues of inheritance, personal and family law, would be considered *dār al-ṣulḥ*.

We would now like to proceed to define in more detail the criteria which jurists use for determining the political-legal status of states. Of the six above mentioned *diyār*, we will concentrate on only three—*dār al-Islām*, *dār al-ḥarb* and *dār al-ṣulḥ*—as the other three *diyār*—*dār al-shirk*, *dār al-kufr*, *dār al-muwādaʿa*—are subsumed in them. But before we go any further, we would like to make it clear that these criteria and the terminology used are not explicit in the Qur'ān and *aḥādīth* but have been obtained by jurists through the process of *ijtihād*.

The earliest scholars applied the terms '*dār al-Islām*' and 'our *dār*' to those lands that were populated by Muslims and in which Islamic Law was applied, while *dār al-kufr* and *dār al-ḥarb* are those lands where non-Muslims hold the reins of power.[84] Kāsānī states, 'There is no difference of opinion amongst our companions in that *dār al-kufr* becomes *dār al-Islām* by the dominance of Islamic Law in it.'[85]

There is, however, a difference of opinion when the situation is reversed, that is, when *dār al-Islām* becomes *dār al-kufr*. Kāsānī here says, 'They [the *fuqahā'*] differ [in their view] as to when *dār al-Islām* becomes *dār al-kufr*. Abū Ḥanīfa states it only becomes *dār al-kufr* under three conditions: firstly,

[84] Raḥamānī, *Jadīd fiqhī masā'il*, vol. 4, p. 65.
[85] ʿAlā al-Dīn Kāsānī, *Badā'iʿ al-ṣanā'iʿ fī tartīb al-sharā'iʿ*, vol. 9, p. 519.

when the dominant law is non-Muslims; secondly, when it [a *dār al-Islām*] aligns itself with a *dār al-kufr*; and thirdly, when any *amān* granted by the Muslims of this state, which has now become *dār al-kufr*, is no longer in force. Abū Yūsuf and Muḥammad state that it becomes *dār al-kufr* when the dominant law is non-Muslims.'[86]

Ibn ᶜĀbidīn corroborates what Kāsānī has said above.[87] The consensus of Ḥanafī scholars affirms Abū Ḥanīfa's view. It is to be noted that, in both the quotations above, Kāsānī does not use *dār al-ḥarb* as the antithesis of *dār al-Islām*. Therefore it could be that the two terms were used interchangeably or rather, as we have argued, that *dār al-kufr* is the more accurate antithesis of *dār al-Islām* according to the traditional view.

Furthermore, *dār al-ḥarb* can have two applications: firstly, it refers to a country with whom there is no peace treaty or armistice, or with whom diplomatic ties have broken down, or when the non-Muslim state is regarded as a threat to the Muslim state, or when a non-Muslim state is at war with a Muslim state. Secondly, it refers to a state which does not recognise the rights of its Muslim citizens, which prohibits Islam, and in which Muslims are required to assimilate completely into the indigenous non-Muslim population.

As to *dār al-ṣulḥ*, it is defined as a country in which the power lies with non-Muslims and yet Muslims are allowed to practice their faith, their rights are protected and they are treated as equal citizens.[88]

From the above definitions, it is easy to see that a non-Muslim country can be regarded as *dār al-ḥarb* by one Muslim country, as *dār al-kufr* by another and as *dār al-ṣulḥ* by a third, each independent Muslim state having its own relationship with the non-Muslim state.

We will now summarise the legal rulings for the application of *dār al-Islām*, *dār al-ḥarb* and *dār al-ṣulḥ* to a country:

Rulings for the application of *dār al-Islām*:

1. The application of and obedience to all individual and community Islamic laws.
2. The ability to accept immigrants from *dār al-ḥarb*.
3. The financial assistance and support of poor and helpless Muslims in *dār al-ḥarb*.

86 Ibid.

87 Ibn ᶜĀbidīn, *Radd al-muḥtār ᶜalā durr al-mukhtār*, vol. 3, p. 277.

88 Raḥamānī, *Jadīd fiqhī masā'il*, vol. 4, p. 75.

4. The furthering of the influence of Islam beyond the borders of the state.[89]

According to the traditional viewpoint, as Muslims living in Western countries are only in a position to carry out the third point and, to some extent, the fourth, Western countries cannot be regarded as *dār al-Islām*.

Rulings for the application of *dār al-ḥarb*:

1. A *dār al-ḥarb* state is outside the borders of a *dār al-Islām* state.
2. As it is not possible to practice Islamic Law in *dār al-ḥarb*, its applications are suspended and Muslims living in a *dār al-ḥarb* state are considered not culpable for not applying the Law.[90]
3. Where Muslims are not permitted to openly study and practice their faith in *dār al-ḥarb*, then any shortcomings in their knowledge of Islam is excused.
4. When the citizens of *dār al-ḥarb* are in a state of war against a Muslim country, then, in principle (but there are conditions for this), their lives and property are open to attack by the Muslims of the state they are at war with.
5. It is not permissible for Muslims living in *dār al-ḥarb* to trade in weapons as these weapons can be used against Muslims.[91]
6. It is not permissible to allow a citizen from *dār al-ḥarb* to stay in *dār al-Islām* for longer than a year even if he requests citizenship. The *jizya* (poll tax) becomes applicable on a person from an enemy state who has taken refuge in a Muslim state (a *musta'min*) if he stays for longer than a year.[92]

It is quite clear from the above that *dār al-ḥarb* is a hostile, enemy state and not a 'normal' non-Muslim state. As it is at best complicated for Muslims to live in a state qualified as *dār al-ḥarb*, the necessity for these Muslims to emigrate becomes an obligation. Ibn Qudāma gives three rulings for this:

1. Those for whom migration is necessary: individuals who cannot practice their faith openly and have the ability to emigrate.
2. Those for whom migration is not necessary: individuals who are

[89] Ibid., p. 76.

[90] Ibn ʿĀbidīn, *Radd al-muḥtār ʿalā durr al-mukhtār*,vol. 3, p. 155.

[91] Aḥmad al-Sarakhsī, *Kitāb al-mabsūṭ* (Beirut: Dār Iḥyāʾ al-Turāth al-ʿArabī, 2002), vol. 10, pp. 87-88.

[92] ʿAbd al-Jalāl al-Marghīnānī, *al-Hidāya* (Multan: Maktabat al-Sharika al-ʿIlmiyya, 1999), vol. 1, pp. 585-86.

unable to emigrate either due to illness, or due to the inability of their wives or children to do so, or who are forced to stay.[93]

3. Those for whom emigration is not necessary but is praiseworthy: individuals who may openly practice their faith and perform the compulsory aspects of Islam and who have the ability to emigrate but decide to live in *dār al-kufr*.[94] For example, al-ʿAbbās, the uncle of the Prophet, stayed in Mecca after becoming a Muslim and did not emigrate to Medina with the other Muslims; also, when Nuʿaym b. al-Najām wanted to migrate his tribe, the Banū ʿAdā, approached him and said, 'Stay with us and you can keep your faith and we will protect you from those who intend to harm you and we will mutually look after one another.' He stayed with them for a while after the Hijra.[95]

Islamic Law and Islamic identity is virtually non-existent within *dār al-Ḥarb* as arguably the Muslim is outside the remit of Muslim legislators and therefore there is very little that differentiates the Muslim from the non-Muslim. Zaylaʿī says, '[There is no *ribā*] between a non-Muslim enemy and a Muslim there. That is, there is no *ribā* between them in *dār al-ḥarb*. Equally, if in *dār al-ḥarb* they conduct any transaction considered illegal [by Islam] then it is legal. This is the opinion of Abū Ḥanīfa and Muḥammad [Shaybānī], whereas Abū Yūsuf and Shāfiʿī say it is impermissible as the Muslim has been afforded security on the grounds that he would not take their wealth except by correct transaction and this transaction is corrupt.'[96]

In summary, it is clear that *dār al-ḥarb* is a non-Muslim state which either persecutes Muslims or with which a Muslim state is at war and where all ceasefires and truces are absent. Yet, even in such situations the traditional approach permits a combatant Muslim to travel to an enemy state and an enemy combatant to be allowed into a Muslim state. What the Law books were discussing was a reality 'on the ground' rather than a relationship that a Muslim state has or should have with a non-Muslim state. As in *dār al-ḥarb* Muslim citizens would not be allowed to practice their faith openly, celebrate

[93] In our era, the obstacles for citizens to move between countries will also apply.

[94] Note the use of *dār al-kufr* rather than *dār al-ḥarb* as has been discussed previously.

[95] Ibn al-Qudāmā, *al-Mughnī maʿa al-sharḥ al-kabīr* (Beirut: Dār al-Kitāb al-ʿArabī, 1983), pp. 514-15.

[96] ʿUthmān al-Zaylaʿī, *Tabyīn al-ḥaqā'iq: sharḥ kanz al-daqā'iq* (Beirut: Dār al-Kutub al-ʿIlmiyya, 2000), vol. 4, p. 476.

their festivals, ritually slaughter animals or build places of worship, and as the state would openly deny the faith of its Muslim citizens and require them to assimilate at all costs, Western countries cannot be termed *dār al-ḥarb*.

Rulings for the application of *dār al-ṣulḥ*:

1. A *dār al-ṣulḥ* state is outside the borders of a *dār al-Islām* state.
2. Unlike Muslims living in *dār al-ḥarb*, Muslims living in *dār al-ṣulḥ* will not be excused ignorance of Sharīʿa rulings and applications.
3. The dealings between Muslims in *dār al-ṣulḥ* and between Muslims and other non-Muslim citizens cannot be settled outside *dār al-ṣulḥ* or in the courts of a *dār al-Islām* state.
4. It is not necessary for Muslims to emigrate from *dār al-ṣulḥ*.
5. It is permissible to defend a *dār al-ṣulḥ* and to assist the majority population there. For example, the Companions assisted the Negus in Abyssinia against his enemies. In the case of offensive, as opposed to defensive, war, Muslims should avoid being involved if it is an unjust war,[97] especially when the war is against a Muslim state.
6. As Muslims in *dār al-ṣulḥ* live in peace and security, then the lives and property of non-Muslims are inviolable.
7. Un-Islamic practices, like usury or trading in alcohol, in order to gain wealth, are impermissible for Muslims living in *dār al-ṣulḥ*.[98]

In summary, *dār al-ṣulḥ* is any state in which Muslims are free to practice the tenets of their faith and law and are in a position to invite others to Islam. Therefore, we conclude that according to the traditional approach Western countries are *dār al-ṣulḥ*.

Finally, one key point to stress is that the process by which jurists decide on the ruling to be applied to a state was, and is, based on the state's attitude towards Islam and Muslims; hence it is a reactionary ruling. Therefore, the ruling issued by jurists is dependent on the stance of a state. As it has been stressed throughout this study, when expounding the traditional view, rulings are not issued in a vacuum but the context and the reality 'on the ground' are absolutely essential and have to be considered before deciding on the legal position.

[97] This is equally applicable in the case of a Muslim state waging an unjust war.

[98] Raḥamānī, *Jadīd fiqhī masā'il*, vol. 4, pp. 81-82.

CHAPTER VI

Applications of Traditional Islamic Law: Ḥanafī *Fiqh* in the West

THE MAJOR CONCERN of our work is the situation of Muslims living as a minority. How do Muslims remain true to their faith in the absence of a Muslim government, whether this be in Western countries or in Muslim countries that do not make allowances for the essentials of Islam? Ibn al-Humām states, 'When there is no sultan or a person of authority in place, as is the case now in some Muslim lands, such as Cordoba, Valencia and Abyssinia where the reins of power are in the hands of non-Muslims, then the Muslims, who reside there under an agreement to pay a tax, are responsible for choosing a person to lead them. The person chosen is to carry out the responsibility of *walī* (ruler). He should either act as a judge himself or select another person to judge in order to settle the legal disputes among the Muslims. Also, an imam should be appointed to lead the Friday congregational prayer.'[1] From this it is clear that, in both of the above cases, it is the Muslim community's responsibility to ensure that various institutes are established and individuals appointed in order that all necessary religious forms are upheld.

In the previous chapter, we saw that traditional *fiqh* categorises Western countries in general as *dār al-ṣulḥ*. This chapter will investigate the application of Ḥanafī Law within the context of the West, including the concept of citizenship which is novel to Islamic law.

The main argument levelled against traditional Islam is that it is out of date and irrelevant to our modern lives. Traditional Law is regarded as inflexible, unable to take into consideration the culture and customs of peoples, and it does not grant the means for communities to integrate into a non-Muslim society.

[1] Kamāl al-Dīn Ibn Humām, *Sharḥ fatḥ al-qadīr* (Beirut: Dār al-Kutub al-ʿIlmiyya, 1995), vol. 7, p. 246.

Our study challenged these hypotheses and demonstrated that the traditional law possesses, both theoretically and practically, the ability to adapt to different times and situations. In this present chapter, we will focus on applications of the traditional approach to situations that face Muslims in the West today. We have chosen the examples below in order to illustrate the breadth, scope, applicability and feasibility of this interpretive model in facilitating the existence of Muslims within a secular, democratic society and allowing them to remain true to their faith.

In the chapters above, we have detailed the methodology which allows a *muftī* to issue *fatāwā* based on the Ḥanafī School. We will summarise these here as: firstly, *taqlīd*, the interrogation of accepted texts within the School to locate an answer; secondly, and only when an answer is not found in the accepted texts, the *muftī* would perform *ijtihād fī'l-madhhab* (the deductive reasoning within the Schools of Law) and utilise all methodologies available in order to provide a *fatwā*. One area of traditional Law which is particularly relevant is *istiḥsān*—to seek the spirit of the Law rather than a strict lexical interpretation; this concept in conjunction with the *ʿurf* of local Muslim communities will contribute to provide the rulings for Muslims in Western countries. It must be stressed that the *fatāwā* are issued by *muftī*s and are legal advice; enforcement is not within the remit of the *muftī*. To assist the *muftī* to arrive at a *fatwā*, recourse can be made to a number of legal maxims. Those that are particularly helpful to the situation of Muslim minorities are the following:

1. Matters are according to their objectives.
2. That which is established by necessity is limited to its requirements.
3. A greater harm is removed by a lesser harm.
4. Harm must be removed.
5. Necessity permits the [usage of the] impermissible.
6. The lesser of the two harms is the one to be chosen.

In order to demonstrate the potential and flexibility of traditional Islamic Law as applied by the Ḥanafī School, a number of situations relevant to the lives of Muslims living as minorities will be put forward: employment, food products, medicines and medical interventions, inheritance, financial transactions and political participation.

Employment: Working with Illegal Products/Services

Among the prohibitions under Islamic Law, there are two in particular that are known widely: the prohibitions of alcohol and the prohibitions of usury/interest (*ribā*). The majority of countries worldwide not only permit both and but have them integrated into their social and economic fabric. Their widespread use and application are, therefore, of significant concern to Muslims.

Handling Alcohol

Jurists have extensively discussed the illegality of alcohol and the exceptional circumstances under which it can be used. It is stated in *Radd al-muḥtār* that:

> It is illegal to take benefit from it [alcohol] even if he is giving it to animals to drink, or in order to irrigate the earth, or [to use] in order to beautify, or in medicine, or [mingled with] oil or food, or other than that except for *takhlīl* (converting to vinegar), or due to fear of [dying from] thirst [but then only that amount which is] necessary [to sustain life] because if he were to drink more and become intoxicated then *ḥadd* punishment[2] would be applicable. It is not permissible to trade [in alcohol] due to the *ḥadīth* narrated in Muslim, Indeed He Who has made its drinking illegal has made trading in it illegal.[3]

Furthermore, it is stated in *Badā'iʿ al-ṣanā'iʿ fī tartīb al-sharā'iʿ*:

> It is illegal for a Muslim to own it [alcohol], or to pass its ownership to a third party by means like buying and selling and any other [means]. This is because all these are [means] of benefiting from alcohol and to benefit from it is illegal for Muslims.
>
> It is narrated from the Prophet (may God bless him and grant him peace) [when the verse for the prohibition of alcohol was revealed] that he said, 'O People of Medina, indeed God has without doubt revealed the illegality of alcohol. So, whoever has heard this verse and he has in [his] possession some alcohol, then he should not drink it nor should he sell it.' So they spilt it in the streets of Medina.[4]

Not only is alcohol regarded as an illegal product it is also regarded as *najisa ghalīẓa* (gross impurity).[5] Marghīnānī stipulates:

> [Alcoholic substances] in themselves are illegal and not because of their ability to intoxicate which it is not a condition [for their illegality]. There are some who state regarding their actual illegality, "It is the intoxication

[2] The legal punishment for drinking alcohol outside exceptional circumstances.

[3] Ibn ʿĀbidīn, *Radd al-muḥtār ʿalā durr al-mukhtār*, vol. 5, p. 319.

[4] Kāsānī, *Badā'iʿ al-ṣanā'iʿ fī tartīb al-sharā'iʿ*, vol. 6, p. 437.

[5] Ibid.

> which causes it to be illegal because corruption is caused by it and that is not allowing [an individual] to remember God." [This position] is disbelief in Islam as it rejects the Qur'ān. For He has referred to it as *rijs* and *rijs* is that which is illegal in itself. The *mutawātir sunna* states that indeed the Prophet made alcohol illegal and the consensus of *ijmāʿ* agrees.[6]

From all the above, it would seem that to work with alcohol in any capacity is illegal. However, Ibn ʿĀbidīn, when discussing the relations with non-Muslims, details the permissibility for transporting alcohol for a non-Muslim:

> It is permitted ...to transport wine for a non-Muslim. Zaylaʿī said, "This is according to him [Abū Ḥanīfa]. His two companions [Abū Yūsuf and Shaybānī] said that it is reprehensible (*makrūh*), because the Prophet (may God bless him and grant him peace) cursed ten [types of individuals][7] with regards to wine, and he included amongst them the one who transports it. Abū Ḥanīfa's reasoning is that the hiring is for transporting [which in] itself is neither a sin nor a reason for it. Rather, the sin only occurs through the action of a willing actor, and drinking is not necessarily brought about by the transportation, because it could be for disposal or to transform into vinegar. Therefore this is similar to being hired to press or cut grapes. As for the *ḥadīth*, it is interpreted to mean transporting with the intention of sin." Zaylaʿī then said, "The same difference exists [between Abū Ḥanīfa and his two companions] if he is hired with a vehicle in order to transport wine upon it, or if he is hired to herd pigs. In such cases, the wages are permissible according to Abū Ḥanīfa, and reprehensible according to the other two."[8]

A particular example where it is possible for Muslims today to come into regular contact with alcohol and other products prohibited by Islamic Law is working at checkouts in supermarkets. A literal approach when analysing

[6] Marghīnānī, *Hidāya*, vol. 2, p. 493.

[7] Tirmidhī quotes this *ḥadīth* from Anas b. Mālik who said: 'The Messenger of God (may God bless him and grant him peace) cursed ten types of individuals with respect to alcohol, the one who crushes [the grape], the one who requests the crushing, the drinker, **the one who carries it**, the one who requests its carrying, the one who serves it, the one who trades in it, the one who benefits from its sale, the one who purchases it and the one for whom it is purchased.' Emphasis added. See Muḥammad ʿUthmānī, *Buḥūth fī qaḍāyā fiqhiyya muʿāṣara* (Karachi: Maktabat Dār al-ʿUlūm, 2006), vol. 1, p. 338.

[8] Ibn ʿĀbidīn, *Radd al-muḥtār ʿalā durr al-mukhtār*, vol. 5, p. 277

the source texts would state that this is an impermissible activity, since the Muslim would be committing a sin and, in order to avoid sinning, would have to leave his/her employment. The liberal approach would be to reinterpret the sources, namely the particular verses and *aḥādīth*, in order to argue for permissibility; this may prove very difficult, but as there are limited practical applications of the liberal approach, in both academic and in religious circles, it is not possible to comment further. The traditional Ḥanafī approach would be for the *muftī* to issue a *fatwā* according to Abū Ḥanīfa's position and to state that, in such a situation, it would be permissible for a Muslim to handle alcohol and other prohibited products as they themselves are not intending to sell the prohibited products.

In fact, one can derive a key principle or legal maxim from a statement by Zaylaʿī, which can have a wide application: '*Lā ba'sa bihī liannahū lā mʿaṣiya fī ʿayn al-ʿaml*,'[9] which translates as 'It is permissible because there is no sin in the actual specific action.' This principle can be applied in many forms of employment, transactions and investments covering a wide range of activities. Notwithstanding the above, it must be added that *taqwā* requires the individual to avoid handling alcohol and other prohibited products if this is possible. The above maxim is applied to the following section.

Usury/Interest (Ribā)

The principle concerning employment in a bank, or any other financial institution which deals with interest, is that any work or job which entails being directly involved in interest-based transactions will be unlawful. Therefore, the person who is involved in setting up interest-based accounts, recording them and promoting them, would be sinning.

Working in a bank or other such institution includes different activities and responsibilities. Here are two positions and their legality:

1. Working in a bank as a call attendant and answering telephone calls would be legal as long as the job is based on discussing general matters regarding a customer's account and giving information and advice to the customer in a general manner. However, if the job is specifically based on interest-based transactions, or dealing with customers who are specifically involved with interest, then this would be considered illegal as that specific activity is illegal.

[9] Ibid.

2. Designing and producing computer software or making computer programmes for the bank would also be legal. However, designing programmes that are exclusively used for usurious transactions would be considered illegal.

Other Employments/Services

Zaylaʿī's principle, that a thing is permissible when there is no sin in the specific action, can be applied to a number of other situations, e.g: a cab driver taking a fare to a nightclub, a plumber fixing a boiler at a pub, or a woman hiring out her function hall for a party where alcohol will be served. Here the possibility that the activity may be prohibited comes from the Qur'ānic verse, *wa-lā taʿāwanū ʿalā al-ithm wa'l-ʿudwān* (Q.v.2), 'do not assist one another in sin or evil.' To apply the literal model would make the above activities impermissible as they involve assisting a third party in something which is illegal according to Islamic Law. However, when the above activities cannot be avoided, then Zaylaʿī's traditional position would make it possible for a Muslim to earn his/her living and still remain within the legal limits of their faith.

Food Products

Meat and Meat Products

Many Muslim-minority communities are fortunate in that they live within a short distance of religious and cultural amenities, one being the presence of butchers who provide *ḥalāl* meat and poultry. However, there are small clusters of Muslims who do not have access to these facilities. What should they do? Should they buy meat from their local supermarket and recite the Name of God at the time of eating, or abandon meat altogether as the liberal and literal models suggest? Ibn ʿĀbidīn says, 'Shaykh al-Islām states that they [the Muslims] should not eat the slaughtered animals of the People of the Book if they [the Christians] believe that the Messiah is God, or that Uzayr is God [according to some Jewish sects]…; the *fatwā* is based on this. However, upon close scrutiny of the evidence, it is [more] suitable for eating…to be permissible. He states in *al-Baḥr*,…that the meat slaughtered by a Christian is legal, absolutely, irrespective of whether he believes in the

Trinity or not; and this is due to absolute evidence from the Qur'ān.'[10]

Kāsānī adds:

> 'Hence the slaughter [i.e. the slaughtered meat] of a *kitābī* (Jew/Christian) will be [permissible to] consume when the slaughtering was not [actually] witnessed…, or when he hears and witnesses from him the name of Almighty God alone; because if he does not hear anything from him then it will be assumed that God's name was invoked…, assuming good of him [*the kitābī* butcher] like one would a Muslim [butcher].
>
> If he [the Muslim] hears him mention God's name but he means by God the Messiah, upon him be peace, they [the jurists] say [it is permissible to] consume [the animal] because this *tasmiyya* is like the *tasmiyya* of the Muslims except when he stipulates and says, 'In the name of God who is the one of three,' then it will not be *ḥalāl*.
>
> Indeed it is narrated from our master ᶜAlī, may God be pleased with him, that he was asked about the slaughter of the People of the Book and what they said [at the time of slaughter]. He replied, "Indeed God has made legal their slaughter and He knows what they say."
>
> When he [actually] hears him invoke only the Messiah, upon him be peace, or the invoking of God and the Messiah, then the slaughter should not be consumed.
>
> As, this has been transmitted from our master ᶜAlī (may God be pleased with him) and none [of the Companions] have opposed him, it is [considered] *ᶜijmāᶜ*.
>
> Also, the Almighty's statement, *[Illegal is] that [slaughter] upon which other than God's name is invoked* (Q. v.3), and this is the invoking of other than God's name so it will not be [permissible to be] consumed.'[11]

Summarising the two jurists: in most cases, the individual who will consume the meat is not present at the time of slaughter, therefore he or she will not know who was invoked at the time of slaughter. Kāsānī puts forward a statement made by ᶜAlī, when he was asked if the slaughter of the 'People of the Book' [i.e. Jews and Christians] is permissible as they invoke the Messiah or the Trinity at the time of slaughter; ᶜAlī's answer was

[10] Ibid., vol. 2, p. 314.

[11] Kāsānī, *Badā'iᶜ al-ṣanā'iᶜ fī tartīb al-sharā'iᶜ*, vol. 6, pp. 229-30. The above argument is rather complex but the key to it is the actual hearing: if you do not hear other than God invoked then the meat is assumed to be *ḥalāl*, if you clearly hear other than God invoked then it is no longer *ḥalāl*.

that it is permissible. Hence, Muslims would be permitted to eat the slaughtered animal of Christians and Jews. Now, this situation is not applicable to meats from supermarkets as their owners' faith (if they profess to one) is not known. It would be applicable to local butchers who profess their faith to be one of the two other Abrahamic faiths. However, ritual slaughter as it was formerly practiced within the Christian world[12] no longer exists in most Western countries; therefore, unless a Christian butcher adopts the procedure of cutting certain arteries in order to allow the blood to drain out of the animal, their meat will be excluded. Kosher meat is permissible in the absence of *ḥalāl* meat as to this day it is still slaughtered according to religious principles.

In conclusion, in the absence of *ḥalāl* meat, Muslims have the option of consuming meat slaughtered by the 'People of the Book'. In most Western countries today, this means consuming kosher meat. Muslims may also choose to practice *taqwā* and, in the absence of *ḥalāl* meat, become vegetarians.

Additives

Shoppers, in particular Muslims, staring at the ingredients of food products are becoming a common sight within the aisles of supermarkets. Complicated food preservatives and colours mean that the average person has to be a food technology expert in order to identify the original source materials for these substances. As this is not a viable possibility, the traditional approach of *inqilāb al-ʿayn* may be applied. The literal translation of *inqilāb al-ʿayn* is 'the transmutation of the substance', and it means the purification of an illegal substance in order to make it legal through the chemical transformation of the original material into a new substance. Ibn ʿĀbidīn gives the example of vinegar, which is a legal product, and whose original substance is often wine or other fermented liquids.[13] The transformation of wine from one substance to another means that it is no longer the original substance and the secondary product is then *ḥalāl* as it is now considered to be completely different from the original one.

Ibn ʿĀbidīn quoting the text of *al-Mujtabā* says: 'The impure olive oil can

[12] This was confirmed in a telephone discussion on 26 May 2008 with Dr P. Lewis (advisor to Bishop of Bradford).

[13] Ibn ʿĀbidīn, *Radd al-muḥtār ʿalā durr al-mukhtār*, vol. 1, p. 230.

be used to make soap and the *fatwā* will be passed that it [the soap] is pure because it has [chemically] changed. According to Muḥammad [Shaybānī] [chemical] change purifies. The *fatwā* is necessary due to *balwā* (necessity). It is apparent [from this] that the fat of a dead animal is similar [to the impure olive oil] as it is considered to be *najis* (impure) [in itself] and not *mutanajjis* (that which makes others impure).'

From the above it is possible to conclude that in cases of necessity (*balwā*), if the substance of a product is chemically transformed then it becomes legal for use or consumption. This ruling would apply to all the substances that Muslims need to check for, such as: food additives, for instance colourants and preservatives; soaps, toothpastes, creams, moisturisers and cleansers made from animal fats, oils and other raw materials, which are deemed impure in their original form.One substance that is of particular concern to Muslims is gelatine because of its animal source. Gelatine, or under its commercial label, E441, is used in a large number of food and non-food products, and is therefore difficult to avoid. The fact that the exact source of the gelatine is not usually stated only compounds the difficulty. Gelatine's most common use is as an emulsifier in food, pharmaceutical and cosmetic manufacturing. It is an irreversibly hydrolysed form of collagen. In more detail, gelatine is a protein produced by partial hydrolysis of collagen extracted from the bones, connective tissues, organs and some intestines of animals such as cattle and horses. The natural molecular bonds between individual collagen strands are broken down into a form that rearranges more easily. It melts when heated and solidifies when cooled; when mixed with water, it forms a semi-solid colloid gel. There are chemical differences between collagen and gelatine, for instance differences in possession of triple-helix structure, molecular weight and distribution, functionality and reaction activity. Zhang Zhongkai *et al* have carried out in-depth research in defining these substances and have clearly found them to be different. They state: 'Only collagen possessed the triple helical conformation. It exhibited many properties distinct from gelatine and collagen hydrolysate, such as high molecular weight and narrow molecular distribution, basic isoelectric point, triple helix to coil translation in the process of denaturation, high resistance to protease, and ability of fibril formation.'[14]

[14] Zhang Zhongkai, Guoying Li and Bi Shi, 'Physicochemical Properties of Collagen, Gelatin and Collagen Hydrolysate derived from Bovine Limed Split Wastes', *Journal of the Society of Leather Technologists and Chemists* (vol. 90, 2006), p. 27.

Therefore the literal approach would not permit the consumption of E441 as its original substance is illegal. The liberal approach would generally argue that as it is difficult for Muslims living in the West to avoid all these products, they should be legalised. The traditional approach is as expounded above. A Muslim may still choose to avoid these products in order to adopt *taqwā*.

Medicines and Medical Interventions

Medication Based on Prohibited Substances

Advances are being made in medical sciences at an incredible speed and with surprising uses for materials and compounds. The question which arises is, can Muslims make use of medicines which contain prohibited materials? Ibn ʿĀbidīn discusses this very dilemma when determining the purity, or otherwise, of urine and more generally illegal materials:

> [Shaybānī's] states that there is a difference of opinion regarding the use of illegal materials for medicinal purposes because in *al-Nihāya* and *al-Dhakhīra* it is permissible if it is known that there is a cure in them and no other medicine is known; and the *al-Khāniyya* [is also of the view of permissibility based upon] the meaning of his statement (may God bless him and grant him peace) as narrated by Bukhārī, "Indeed God did not place your cures in that which he made illegal for you."'[15] Therefore, there is no problem [in consuming] that which possesses a cure within it. This is similar to the permissibility of alcohol out of necessity for the one dying of thirst. The author of *al-Hidāya* has also adopted [this principle].[16]

Ibn ʿĀbidīn further elaborates on the use of prohibited materials for curing illnesses, especially the use of alcohol:

> [It is stated] in *al-Tahdhīb* that it is permissible for a sick person to drink urine or blood or consume carrion for medicinal purposes when a Muslim doctor informs him that the cure is in it and he does not find any [cure] from other permissible [medication]. As has already been mentioned, if there is no alternative then the meaning [of the above mentioned *ḥadīth*] is understood that indeed Almighty God has given permission for you to

[15] Though this *ḥadīth* can be interpreted to mean that that which is illegal does not have in it a cure for you and thus must not be used even in illness, the jurists have interpreted it to mean that if something possesses a curative quality then even though it may be illegal on other occasions it is legal for the curing of illness.

[16] Ibn ʿĀbidīn, *Radd al-muḥtār ʿalā durr al-mukhtār*, vol. 1, p. 154.

> utilise it for medicinal purposes as He has made for every illness a cure. So if there is a cure in this illegal material and you know it is a cure then the illegality of its use will be removed.... [For example,] there is nothing wrong in drinking that which intoxicates the mind so that a gangrenous sore, or the like, can be removed as is stated in *al-Tātarkhāniyya*.[17]

The traditional interpretation of Islamic Law makes things permissible in order to preserve life or to improve the condition of someone's life. Its pragmatism and realism is apparent in that a material which is absolutely and unequivocally prohibited in the Qur'ān and *aḥādīth* is no longer so under exceptional circumstances. To summarise, if there is no permissible form of cure, then it would be permissible to take medication which consists of prohibited substances. In fact, not only would it be permissible, it would be necessary for the sake of preserving life, which is the higher purpose. For example, morphine can be used as an anaesthetic during operations and for pain control. As it is common practice for doctors in a country such as Britain to take into consideration the individual's belief, and in the absence of a Muslim doctor capable of judging which medicines with prohibited substances he or she may use, a non-Muslim doctor, supported by advice from a religious expert, may make such decisions.

Blood Transfusion and Organ Transplantation

It is common practice in many operations for blood supply to be held on standby in case of emergency; however, the question which arises is whether it permissible for a Muslim to accept this blood? Even more so, is it permissible for Muslims to donate and to be the recipients of organs? The primary consideration given by jurists is to the sanctity of the human body. The human body is considered a gift from Almighty God and it must be maintained and used for the purposes of this life and the next. Are we then permitted to donate a part of the body when ultimately we are not its proprietors?

According to Ibn ʿĀbidīn, the *ʿilla* making the use of human body parts prohibited is because the human body should be treated with respect, dignity and honour, irrespective of whether the person is alive or dead.[18] But this is a general *ʿilla* and, if one looks more deeply into the matter, one will see that the illegality is exclusively directed against situations that disgrace and dishonour the

[17] Ibid., vol. 5, p. 275

[18] Ibid., vol. 1, p. 150.

human body and its use for purposes other than what it was created to serve.[19] Now, organ transplantation is a means by which a human organ is used for its exact purpose but in another person's body. With respect to blood transfusion, one finds within the accepted texts that to give and receive human milk in order to sustain life is permissible but, 'according to the correct view, because it is part of a human, to take benefit from it without necessity is illegal.'[20] If one applies *qiyās* to human milk, then the donating and receiving of blood will be permissible as it is only utilised times of extreme emergency and necessity.

Nawᶜ (bodily fluid)	*Jins*	*ᶜIlla*
human milk	sustains life	permissible with necessity (*aṣl*)
human blood	sustains life	ruling transfers (*farᶜ*)

In summary, the reasoning behind the impermissibility of utilising body parts is the honour and respect for the gift from God that is the human body. However, this is limited to situations in which the human body part is utilised in a dishonourable way. In the case of organ transplantation and blood transfusion the honour and respect of human life is the very reason which brings about this action and the body part is not degraded in any way, but rather is utilised for the very purpose for which it was created. Therefore, in this case one adopts *istiḥsān* and reaches the conclusion that the purpose or *ᶜilla* behind organ transplantation is the preservation of life, which overrides virtually any other legal edict. One may also adopt the legal maxims, 'It is obligatory upon the Muslim that he removes the means of destruction from himself,' and 'The lesser of the two harms is the one to choose,' and other such maxims. Therefore, when there is no other alternative it is possible to receive blood transfusions and to donate and receive body parts in order to improve and sustain life.

Immunisation

Immunisation is a method of protecting mostly children but some adults too, and as a result the wider population, from various diseases by facilitating the production of antibodies which increase immunity to particular diseases. Vaccines are formed by utilising the pathogen—which is the very organism that

19 Ibid.
20 Ibid., vol. 2, p. 438.

produces the disease—but altering it before it is administered. This can be done in three ways: by weakening or attenuating the pathogen so it does not cause complicates (polio and MMR vaccines are made in this way), extracting that part of the pathogen which brings about the immune response (Hib vaccine is made by this method); and by destroying the pathogen by heating or using formalin (whooping cough vaccine is made this way). Other components are added before the vaccine is administered. Their purpose is to stimulate the immune system in order for it to produce antibodies.

Certain diseases are passed from human to human and therefore if a significant portion of the community is immunised then it is difficult for the disease to be passed on. This is referred to as 'herd immunity'. For instance, measles is highly infectious; if no children were immunised, then virtually all would be infected. However, if 90% of children were vaccinated it would stop the disease spreading and if 95% were vaccinated then it would eventually be eliminated.[21]

Islam not only permits but rather makes it compulsory to find ways of caring for and curing the body and mind. However, that is after a person has been diagnosed with a certain illness. The argument against immunisation adopted by many who hold the literal approach is that one is attempting to 'cure' oneself in the absence of an illness or, worse still, actually administering the disease itself (through use of the pathogen). Their argument is that one may or may not contract a particular disease, and as there is a possibility of not contracting it then one should wait for one's fate rather than second-guessing one's destiny. Putting it another way, we should leave it in God's hands until He decides and then take reactionary steps. However, this premise is flawed as there are many examples in Islam where a person is required to perform preventative action rather than retrospective action. For example, the maxim: 'It is obligatory upon the Muslim that he removes the means of destruction from himself,' implies that one should act prospectively and not only retrospectively.

There are a number of legal maxims make immunisation permissible but not necessary:

1. The origin in anything is permissibility.
2. A greater harm is removed by a lesser harm.
3. Harm must be removed.
4. It is obligatory upon the Muslim that he removes the means of destruction from himself.

[21] Department of Health, Immunisation Information, see http://immunisation.dh.gov.uk/.

5. Averting harm is superior to giving benefit.
6. The specific harm will be acted upon in order to remove the general harm.
7. The lesser of the two harms is the one to choose.
8. Matters are according to their objectives.

In conclusion, the literal approach is that, on one hand, immunisation is injecting a child or adult with a disease, and, on the other hand, there is no illness to cure, thus immunisation is deemed impermissible. The liberal approach would possibly utilise the principle of the preservation of life and argue for its permissibility; again we have nothing further to add here as no documentation exists on this. Finally, according to the traditional model, not only is it permissible to immunise oneself or one's children against diseases, but it is necessary. The reason for this is that when one does not immunise then one is risking one's own life and the lives of others and this itself is impermissible. It should be added that there are a number of forms of immunisation and that we are here only referring to the principle of immunisation.

Inheritance

In the event of death, Islam requires the transfer of the individual's estate to his or her heirs as the wealth now belongs to them and is distributed among them according to proportions detailed explicitly in the Qur'ān (with further additions found in the *Sunna* and clarifications from the *fuqahā'*). There are two processes by which wealth is transferred: one is bequest (*waṣīyya*), defined as 'the leaving of property to a person or other beneficiary by a will'; and the other is inheritance (*mīrāth*), defined as 'to receive money, property or a title, as an heir at the death of a previous owner/holder.'[22]

A question which arises due to the significant number of Muslim converts is: does Islam permit money and the like to be inherited from a non-Muslim parent, or can a non-Muslim inherit from a Muslim relation? Zaylaʿī says this about *waṣīyya*: 'A Muslim can make a bequest to a non-Muslim (*dhimmī*) and vice versa; it is permissible that a Muslim bequeaths to a non-Muslim and a non-Muslim to a Muslim.'[23]

An explanation for why it is permissible is found in *Hidāya*:

'It is permissible that a Muslim bequeaths to a non-Muslim and non-Muslim

[22] Judy Pearsall (ed.), *The Concise Oxford Dictionary* (New York: Oxford University Press Inc., 1999).

[23] Zaylaʿī, *Tabyīn al-ḥaqā'iq*, vol. 7, p. 379.

> to a Muslim firstly because of the Almighty's statement, *God does not prohibit you from those who do not fight you in religion* [Q.LX.8] and secondly because due to the agreement with *dhimmīs* they are as equal as Muslims in transactions. That is why it is permissible to be mutually beneficial to one another in the life of this world and in what comes after death. In *al-Jāmiʿ al-ṣaghīr* bequeathing to *ahl al-ḥarb* (hostile non-Muslims) is completely void due to the Almighty's statement, *Indeed God only prohibits you from those who fight you in religion.* [Q.LX.9]'[24]

As there is the potential that the wealth of a non-Muslim may have been gained by means which are prohibited in Islam, for example through usury, Kāsānī explains, 'It is correct for a non-Muslim to bequeath wealth to a Muslim. Do you not see that it is correct to trade with a non-Muslim and to receive gifts from him, hence receiving a bequest is the same.'[25]

With respect to *mīrāth*, Zaylaʿī puts forward the School's position,: 'The difference of religion stops inheritance, what is meant by it is the difference between Islam and other than Islam. This is due to his statement upon him be blessings and peace, "There is no inheritance between a Muslim and non-Muslim and between a non-Muslim and Muslim."'[26]

In summary, at death the transfer of wealth between Muslims and non-Muslims may take place by way of bequest but not by way of inheritance. It is acceptable for a Muslim to receive and make bequests to and from non-Muslim relations, in particular to parents, however one cannot inherit from them according to the view as it exists. All bequests can be made through the writing of a will. As Muslims are permitted to deal with all communities in lawful ways, earnings from sources not approved by Islamic Law do not prevent the Muslim from accepting a bequest.

Financial Transactions

Non-contact Sales

The internet has allowed communication and the transfer of information to increase by levels which were unthinkable a few decades ago. This has brought about many solutions but also a certain number of problems, or more correctly, challenges for Muslims to ensure they stay within the legal guidelines

[24] Marghīnānī, *Hidāya*, vol. 2, p. 657.
[25] Kāsānī, *Badāʾiʿ al-ṣanāʾiʿ fī tartīb al-sharāʾiʿ*, vol. 10, pp. 485-86.
[26] Zaylaʿī, *Tabyīn al-ḥaqāʾiq*, vol. 7, p. 490.

for transactions. One example is the use of the internet to buy and sell either directly or through auctions. The books of *fiqh* do not stipulate that the product of sale/purchase must be 'seen' during the transaction. The key point is that disputes should be avoided and, for the sale to proceed according to Islamic principles, the condition of the product must be clearly described.

Chapter 2 of Section 5 of the *Majallah*, which discusses the rescission of a sale, stipulates the conditions and level of description required when a product is being sold:

> 197. The thing to be sold must exist. [Products cannot be made to order except where there is a *ʿurf* for this, for instance clothes made to order].
> 198. It is necessary that the delivery of the thing being sold be possible. [Hence, the sale of a flock of birds in flight would not be legal].
> 199. It is necessary that the thing being sold should be *māl mutaqawwim*. *Māl mutaqawwim* is one of two things: the first is that the Law considers it legally sound to utilise, and the second means acquired property. For example, a fish in the sea is not *māl mutaqawwim* [as fish are not the possession of one person] when it [the fish] is caught and taken it is *māl mutaqawwim*.
> 200. It is necessary that the buyer should know the thing sold. [An accurate description or a good quality picture would bring about this condition in internet sales].
> 201. The thing sold is identified through a description of its qualities and state, which will distinguish it from other things.[27]

Therefore, any transaction which takes place without the actual existence of the product or in the absence of physical contact between the buyer and seller would be legal as long as the above conditions are met; the transaction and the ownership of the product would upon payment be transferred from the seller to the buyer.

Currency Trading

The historical shift from the use of gold and silver coins to paper currency was because paper currency is a safer and more pragmatic approach in financial transactions. Based on this fact, religious scholars, along with financial institutions and the general public, acknowledged paper currency as representing

[27] C. Tyser, D. Demetriades and I. Effendi, *The Mejelle: Being an English Translation of Majallah el-Ahkam-l-Adliya and a Complete Code of Islamic Civil Law*, p. 27; with grammatical changes where required and my additional text in square brackets.

gold and silver. However, paper currency was not regarded as something that had a value in itself, but was merely a certificate or promise indicating that its possessor has gold and silver, deposited in a bank, to the value of the note.

However, should we accept that paper currency today has become a medium of transaction in itself? Does it now have a value in itself as it has taken the place of gold and silver, and as the promise to pay gold and silver which appears on paper notes is now meaningless and of no significance? It is not possible to walk into a bank and request the equivalent in gold or silver of paper currency. In addition, paper currency is accepted and acknowledged as money throughout the world. The conclusion is that paper currency no longer 'represents' gold or silver, it has replaced gold and silver and it is now considered legal tender and a medium of transaction in itself.[28]

Before discussing the specific transaction of trading in currencies, it is relevant in terms of background information to discuss the concept of *ribā*. Marghīnānī says:

> He [Qudūrī] states *ribā* is illegal in every product sold by volume or weight if it is traded in its *jins* [genus] with excess. Hence the *ʿilla* according to us is [that a product sold] by weight or volume and of the same *jins* and an [excess] amount is specified [above and beyond that] which is included [in the transaction]. The origin is due to the *mashhūr ḥadīth* which is his statement upon him be peace, "Wheat for wheat, like for like, hand-to-hand and the extra is *ribā*," and he counted six things: wheat, barley, dates, salt, gold and silver.[29]

Marghīnānī then defines what the jurists term *ribā*: '*Ribā* is the additional earning of one of the two parties in a transaction when [one party offers] nothing in exchange for what is included in it [i.e. the terms of the transaction].'[30]

Therefore, based on the above brief explanation, trading in the currency of the same country with an increase for one of the parties as a condition of the transaction is considered *ribā* and is prohibited. For instance, exchanging one GBP for two GBP is unlawful. However, it is not necessary, as is the case with exchanging gold for gold, that both parties take possession of the currency they have exchanged in the same *majlis* (transaction session). The reason is that for Muslim jurists paper currency is not treated like gold and silver; but rather as

[28] For a discussion on paper currency see ʿUthmānī, *Buḥūth fī qaḍāyā fiqhiyya muʿāṣara*, vol. 1, pp. 143-168.

[29] Marghīnānī, *al-Hidāya*, vol. 2, p. 77.

[30] Ibid. For example, if party A voluntarily gives extra without it being a condition of the transaction or without a request it is not considered to be *ribā*.

legal tender and as such a medium of exchange. Also, it was not included in the list mentioned by the Prophet. Therefore the condition of exchanging within the same transaction session does not apply to currency. Having said that, one party must take possession during the transaction session before *iftirāq* (separating and departing), as debts on either side are not permitted.

It is obvious that if the currency were exchanged at par value, say an exchange of one GBP for another, then this is without doubt legal as even though the currency is the same no 'excess' (*ribā*) is being made by either party.

As to the exchanging of currencies of different countries, this is legal even with excess on one side. For instance, exchanging one GBP for two Euros. The reasoning is that the *jins* (genus) of both currencies is different, and when exchanging items of varied nature, it is not illegal to have excess on one side. In other words paper currency is not one of the six items mentioned in the *ḥadīth*, where the items must be like for like and hand to hand. As the trading of currencies does not have to be hand to hand then one party may depart after the completion of the transaction still in debt to the other, but due to the fact that if it is a currency of the same type, for instance one British pound for two, then it would have to be an equal transfer as no excess will be allowed, because that would be *ribā* and therefore illegal.

In summary, it is permitted to trade in currencies of different countries and to make profit from such trade. However, it is necessary for one of the parties to take possession of the amount at the time of the transaction and before the two parties separate because debt on both sides is not permitted according to the *ḥadīth*. Note that this permissibility is in normal circumstances, as trading in currencies must be conducted at a rate which is determined by the government. By comparison, to trade at a different rate from that which is set by the government will not be permitted, although it will not be considered as *ribā*. This is because it contravenes the law of the land, and Islam does not permit this. Thus, if the government fixes a rate of exchange for the British pounds against the euro, then, from an Islamic perspective, it will be illegal to trade on the black market at a different rate.

The above has shown the application of Islamic Law to a relatively new area of finance. It demonstrates that traditional *fiqh* is able to deal with contemporary concepts and that the use of traditional methodologies can grant confidence that such transactions are still in conformity with religious source texts.

Political Participation

Political scientists have recently started to conduct work in the area of Muslim minorities' political participation and this trend looks set to continue.[31] However, from the perspective of traditional Islamic Law there is very little to be found on the subject as the traditional texts were almost exclusively written either when Muslims were in a majority or on the basis of a conflict with a *dār al-ḥarb*, and never entered into the political participation of a Muslim minority living peacefully within a non-Muslim majority. Therefore, this is an area where *ijtihād* is required. The following two sections are an attempt at this essential area of research. In Chapter V, we discussed political-legal jurisdictions, here we will specifically address citizenship and the election process. The key legal maxim that influences the direction of this discussion is: 'The origin in anything is permissibility.'

Citizenship of a Non-religious State

If we take the example of Britain, it is in practice a secular state and it allows its citizens, Muslims and non-Muslims alike, to be involved in all aspects of its identity and development. Muslims and non-Muslims are equal partners in all matters, ranging from deciding who administers the country, to the paying of taxes to provide public services, the development the economy, the assistance in humanitarian projects across the world. Britain can be described as a programmatic secular state which is neither anti-God nor does it challenge people of faith but rather allows believers and non-believers a space to live their lives according to their views, but not to the detriment of agreed universal principles. As we have seen above, Islam does not prohibit working, trading or living amongst non-Muslims; the prohibition is limited to those states that are hostile to Muslims and even here there are exemptions. This is clearly observable from the following Qur'ānic verses in which God reveals what relations between Muslims and non-Muslim should be: *God does not prohibit you from those who do not fight* [*or 'are hostile to'*] *you on account of religion and do not exile you from your homes; deal with them kindly and justly, verily*

[31] Andrew March, *Islam and Liberal Citizenship: The Search for an Overlapping Consensus* (New York: Oxford University Press, 2009) and 'Sources of Moral Obligation to non-Muslims in the "Jurisprudence of Muslim Minorities" (*Fiqh al-aqalliyyāt*) Discourse', *Islamic Law and Society* (vol. 16, 2009), pp. 34-94.

God loves those who deal with equity. God only prohibits that you befriend those who fight against you on account of religion and exile you from your homes or they assisted in exiling you; for whomsoever befriends them then they are wrongdoers. (Q.LX.8-9) Therefore, the original ruling is that relations are permissible with non-Muslims and by extension this can be interpreted as permission to integrate as a minority.

From a legal perspective, the concept of citizenship is a social contract[32] between the citizen and the state; the state offers services and benefits, for instance, emergency services, national health and protection against an external enemy; whilst the citizen agrees to pay taxes, to be law abiding and to contribute to the benefit of the state. We have seen above that Madani[33] proposed the concept of *qawmiyya muttaḥida* (composite nationalism) which was not rejected by religious scholars except when his argument was misunderstood to mean 'assimilation'.[34] Thus there is no religious impediment to Muslims being full citizens of Britain and partaking fully in all activities, which are permitted by Islam.

One question that does arise is how can Muslims retain their religious identity and avoid potential conflicts with the secular societies they live in? In answer, one can say that this is not a new phenomenon as, for example, the Catholic Church has coexisted alongside the concept of nation-states in recent centuries with relatively little conflict. Based on this example, Muslims, both minorities and majorities, can come together under the umbrella of the *umma* through a leadership that caters for their religious needs—an Islamic Legal Council—which consists of the main Schools and theologies accepted by the majority, who will administer the Law and work in conjunction with representatives from each nation so as to take into consideration the laws of each state and the specific requirements of the different Muslim-minority communities. As a result, religious rulings will be debated, agreed upon and then issued by the Council taking into consideration both the laws of the states and the particular needs of a Muslim community; thus the potential for conflict would be minimised and there would be greater understanding and co-operation among all parties.

[32] The concept of a social contract theory is discussed by a number of philosophers in particular Plato, Rousseau and Locke (see Bryan Greetham, *Philosophy*, Hampshire: Palgrave Macmillan, 2006, pp. 345-356).

[33] Hussain Madani, '*Mas'ala Qawmiyyat aur Islam*' in Madani, *Maqālāt Siyāsiyya* (Karachi: Majlis Yādgār Shaykh al-Islām), pp. 295-374.

[34] Zafar ʿUthmānī, *Aʿlā al-sunan*, vol. 2, pp. 688-713.

Participating in Elections[35]

Being a democratic society, Britain allows its citizens to choose their leadership and this leadership is in turn there to serve the needs of the electorate. The government's role is manifold: it needs to maintain social order amongst its citizens, provide education and health facilities, make arrangements to cater for the weak and less able of society, protect the interests of the state abroad, provide protection to its citizens, and all this without any prejudice due to religious, ethnic or social differences. It is not a religious role and the major political parties do not profess to or promote a religious agenda. In addition, they do not intentionally disregard or and negatively target the religious beliefs of faith groups. In summary, the process of voting in Britain is not based on religious grounds and as a result elections are not won or lost on the basis of one's faith. For instance, when an individual votes for a particular political party, it does not necessarily mean that the individual agrees completely and wholeheartedly with all its beliefs, ideologies and policies, but rather the intention is that the candidate and/or political party will be of help to the community as a whole. For instance, if a non-Muslim citizen votes for a Muslim candidate that does not mean that the citizen accepts all the beliefs of this local councillor but that the vote is based on his/her potential at delivering a programme and his/her past track record. Therefore, with respect to local elections, each candidate should be evaluated upon his/her aspirations, aims and activities on behalf of the individual's local area and, on a national level, the party's policies should be assessed on the basis of its overall programme.

One must bear in mind the importance and gravity of selecting an individual to represent the community and likewise, on a larger scale, selecting a political party. Thus, serious thought and careful consideration must be given when making a selection as the voter is choosing a person and bearing witness that this person/political party is deemed the best for serving the community's national and international needs and fulfils the rights of members of the public, so therefore voting must not be treat lightly. Muslims who are in a position to vote must do so to the best of their ability; giving false witness or treating one's responsibility for selecting leaders lightly is a grave sin. As for Muslims elected to positions of power, there is a religious obligation on those

[35] For recent research on the topic, see Dilwar Hussain 'Muslim Political Participation in Britain and the "Eurpeanisation" of *Fiqh*', *International Journal for the Study of Modern Islam* (vol. 44, No. 3, 2004), pp. 376-401.

individuals representing others to fulfil their tasks with diligence, not to abuse power, nor to usurp the rights of others and not to shirk one's responsibilities when so elected.

Therefore, to vote for a particular candidate or political party in Britain is permissible as the origin in anything is that it is permissible until Islamic Law interprets from the sources that it is no longer so.

CONCLUSION

Due to mass migration over a number of decades, many Muslims find themselves today residing as a minority in Western secular nations and as a result search for answers in order to live within these societies and remain true to their faith. The purpose of this study was to counter the idea that there are only two possibilities for Muslim minorities: isolation or assimilation; and also to refute the image of traditional Islamic Law as outdated, irrelevant and too inflexible to be utilised in the twenty-first century, especially where Muslims are in a minority.

The study has argued that adopting the isolationist position is not sanctioned by traditional Islam except when the state or the majority non-Muslim population adopt a hostile stance towards Islam and Muslims; and that this should only be a reactionary measure required when the faith and identity of Muslims is under attack. The assimilationist model equally has been rejected as this reduces Islam to a mere belief system with only relatively limited rituals or legal system and virtually no identity. Traditional Islam, as interpreted by this study, advocates an integrationist model whereby Muslims can fully integrate within the wider non-Muslim society and at the same time retain their Islamic faith and identity.

As very little academic research has been conducted on the theory and applications of traditional Islamic Law for minority-status Muslims, this study has introduced the subject of *fiqh* and its methodology and attempted to demonstrate that there are an abundant number of processes and methods which a jurist can employ in order to arrive at legally-sound rulings applicable to Muslims living as minorities. Our aim has been to show Islamic Law, as interpreted by the Ḥanafī School of Law, to be a multifaceted, complex legal system, consisting of rationally sound theory and practice, detailed discourse analysis methodology, legal maxims and principles, which take into account both the individual's situation and the society's culture and customs. The research has also shown the applicability of this model to a number of different contemporary cases. Rather than being found wanting, it has demonstrated the robustness and flexibility of traditional Islamic Law, which allows Muslims to remain as Muslims in a secular environment whilst maintaining a link to the sources of their religion and its legal rulings.

In addition, we have concluded that, contrary to how others have chosen to interpret it, the position of traditional Law is that non-Muslim countries are not *dār al-ḥarb* but *dār al-ṣulḥ*; and that the majority of countries in the West can be categorised as such. This interpretation was employed in order to determine the applications of the Law to particular cases occurring for Muslims living in Western countries.

We hope that this study will encourage others to investigate further the principles and applications of traditional Islamic Law and the possibility of aspects of Islamic family Law being accepted and even integrated into the legal systems of Western countries.

APPENDIX

Ibn ᶜĀbidīn's *ᶜUqūd rasm al-muftī*

IBN ᶜĀBIDĪN'S *ᶜUqūd rasm al-muftī* (Chaplets of the Muftī's Task) is a concise and clear overview in poetic form by one of the greatest of Ḥanafī legal scholars. It details the procedure a jurist adopts when determining the Ḥanafī School's position. In the translation below, we have adopted the same style as Normal Calder[1] in which he asserts the poem to be an *urjūza* (transmission). which is made up two rhyming hemistyches, each of three *juz'* (parts). Calder adopts an iambic pentameter in his translation, without rhyme. I have translated the poem in a manner that is closer to the text; hence I have lost most, if not all, of its poetry, which Calder retains well. I have also included the translation of two lines, namely 23 and 24, which Calder has omitted. I have also added explanatory notes where necessary. *ᶜUqūd rasm al-muftī* aptly encapsulates and summarises most of what has already been discussed of the approach of the Ḥanafī School in the main text of this work.

In God's name, Legislator of rulings,
and with His praise I start my poem.
Then blessings and peace for eternity
Upon the Prophet who preceded us with guidance
And on his House and honourable companions,
Through long ages and the passing of years.
[And now] the sinning, needy slave of God
Muḥammad b. ᶜĀbidīn seeks
The ability from his Lord, the One, the Generous
And success in acceptance of the aims (5)

[1] Norman Calder, 'The ᶜ*Uqūd rasm al-muftī* of Ibn ᶜĀbidīn', *Bulletin of the School of Oriental and African Studies* (vol. 63, no. 2, 2000), pp. 215-28.

Ibn ʿĀbidīn starts his poem by praising God, sending salutations upon the Prophet and asking God for forgiveness and assistance in this work.

And in the composition of an ordered jewel
    A necklace rare of splendid pearls.
I named it 'Chaplets on the Muftī's Task'
    Required by those who perpetrate or issue *fatwā*
And now I begin the task
    In need of the Grace from the sea of Providence. (8)

He states that the poem is for those who issue *fatāwā* and, by describing it as a 'necklace rare of splendid pearls', he believes it to be invaluable and essential for the *muftī*.

Know that it is necessary to follow that which
    Has been prioritised by the *ʿulamā'*
Or that is in the *Ẓāhir al-riwāya* [The Books of Manifest Transmission]
    and So know, nothing opposing has been prioritised (10)

He introduces the *Ẓāhir al-riwāya,* which he considers the standard for those scholars who wish to issue *fatwā*.

The Books of Manifest Transmission arrive at
    Six, and by *uṣūl* also I have named
Authored them Muḥammad al-Shaybānī
    Detailed in them the School of al-Nuʿmānī
al-Jāmiʿ al-Ṣaghīr and *al-Kabīr*
    And *al-Siyar al-Kabīr* and *al-Ṣaghīr*
Then *al-Ziyādāt* with *al-Mabsūṭ*
    Transmitted by an authoritative chain
Also for him is *al-Nawādir*
    Its transmission is in books not manifest
And after them the matters of *al-Nawāzil*
    Deduced them our Elders with evidence (16)

One can conclude from this that for Ibn ʿĀbidīn there are three type of texts: the *Ẓāhir al-riwāya,* which is the dominant view; *Nawādir,* which has not reached us with sound transmission; and *Nawāzil,* which are further deductions in the form of *fatāwā* by scholars who followed the founders.

Better known is *al-Mabsūṭ* by *al-Aṣl*
    That is because it is the first of the six he authored
Al-Jāmiʿ al-ṣaghīr was after it so that
    What it contains is prioritised over *al-Aṣl*
The last of the six, which he authored, was
    Al-Siyar al-kabīr so it is relied upon (19)

The six books of Shaybānī are named and also the order in which they should be consulted.

Combined the six books in *al-Kāfī*
    Did al-Ḥākim al-Shāhid, so it is sufficient.
Its finest commentary is his who is like the Sun
    Al-Mabsūṭ, of the Sun of the Imāms al-Sarakhsī
Relied upon transmission cannot act
    In opposition to it nor to deviate.
So grasp *al-Mabsūṭ* of al-Sarakhsī for indeed (23)[2]
    It is the sea and the scattered pearls of its matters.
And do not rely except upon it for indeed
    Reply according to it for the enquiring questioner. (24)

The six books are thus gathered together and entitled *Kāfī* with a subsequent commentary by Sarakhsī called *Mabsūṭ*; hence it is the most authoritative text in the Ḥanafī School.

Know that indeed from Abū Ḥanīfa
    Arrives the narrations and source of excellence.
From these he chose some and from the remainder
    The fellow jurists chose some.
So there is not from other than him the answer
    As have the companions testified upon it.
Whenever one does not find from him a choice
    Then the view of Yaʿqūb [Abū Yūsuf] is preferred.
Then Muḥammad [Shaybānī] for his view is sound
    Then Ẓufar and Ibn al-Ziyād al-Ḥasan.
And it is said there is a choice in issuing a *fatwā*
    If the Imām disagrees with his two companions.

[2] This section is omitted from Calder's translation, hence the numbering of lines will differ between the two translations from here on.

And it is said the one with stronger evidence is prioritised
But that is for the muftī possessing *ijtihād*. (31)

Ibn ʿĀbidīn discusses the founders of the Ḥanafī School and, where there is a difference of opinion, the procedure by which the *muftī* will prioritise one opinion over another. In Lines 31 and 32 it is quite clear from Ibn ʿĀbidīn's words that there was a possibility for a *muftī* to exist who possessed the skills of *ijtihād* to such an extent that the *muftī* was legally qualified to investigate and then to decide on which of the three main founders had the stronger evidence, if they disagreed, and then to act upon the opinion of the one he determined had the stronger evidence:

However in our time there is no preference based on evidence
So there is no verdict except an opinion based on order.
That which is based on other [than order] is not preferred by them
So will be accepted that which was clear to them.
For indeed we observe that they have prioritised
The view of some of his companions and made it prevail,
For instance that which they have prioritised for Ẓufar
His view in seventeen rulings (35)
Then if you do not find a transmitted view
From our *ʿulamā'*, of learned authority,
And if differ those who came after
Then will be prioritised the majority.
Like al-Ṭaḥāwī and Abū Ḥafṣ al-Kabīr
And Abū Jaʿfar and the famous Abū al-Layth.
And when you do not find from them
A verdict and there is a need for response
Then the muftī should make effort and make *ijtihād*
And he should fear the power of his God on the Day of Judgement.
Those who do not have the ability [should desist]
Except the wretched loser of all (41)

Once all reliable views have been investigated and still no answer obtained, then those qualified should perform *ijtihād* in order to seek the answer directly from the source texts:

And here some principles that are excepted
Defined by those who are qualified to rule:

In every section on ritual worship is prioritised
The view of the Imām, absolutely, unless it is not sound
Then transmission from him is not adopted
Like performing *tayammum*[3] when fermented date water is present.
And in all rules pertaining to the judge's office
the view of Abū Yūsuf is selected. (45)
And in matters of inheritance then indeed
the *fatwā* is based on the view of Muḥammad [Shaybānī]
And they prioritise *istiḥsān* over *qiyās*
Except in matters where there is obscurity.
The Manifest Transmission is not to be transgressed from
Towards an opposing view which is quoted.
It is not correct to deviate from the transmitted
When arrives knowledge with transmission
And every verdict that wards off disbelief
From a Muslim, must be accepted, even if weak. (50)
And everything, which the *mujtahid* abandons
Becomes like abrogation so something else is required.
And every verdict in the *mutūn* that comes
That is sound whenever it comes
So it is prioritised upon the *shurūḥ* (commentaries) and the *shurūḥ*
Upon the *fatāwā* are ranked higher
As long as there is not other than it a correct view
So most sound is that which is described. (54)

One observes that Ibn ʿĀbidīn attempts to keep a strict order of preference between *mutūn*, *shurūḥ* and *fatāwā*. However, as we have documented this was not the actual case and we observe that *fatāwā* made their way into the commentaries and so became the practised view, with the *mutūn* regarded as academic and taught in Islamic institutes.

The best of statements is in *al-Khāniyya*
And *Multaqā al-Abḥār*
And, in other than these two, rely on that which they put last
In terms of proof for that is the established way.

[3] *Tayammum* is considered as 'dry ablution', a ritual preparation before worship. According to some scholars water from fermented dates is considered as water and not juice, hence permissible to use for ablution.

It is the custom in *al-Hidāya*
And such similar works.
Likewise when they adopt one view and give reasons
And disregard others, so choose it.
Whenever you find two views and indeed
One is deemed sound then that is relied upon.
With words like, 'upon it is the *fatwā*', 'closer'
'Clearer', 'chosen' and 'more fit'
'Sound', 'more sound', 'more secure than it'
and some say, 'its opposite is most secure'
Similarly, 'upon it *fatwā* is issued', 'upon it is the *fatwā*'
And these two are stronger than all the others.
If you find two sound views reported
Then choose the one you wish for both can be relied upon
Except if they are 'sound' and 'more sound'
Or it is said 'one upon *fatwā* is passed' then that is prioritised
Or it is in the *mutūn* or the verdict of the Imām
Or it is a Manifest Transmission or the great
Have adopted it or it is *istiḥsān*
Or it increases for the benefit of *waqf* (endowments)
Or it is a view that is more suited to the era
Or it is clearer in proof.
This is when there is a conflict in sound views
Or there is no verdict of the sound view
So take the view that is prioritised
From that you have come to know, so that is the best.
Act upon the understanding of the transmissions
That which does not oppose the established view.
Custom in Law is considered
And so upon it a ruling can be established.
It is not permitted to act upon a weak [transmission]
Nor is it permissible to respond by it to a questioner.
Except him who acts upon it through *ḍarūra* (necessity)
Or one whose knowledge is renowned.
But not for a judge for he cannot adjudicate in this way,
And if he does his judgement does not stand.
Especially our judges as they are restricted

To the School's view as they are performing *taqlīd* (75)
Is completed now what I composed in verse
And all Praise be to God and this is the best of endings.

In this last section one can observe a potential cause for the confusion which exists with respect to *taqlīd*: judges have to perform *taqlīd* as they are not in a legal position to abandon the School's view and pass judgements on their own *ijtihād*. Whereas a jurist has the legal capacity to perform *ijtihād* when required which subsequently has the possibility of becoming the School's view once consensus has been achieved. Once the School's view has changed then the judge would have to pass judgement according to the new view rather than the former as the judge is not in a position to choose but must perform *taqlīd*.

GLOSSARY

ʿāda: habit.
ahl al-ḥall wa'l-ʿaqd: individuals in charge of community affairs.
ʿālim (pl. *ʿulamā'*): religious scholar.
amān: state security or civil order.
ʿāmm: a general term or ruling that is not specified or qualified.
aṣḥāb al-takhrīj: jurists who can derive laws from legal principles, see also *mujtahid fī al-madhhab*.
aṣḥāb al-tarjīḥ: jurists who settle individual issues on the basis of already established precedents, see also *mujtahid fī al-masā'il*.
aṣl: root, origin, source.
āya (pl. *āyāt*): verse of the Qur'ān.
bayān: explanation.
bidʿa: illegitimate innovation; an illegal development or introduction of practice which is not sanctioned by the Sharīʿa.
dalālat al-naṣṣ: inferred or implied meaning of text.
dalīl: proof, indication, evidence.
dār al-daʿwa: the domain or abode of those accepting the call (to Islam).
dār al-ḥarb: enemy country, area or territory; domain of war.
dār al-ijāba: the domain or abode of response to the call (to Islam).
dār al-Islām: Muslim country, area or territory.
dār al-kufr: non-Muslim or infidel state.
ḍarar: harm, prejudice.
ḍarūra: necessity which brings about ease in the application of law; Sharīʿa-compliant necessities.
dhimmī: a non-Muslim person who lived in a Muslim state.
faqīh (pl. *fuqahā'*): one who is learned in *fiqh*, namely a jurist.
farḍ: compulsory.
farʿ (pl. *furūʿ*): generally a branch or subsidiary of *fiqh*; in *qiyās* a new case.
fatwā (pl. *fatāwā*): edict issued by a religious scholar; juristic opinion.
fiqh: the study of Islamic law; the study of how to construct and pass laws in Islam; jurisprudence.

ghālib al-ra'y: prevailing speculative opinion.
ghayr madkhūl biha: new bride, in a still unconsummated marriage.
ghayr muqallid: a person (or a school) who does not follow a traditional School of Law.
ghusl: ritual purification.
ḥadīth (pl. *aḥādīth*): the written record of the saying and actions of the Prophet Muḥammad.
ḥadīth mashhūr: a *ḥadīth* originally transmitted by only two or three of the Companions of the Prophet which, on their authority, in the next two generations became widely transmitted.
ḥadīth mursal: 'disconnected' *ḥadīth*; that is, a *ḥadīth* that can be traced back only to a Companion and not to the Prophet himself.
ḥadīth mutawātir: a *ḥadīth* transmitted by a large number of narrators of the first three generations of Muslims and thus judged to be the most sound of all categories of *ḥadīth*.
ḥadīth wāḥid: a *ḥadīth* transmitted by only one or possibly two or three narrators of the first three generations of Muslims.
ḥāfiẓ al-ḥadīth: a memoriser of *ḥadīth*.
ḥāja: need.
ḥaqīqa: real, original, literal meaning.
ḥaraj: difficulty.
ḥalāl: lawful, permitted.
ḥarām: absolutely prohibited.
ḥīla (pl. *ḥiyal*): legal device, stratagem.
ḥudūd: corporeal punishments which are solely legislated by revelation.
ḥukm (pl. *aḥkām*): judicial ruling.
ibāḥa: permissibility.
ᶜibārat al-naṣṣ: explicit meaning of text which is understood from the words of the text.
ᶜidda: the waiting period for a woman following the end of marriage by death or divorce.
ijmāᶜ: consensus of jurists on an issue.
ijtihād: independent reasoning by a qualified jurist to obtain legal rulings from the sources of the Sharīᶜa.
ᶜilla (pl. *ᶜilal*): effective cause of a particular ruling.
ᶜilm al-kalām: the study of theology.
iqtiḍā'at al-naṣṣ: what is required from a text in order to arrive at a sound understanding.

ishārat al-naṣṣ: an alluded meaning in a text.
isnād: the chain of narrators who transmit a *ḥadīth*.
istiḥsān: juristic preference, or reasoning based on equity and fairness.
istinbāṭ: rational deduction.
jins: species, type.
jizya: poll tax.
juz': parts.
kaffārat al-yamin: expiation of an oath; *k. al-zihār*: of a divorce; *k. al-qatl*: of a murder.
khabar: usually a synonym for *ḥadīth*. See all entries for *ḥadīth* above.
khafī: hidden, obscure, unclear words.
khāṣ: a word or text which conveys a specific meaning.
kharāj: land tax.
kināya: allusion, allusive meaning.
liʿān: imprecation; a form of divorce.
madhhab (pl. *madhāhib*): School of Law.
mahjūr: abandoned word or term.
mahr: dowry.
majāz: metaphorical, allegorical.
makrū: reprehensible.
mandūb: commendable, praiseworthy.
masā'il (sing. *mas'ala*): transmitted legal opinions.
millat: religion or Sharīʿa or *the way of life*.
mīrāth: inheritance.
muʿāmalāt: dealing with social affairs.
mu'awwal: interpreted beyond the obvious meaning of the text.
mubāḥ: permissible.
mufassar: clarified, exposited.
muftī: one legally qualified to issue *fatāwā*.
muḥkam: a word or text conveying a clear and unequivocal meaning.
mukhtaṣar: abridgement, summary; juristic manuals composed for teaching purposes.
mujmal: ambivalent, ambiguous, especially when referring to unclear words.
mujtahid: a jurist capable of conducting *ijtihād* at the highest level.
mujtahid fī'l-madhhab: a jurist who performs *ijtihād* according to a legal School's *uṣūl al-fiqh*.
mujtahid fī'l-masā'il: a jurist who decides on issues on the basis of the transmitted

legal opinions of his School.
mukallaf: required by Law.
muqallid: one who follows another due to the other's knowledge of the Law.
muqayyad: confined, qualified.
mushkil: difficult, a category of unclear words.
mushtarak: homonym.
mustaʿmal: applied term.
mutaʿadhir: unfeasible.
mutaʿallaqāt al-nuṣūṣ: textual indications.
mutaqābil: antonym.
mutaqaddimūn: the earliest scholars.
mutashābih: intricate, unintelligible, a category of unclear words.
muṭlaq: absolute, unqualified.
mutūn mu'tabara: foundational or accepted texts of the Ḥanāfī School of Law.
najisa ghalīẓa: gross impurity.
naṣṣ (pl. *nuṣūṣ*): a clear text; especially a *ḥadīth mutawātir* or verse of Qur'ān.
nawʿ: type.
nikaḥ: marriage or family law.
niyya: intention.
qāḍī: judge.
qatʿī: definitive, decisive.
qawāʿid -Sharīʿa: principles of Sharīʿa Law.
qawāʿid fiqhiyya: principles extracted from Islamic Law by the *fuqahā'* to form a general rule or legal maxim.
qawm: a group of men, or men and women, whether Muslims or non-Muslims.
qawmiyya muttahida: composite nationalism.
qiyās: analogy, analogical reasoning, syllogism.
ribā: usury or interest; literally, 'excess'.
rukhṣa (pl. *rukhaṣ*): legal dispensation.
rukn: essential part.
sabab: way.
sadaqa: a tithe.
ṣarīḥ: unequivocal.
Sharīʿa: the legal aspects of the Islamic revelation.
Sharṭ: condition.
shurūḥ: commentaries.
Sunna: the example of the Prophet Muḥammad.

Sūra (pl. *Suwar*): chapter of the Qur'ān.
Tābiʿūn: the generation coming directly after the Companions of the Prophet.
tadrīj: transience.
taʿlīl: ratiocination; search for the effective cause of a ruling.
ta'wīl: interpretation.
takhrīj: to derive laws by reasoning on the basis of legal principles; *t. al-manāt*: identifying the causes (for a ruling).
takhṣīṣ: specification or deriving special applications from general rules.
taqlīd: adhering to a School's doctrines. This applies to all those who are not qualified to engage in deductive and analogical reasoning.
talāq: divorce.
tarjīḥ: to prioritise a view as the dominant view of the School of law.
taṣḥīḥ: amending earlier rulings due to changing circumstances.
tasmiyya: naming (of God).
ṭawāf al-ziyāra: an obligatory circumambulation of the Kaʿba specified in the Qur'ān.
tawātur: continuous recurrence and testimony.
tayammum: dry ablution.
ṭuhr: ritual purity.
ʿulamā': see *ʿālim*.
umma (pl. *umam*): worldwide community of Muslims.
ʿurf: societal custom or culture; customary practice.
uṣūl al-fiqh: principles of *fiqh*; legal theory.
ʿushr: a tithe of a tenth.
waqf: religious endowment.
walī: ruler.
waṣiyya: bequest.
yusr: ease.
ẓāhir: clear, apparent.
ẓāhir al-riwāya: the authentic and approved transmissions of the legal opinions within the Ḥanafī School of Law.
ẓālim: in a position to oppress
ẓannī: speculative, hence open to interpretation.

BIBLIOGRAPHY

Abbas, Tahir. *Muslim Britain: Communities Under Pressure*, London: Zed Books Ltd, 2005.

Abd Allah, Umar. *Islam and the Cultural Imperative*, A Nawawi Foundation Paper, 2004.

Abdul Bari, Muhammad. *Race, Religion & Muslim Identity in Britain*, Swansea: Renaissance Press, 2005.

Abedin, Syed. *Islamic Fundamentalism, Islamic Ummah and the World Conference on Muslim Minorities*, CSIC Papers Europe No. 7, Birmingham: CSIC, 1992.

Abou El-Fadl, Khaled. *Islam and the Challenge of Democracy*, Boston: Boston Review, 2003.
——'Islamic Law and Muslim Minorities: The Juristic Discourse on Muslim Minorities from the Second/Eighth to the Eleventh/Seventeenth Centuries', *Islamic Law and Society*, vol. 1, no. 2, 1994, pp. 141- 87.

Abu Saʿīd, Aḥmad b. (Mullah Jewan). *Nūr al-anwār (sharḥ of al-manār) maʿa qamr al-aqmār*, Karachi: Saeed Company, no date.

Abū Dā'ūd. *Sunan*, 2 vols., Multan: Idārat al-Ta'līfāt al-Ashrafiyya, no date.

Affendi, Abdulwahab El-. *Who Needs an Islamic State?* London: Malaysia Think Tank London, 2008.

Afsaruddin, Asma. 'The "Islamic State": Genealogy, Facts and Myths', *Journal of Church and State*, vol. 48, 2006, pp. 153-73.

Aḥmad, Jamīl. *Ajmal al-ḥawāshī ʿalā uṣūl al-shāshī*, Karachi: Kutub Khāna Maẓharī, 1999.

Ahmed, Akbar. *Discovering Islam: Making Sense of Muslim History and Society*, London: Routledge, 2002.
——*Living Islam: From Samarqand to Stornoway*, London: BBC Books, 1993.

Ahsan, Abdullah Al-. *Ummah or Nation?: Identity Crisis in Contemporary Muslim Society*, Leicester: The Islamic Foundation, 1992.

Alwani, Taha. *Towards a Fiqh for Minorities:Some Basic Reflections*, Occasional Papers Series 10, London: The International Institute of Islamic Thought, 2003.

Ameli, S., Faridi, B., Lindahl, K. and Merali, A. *Law & British Muslims: Domination of the Majority or Process of Balance?* British Muslims' Expectations Series, vol. 5, Islamic Human Rights Commission, see http://www.ihrc.org.uk/file/BMEG_VOL5.pdf, 2006.

Ansari, Humayun. *The Infidel Within: Muslims in Britain since 1800,* London: Hurst and Company, 2004.

Anwar, Muhammad. 'Muslims in Western States: The British Experience and the Way Forward', *Journal Institute of Muslim Minority Affairs*, vol. 28, no. 1, 2008, pp. 125-37.

Asad, Talal. *The Idea of an Anthropology of Islam*, Washington: Center for Contemporary Arab Studies, Georgetown University, 1986.
——'Muslims and European Identity: Can Europe Represent Islam?', in Pagden, A. (ed.) *The Idea of Europe: From Antiquity to the European Union*, Cambridge: Cambridge University Press, 2002, pp. 209-28.

Association of Muslim Social Scientists [AMSS]. *Fiqh Today: Muslims as Minorities,* 5th Annual AMSS (UK) Conference Booklet, 2004.

Attia, Gamal. *Towards Realization of the Higher Intents of Islamic Law:* Maqāṣid al-Sharīʿah*: A Functional Approach,* London: IIIT, 2007.

Auda, Jasser. *Maqasid al-Shariah as Philosophy of Islamic Law: A Systems Approach*, London: IIIT, 2008.
——*Maqāṣid al-Sharīʿah: A Beginner's Guide*, Occasional Papers Series 14, London: IIIT, 2008.

Barkhusānī, Muḥammad. *Tashīl uṣūl al-shāshī*, Karachi: Bayt al-ʿIlm, 2004.

Baxter, Kylie. 'From Migrants to Citizens: Muslims in Britain 1950s-1990s', *Immigrants and Minorities*, vol. 24, no. 2, 2006, pp. 164-92.

Bloul, Rachel. 'Anti-discrimination Laws, Islamophobia and Ethnicization of Muslim Identities in Europe and Australia', *Journal Institute of Muslim Minority Affairs*, vol. 28, no. 1, 2008, pp. 7-25.

Bouti, Saᶜīd. 'It is not a Coincidence that the Call to the Jurisprudence of Minorities Meets with the Plot Aiming at Dividing Islam', see: http://www.bouti.net/en/article.php?PHPSESSID=fa65d3e34ef946bad316aa05e5a67840&id=336, 2001.

Bradford Metropolitan District Council [BMDC]. *Bradford Population Forecasts Information Bulletin,* Bradford: The Policy and Research Unit, BMDC, 2000.

Bradney, Anthony. 'The Legal Status of Islam within the United Kingdom', in S. Ferrari and A. Bradney (eds.), *Islam and the European Legal Systems*, Dartmouth: Ashgate, 2000, pp. 181-97.

Brown, Gillian & Yule, George. *Discourse Analysis*, Cambridge: Cambridge University Press, 1983.

Brown, Nathan. 'Shariᶜa and State in the Modern Muslim Middle East', *International Journal of Middle East Studies*, vol. 29, no. 3, 1997, pp. 359-76.

Calder, Norman. 'The *ᶜUqūd rasm al-muftī* of Ibn ᶜĀbidīn', *Bulletin of the School of Oriental and African Studies*, vol. 63, no. 2, 2000, pp. 215-28.

Centre for the Study of Islam and Christian-Muslim Relations [CSIC]. *British Muslims Monthly Survey,* Birmingham: Selly Oak Colleges, 1997.

Chapra, Muḥammad. *The Islamic Vision of Development in the Light of Maqāṣid al-Sharīᶜah*, Occasional Papers Series 15, London: IIIT, 2008.

Choudhury, Ghulam-Wahid. *Constitutional Development in Pakistan*, London: Longman, 1959.

Choudhury, Tufayl. *The Role of Muslim Identity Politics in Radicalisation (A Study in Progress)*, London: Department for Communities and Local Government, 2007.

Churches Committee on Migrant Workers in Europe [CCMWE], Expert Group on Islam, Nielsen, Jorgen. *Islamic Law and its Significance for the Situation of Muslim Minorities in Europe*, Research Papers, Muslims in Europe, Birmingham: Centre for Study of Islam and Christian-Muslim Relations, 1987.

Council on American-Islamic Relations [CAIR]. *Western Muslim Minorities: Integration and Disenfranchisement*, Washington: CAIR Policy Bulletin, 2006.

Crone, Patricia. *Medieval Islamic Political Thought*, Edinburgh: Edinburgh University Press, 2004.

Dale, A., Shaheen, N., Kalra, V. and Fieldhouse, E. 'Routes into Education and Employment for Young Pakistani and Bangladeshi Women in the UK', *Ethnic and Racial Studies*, vol. 25, no. 6, 2002, pp. 942-68.

Denscombe, Martyn. *The Good Research Guide for Small-scale Social Research Projects*, Open University Press: Berkshire, 2007.

Department of Health, 'Immunisation Information', see http://immunisation.dh.gov.uk.

Dikici, Ali. 'The Torshebes of Macedonia: Religious and National Identity Questions of Macedonian-Speaking Muslims', *Journal Institute of Muslim Minority Affairs*, vol. 28, no. 1, 2008, pp. 26-43.

Doi, Abdur-Rahman. 'Duties and Responsibilities of Muslims in non-Muslim States: A Point of View', *Journal Institute of Muslim Minority Affairs*, vol. 8, no. 1, 1987, pp. 42-61.

Dossa, Shiraz. 'Lethal Muslims: White-trashing Islam and the Arabs', *Journal Institute of Muslim Minority Affairs,* vol. 28, no. 2, 2008, pp. 225-236.

Eickelman, Dale and Piscatori, James. 'Social Theory in the Study of Muslim Societies', in D. Eickelman and J. Piscatori (eds.), *Muslim Travellers: Pilgrimage, Migration and the Religious Immigration*, London: Routledge, 1990, pp. 3-25.

Engineer, Asghar. *The Origin and Development of Islam: An Essay on its Socio-Economic Growth*, London: Sangam Books Ltd, 1987.

Esposito, John. *The Islamic Threat: Myth or Reality?* New York: Oxford University Press, 1999.

Fierro, Maribel. 'Islamic Law in al-Andalus', *Islam Law and Society*, vol. 7, no. 2, 2000, pp. 119-21.

Finney, Nissa & Simpson, Ludi. *'Sleepwalking to Segregation?': Challenging Myths about Race and Migration,* Bristol: Policy Press, 2009.

Fishman, Shammai. *Fiqh al-Aqalliyyat: A Legal Theory for Muslim Minorities*, Research Monographs on the Muslim World, Series No. 1, Paper No. 2, Washington: Hudson Institute, Center on Islam, Democracy, and the Future of the Muslim World, 2006.

Forbes, Andrew. 'Thailand's Muslim Minorities: Assimilation, Secession or Coexistence?' *Asian Survey*, vol. 22, no. 11, 1982, pp. 1056-73.

Freamon, Bernard. 'The Emergence of a New Qur'anic Hermeneutic: The Role and Impact of Universities in West and East', in Bearman, Heinrichs & Weiss (eds.) *The Law Applied: Contextualising the Islamic Shariʿa*, London: I. B. Tauris, 2004, pp. 342-60.

Gazi, Muḥammad. *The Shorter Book on Muslim International Law: Kitab al-Siyar al-Saghir*, New Delhi: Adam Publishers and Distributors, 2004.

Gill, Graeme. *The Nature and Development of the Modern State*, New York: Palgrave Macmillan, 2003.

Gilman, Sander. 'The Parallels of Islam and Judaism Diaspora', *Palestine-Israel Journal of Politics, Economics and Culture*, vol. 12, no. 2-3, 2005, pp 61-66.

Gladney, Dru. 'Islam in China: Accommodation or Separation?', *The China Quarterly*, vol. 174, 2003, pp. 451-67.

Gleave, Robert. 'Elements of Religious Discrimination in Europe: The Position of Muslim Minorities', in Konstadinidis, S. V. (ed.), *A Peoples' Europe: Tuning a Concept into Content*, Aldershot: Dartmouth Ashgate, 1999, pp. 95-107.

Gleave, R. and Kermeli, E,(eds.). *Islamic Law: Theory and Practice*, London: I. B. Tauris, 1997, pp. 205-31.

Glynn, Sarah. 'Bengali Muslims: The New East End Radicals?', *Ethnic and Racial Studies*, vol. 25, no. 6, 2002, pp. 969-88.

Graham, William. 'Traditionalism in Islam: An Essay in Interpretation', *Journal of Interdisciplinary History,* vol. 23, no. 3, 1993, pp. 495-522.

Greetham, Bryan. *Philosophy*, Hampshire: Palgrave Macmillan, 2006.

Griffel, Frank. 'Introduction', in A. Amanet and F. Griffel (eds.), *Shariʿa: Islamic Law in the Contemporary Context*, Stanford: Stanford University Press, 2007, pp. 1-19.

Griffiths, John. 'What is Legal Pluralism?' *Journal of Legal Pluralism*, vol. 24, nos. 1-2, 1986, pp. 1-56.

Gulam, Hyder. 'Islam, Law and War', *University of New England Law Journal*, vol. 3, 2006, pp. 187-209.

Hallaq, Wael. *A History of Islamic Legal Theories*, Cambridge: Cambridge University Press, 1997.

——*Law and Legal Theory in Classical and Medieval Islam*, Aldershot: Variorum, 1994.

——*Sharīʿa: Theory, Practice, Transformations*, Cambridge: Cambridge University Press, 2009.
——'Considerations on the Function and Character of Sunnī Legal Theory', *Journal of the American Oriental Society,* vol. 104, no. 4, 1984, pp. 679-89.
——'From Fatwās to Furūʿ: Growth and Change in the Islamic Substantive Law', *Islamic Law and Society*, vol. 1, no. 1, 1994, pp. 29-65.
——'Ifta and Ijtihad in Sunni Legal Theory', in M. K. Masud, B. Messick and D. S. Powers (eds.). *Islamic Legal Interpretation: Muftis and their Fatwas*, Pakistan: Oxford University Press, 2005, pp. 33-43.
——'Logic, Formal Arguments and Formalization of Arguments in Sunnī Jurisprudence', *Arabica*, vol. 37, no. 3, 1990, pp. 315-57.
——'Non-Analogical Arguments in Sunnī Juridical *Qiyās*', *Arabica*, vol. 36, 1989, pp. 286-306.
——'On the Authoritativeness of Sunnī Consensus', *International Journal Of Middle East Studies,* vol. 18, no. 4, 1986, pp. 427-54.
——'*Uṣūl al-fiqh*: Beyond Tradition', *Journal of Islamic Studies*, vol. 3, no. 2, 1992, pp. 172-202.
——'Was the Gate of Ijtihad Closed?' *International Journal of Middle Eastern Studies,* vol. 16, no. 1, 1984, pp. 3-41.

Hamidullah, Muhammad. *The Muslim Conduct of State*, Lahore: Muhammad Ashraf Publishers, 1990.

Hamilton, Carolyn. *Family, Law and Religion*, London: Sweet & Maxwell, 1995.

Haralambos, M. and Holborn, M. *Sociology: Themes and Perspectives*, London: HarperCollins, 2004.

Hasan, Masud al-. *History of Islam*, 2 vols., Lahore: Islamic Publications (Pvt.) Ltd, 2002.

Hellyer, Hisham. 'Minorities, Muslims and Shariʿa: Some Reflections on Islamic Law and Muslims without Political Power', *Islam and Christian-Muslim Relations*, vol. 18, no. 1, 2007, pp. 85-109.
——'Wanton Violence in Muslimdom: Religious Imperative or Spiritual Deviation?', in Malik, A. A. (ed.), *The State We Are In: Identity, Terror and the Law of Jihad*, Bristol: Amal Press, 2006, pp. 93-98.

Henkel, Heiko. 'Rethinking the *dār al-harb*: Social Change and Changing Perceptions of the West in Turkish Islam', *Journal of Ethnic and Migration Studies*, vol. 30, no. 5, 2004, pp. 961-77.

Hofmann, Murad. 'Muslims as Co-citizens of the West: Rights, Duties and Prospects', see http://www.islamonline.net/English/contemporary/2002/05/article3.shtml, 2002.

Horii, Satoe. 'Reconsideration of Legal Devices (*Ḥiyal*) in Islamic Jurisprudence: The Ḥanafīs and their "Exits" (*Makhārij*)', *Islamic Law and Society,* vol. 9, no. 3, 2002, pp. 312-57.

Hourani, George. 'The Basis of Authority and Consensus in Sunnite Islam, *Studia Islamica*, vol. 21, 1964.

House of Lords. [2008] *UKHL 64*, appeal from [2006] EWCA Civ 1531, 2008.

Huntington, Samuel. *The Clash of the Civilizations and the Remaking of the World Order*, New York: Simon & Schuster, 1996.

Husain, Mir. *Global Islamic Politics*, New York: HarperCollins, 1995.

Hussain, Dilwar. 'British Muslim Identity', in M. Seddon, D. Hussain and N. Malik (eds.), *British Muslims between Assimilation and Segregation,* Leicester: The Islamic Foundation, 2004, pp. 83-118.
——'Muslim Political Participation in Britain and the "Europeanisation" of *Fiqh*', *International Journal for the Study of Modern Islam*, vol. 44, no. 3, 2004, pp. 376-401.

Hussain, Hadi. *Imam Abu Hanifah: Life and Work*, English Translation of Allahmah Shibli Nuᶜmani's *Sirat-i-nuᶜman*, New Delhi: Idārat Ishāᶜāt-e-Dīnīyat, 1995.

Hussain, Imtiaz. 'Migration and Settlement: A Historical Perspective of Loyalty and Belonging', in Seddon, et al (eds.) *British Muslims: Loyalty and Belonging*, Leicester: Islamic Foundation & The Citizen Organising Foundation, 2003, pp. 21-34.

Ibn ᶜĀbidīn, Muḥammad. *Sharḥ ᶜuqūd rasm al-muftī*, Karachi: Qadīmī Kutub Khāna, no date.
——*Radd al-muḥtār ᶜalā durr al-mukhtār*, 5 vols., Karachi: al-Maktaba al-Rashīdiyya, 1984.

Ibn Ashur, Muhammad. *Treatise on Maqāṣid al-Shariᶜah*, London: IIIT, 2006.

Ibn Baz, Abdul-Aziz and Uthaymeen, Muḥammad. *Muslim Minorities: Fatawa Regarding Muslims Living as Minorities*, Middlesex: Message of Islam, 1998.

Ibn Humām, Kamāl al-Dīn. *Sharḥ fatḥ al-qadīr*, 10 vols., Beirut: Dār al-Kutub al-ᶜIlmiyya, 1995.

Ibn Nujaym, Zayn al-ʿĀbidīn. *al-Baḥr al-rāʾiq: sharḥ kanz al-daqāʾiq*, Cairo: al-Maṭbaʿa al-ʿIlmiyya, 1893.

Ibn al-Qudāmā, ʿAbd Allah. *Al-Mughnī maʿa al-sharḥ al-kabīr*, 12 vols., Beirut: Dār al-Kitāb al-ʿArabī, 1983.

Ihle, Annette. 'Islamic Morality, Youth Culture, and the Expectations of Social Mobility among Young Muslims in Northern Ghana', *Journal Institute of Muslim Minority Affairs*, vol. 28, no. 2, 2008, pp. 267-288.

Israeli, Raphael. 'The Muslim Minority in the People's Republic of China', *Asian Survey*, vol. 21, no. 8, 1981, pp. 901-19.

Jackson, Sherman. 'From Prophetic Action to Constitutional Theory: A Novel Chapter in Medieval Muslim Jurisprudence', *International Journal of Middle East Studies*, vol. 25, no. 1, 1993, pp. 71-90.
——'Jihad and the Modern World', *The Journal of Islamic Law and Culture*, vol. 7, no. 1, 2002, pp. 1-26.
——'Shariʿah, Democracy, and the Modern Nation-State: Some Reflections on Islam, Popular Rule, and Pluralism', *Fordham International Law Journal*, vol. 27, 2003, pp. 88-107.

Jewan, Mullah. See Abu Saʿīd, Aḥmad b.

Johansen, Baber. *Contingency in Sacred Law: Legal and Ethical Norms in the Muslim Fiqh*, Leiden: E. J. Brill, 1999.
——'Casuistry: Between Legal Concept and Social Praxis', *Islamic Law and Society,* vol. 2, no. 2, 1995, pp. 135-56.

Jokisch, Benjamin. '*Ijtihād* in Ibn Taymiyya's *fatāwā*', in R. Gleave and E. Kermeli (eds.), *Islamic Law: Theory and Practice*, London: I. B. Tauris, 1997 pp. 119-37.

Kamali, M. H. *Principles of Islamic Jurisprudence*, Cambridge: The Islamic Texts Society, 2003.
——*Equity and Fairness in Islam*, Cambridge: The Islamic Texts Society, 2005.
——*Maqāṣid al-Sharīʿah Made Simple*, Occasional Papers Series 13, London: IIIT, 2008.

Kāsānī, ʿAlāʾ al-Dīn. *Badāʾiʿ al-ṣanāʾiʿ fī tartīb al-sharāʾiʿ*, 10 vols., Beirut: Dār al-Kutub al-ʿIlmiyyah, 1997.

Keller, Nuh. 'Which of the Four Orthodox Madhhabs has the most Developed

Fiqh for Muslims living as Minorities?', see, http://www.sunnah.org/fiqh/usul/fiqh4.htm, 1995.
——'Modernism and Fiqh al-Aqaliat', see, http://al-miftah.blogspot.com/2007/09/islam-not-cereal-shaykh-nuh-keller-uk.html, 2007.

Kelly, Paul. 'MacIntyre's Critique of Utilitarianism', in Horton & Mendus (eds.), *After MacIntyre: Critical Perspectives on the Work of Alasdair MacIntyre*, Cambridge: Polity Press, 1994, pp. 127-145.

Kettani, Mohammed. *Muslim Minorities in the World Today*, London: Mansell Publishing Ltd, 1986.
——'Challenges to the Organization of Muslim Communities in Western Europe: The Political Dimension', in W. Shadid & P. S. van Koningsveld (eds.), *Political Participation and Identities of Muslims in Non-Muslim States*, Kampen: Kak Pharos Publishing House, 1996, pp. 15-35.

Khadduri, Majid. *The Islamic Law of Nations: Shaybānī's Siyar*, Baltimore: The Johns Hopkins Press, 1966.

Khalidi, Omar. 'Muslim Minorities: Theory and Experience of Muslim Interaction in Non-Muslim Societies', *Journal of the Institute of Muslim Minority Affairs*, vol. 10, no. 2, 1989, pp. 425-37.

Khan, Asif. *The Fiqh of Minorities: The New Fiqh to Subvert Islam,* London: Khilafah Publications, 2004.

Khir, Bustami. 'Who Applies Islamic Law in Non-Muslim Countries? A Study of the *Sunnī* Principle of Governance of the Scholars (*wilāyat al-ʿulamā'*)', *Journal of Muslim Minority Affairs*, vol. 27, no. 1, 2007, pp 79-91.

King, Michael (ed.). *God's Law versus State Law: The Construction of Islamic Identity in Western Europe*, London: Grey Seal, 1995.

Kohn, Hans. *A History of Nationalism in the East*, New York: Harcourt, 1929.
——*Nationalism and Imperialism in the East*, New York: Howard Fertig, 1969.

Kosmin, Barry. 'Contemporary Secularity and Secularism', in Kosmin & Keysar, *Secularism & Secularity: Contemporary International Perspectives*, Hartford, CT: Institute for the Study of Secularism in Society and Culture (ISSSC), 2007.

Krishna, Gopal. 'Islam, Minority Status and Citizenship: Muslim Experience in India', *Archives Europennes de Sociologie*, vol. 27, no. 2, 1986, pp. 353-68.

Kurdi, Abdulrahman. *The Islamic State: A Study Based on the Islamic Holy*

Constitution, London: Mansell Publishing Limited, 1984.

Laknawī ʿAbd al-Ḥayy. 'Introduction', in Shaybānī, *The Muwatta of Imam Muhammad*, London: Turath Publishing, 1990, pp. 1-49.
——'Introduction', in Shaybānī, *Al-Jāmiʿ al-ṣaghīr maʿ sharḥ al-nāfiʿ al-kabīr*, Karachi: Idārat al-Qur'ān, 2004, pp. 5-66.

Lapidus, Ira. *A History of Islamic Societies*, New York: Cambridge University Press, 1991.
——'The Separation of State and Religion in the Development of Early Islamic Society', *International Journal of Middle East Studies*, vol. 6, no. 4, 1975, pp. 363-85.
——'State and Religion in Islamic Societies', *Past and Present*, no. 151, 1996, pp. 3-27.

Lathion, Stephane. 'Muslims in Switzerland: Is Citizenship Really Incompatible with Muslim Identity', *Journal Institute of Muslim Minority Affairs*, vol. 28, no. 1, 2008, pp. 53-60.

Leiken, Robert. 'Europe's Angry Muslims', *Foreign Affairs*, vol. 84, no. 4, 2005, pp. 120-35.

Lewis, Bernard. *Political Language of Islam*, Chicago: University of Chicago Press, 1988.
——*The Crisis of Islam: Holy War and Unholy Terror*, New York: Modern Library, 2003.
——'Legal and Historical Reflections on the Position of Muslim Populations under Non-Muslim Rule', *Journal Institute of Muslim Minority Affairs*, vol. 13, no. 1, 1992, pp. 1-16.

Lewis, Philip. *Islamic Britain: Religion, Politics and Identity among British Muslims*, London: I. B. Tauris, 2002.

Libson, Gideon. 'On the Development of Custom as a Source of Law in Islamic Law', *Islamic Law and Society*, vol. 4, no. 2, 1997, pp. 131-55.

MacIntyre, Alasdair. *After Virtue: A Study in Moral Theory*, London: Gerald Duckworth & Co. Ltd, 1985.
——*Marxism: An Interpretation*, London: SCM Press, 1953.
——*Three Rival Versions of Moral Enquiry: Encyclopaedia, Genealogy, Tradition*, London: Gerald Duckworth & Co. Ltd, 1990.
——*Whose Justice? Which Rationality?* London: Gerald Duckworth & Co. Ltd, 1988.
——'A Partial Response to My Critics', in J. Horton and S. Mendus (eds.),

After MacIntyre: Critical Perspectives on the Work of Alasdair MacIntyre, Cambridge: Polity Press, 1994, pp. 283-304.

McLoughlin, Sean. 'In the Name of the Umma', in A. Shadid & P. S. van Koningsveld (eds.), *Political Participation and Identities of Muslims in Non-Muslim States*, Kampen: Kok Pharos Publishing House, 1996, pp. 206-28.
——'Mosques and the Public Space: Conflict and Cooperation in Bradford', *Journal of Ethnic and Migration Studies*, vol. 31, no. 6, 2005, pp. 1045-66.

Madani, Hussain. '*Mas'ala Qawmiyyat aur Islam*', in Madani, *Maqālāt Siyāsiyya*, Karachi: Majlis Yādgār Shaykh al-Islām, date?, pp. 295-374.
——*Composite Nationalism and Islam;* translation of *Muttahida Qawmiyat aur Islām*, New Delhi: Ajay Kumar Jain, 2005.

Makdisi, George. *The Rise of Colleges: Institutions of Learning in Islam and the West,* Edinburgh: Edinburgh University Press, 1981.

Makdisi, John. 'Legal Logic and Equity in Islamic Law', *American Journal of Comparative Law,* vol. 33, 1985, pp. 63-92.

Malik, Aftab. 'The State We Are In', in A. Malik (ed.), *The State We Are In: Identity, Terror and the Law of Jihad,* Bristol: Amal Press, 2006, pp. 14-31.

Malik, Maleiha. 'Accommodating Muslims in Europe: Opportunities for Minority Fiqh', *Law and Society*, ISIM Newsletter 13, 2003, pp. 10-11.
——*Muslim Legal Norms and the Integration of European Muslims*, EUI Working Papers, RSCAS 2009/29, San Domenico di Fiesola: European University Institute, 2009.

Manṣūrpūrī, Muḥammad. *Fatāwā nawaysī kay rahnumā uṣūl*, Karachi: Maktaba Nuʿmāniyya, 2001.

March, Andrew. *Islam and Liberal Citizenship: The Search for an Overlapping Consensus*, New York: Oxford University Press, 2009.
——'Sources of Moral Obligation to non-Muslims in the "Jurisprudence of Muslim Minorities" (*Fiqh al-aqalliyyāt*) Discourse', *Islamic Law and Society*, vol. 16, 2009, pp. 34-94.

Marczyk G., DeMatteo D. & Festinger D. *Essentials of Research Design and Methodology*, Wiley: New Jersey, 2005.

Marghīnānī, ʿAbd al-Jalāl. *al-Hidāya*, 2 vols., Multān: Maktabat al-Sharika al-ʿIlmiyya, 1999.

Mason, Andrew. 'MacIntyre on Liberalism and its Critics: Tradition, Incommensurability and Disagreement', in J. Horton and S. Mendus (eds.), *After MacIntyre: Critical Perspectives on the Work of Alasdair MacIntyre*, Cambridge: Polity Press, 1994, pp. 225-244.

Mastura, Michael. 'Legal Pluralism in the Philippines', *Law and Society Review*, vol. 28, no. 3, 1994, pp. 461-75.

Masud, Khalid. 'Being Muslim in a Non-Muslim Polity: Three Alternate Models', *Journal Institute of Muslim Minority Affairs,* vol. 10, no. 1, 1989, pp. 118-28.

Masud, K., Messick, B., & Powers, D.. 'Muftis, Fatwas, and Islamic Legal Interpretation', in Masud, M. K., Messick, B., & Powers, D. S. (eds.), *Islamic Legal Interpretation: Muftis and their Fatwas,* Pakistan: Oxford University Press, 2005.

Maxwell, Rahsaan. 'Muslims, South Asians and the British Mainstream: A National Identity Crisis', *West European Politics*, vol. 29, no. 4, 2006, pp. 736-56.

Menski, Werner. 'Asians in Britain and the Question of Adaptation to a New Legal Order', in Israel M. & Wagle N. (eds.), *Ethnicity, Identity and Migration: The South Asian Context*, Toronto: Toronto University Press, 1993, pp. 238-68.

Meron, Ya'akov. 'The Development of Legal Thought in Hanafi Texts', *Studia Islamica,* vol. 30, 1969, pp. 73-118.
——'The Mejelle tested by its Application', *Israel Law Review*, vol. 5, 1970, pp. 203-15.
——'Research Note: Marghīnānī, his Method and his Legacy', *Islamic Law and Society*, vol. 9, no. 3, 2002, pp. 410-416.

Messick, Brinkley. *The Calligraphic State: Textual Domination and History in a Muslim Society*, Berkeley: University of California Press, 1993.

Michot, Yahya. *Muslims under Non-Muslim Rule: Ibn Taymiya*, Oxford: Interface Publications, 2006.

Miller, Kathryn. 'Muslim Minorities and the Obligation to Emigrate to Islamic Territory: Two *Fatwās* from Fifteenth-Century Granada', *Islamic Law and Society*, vol. 7, no. 2, 2000, pp. 256-88.

Modood, Tariq and Ahmad, Fauzia 'British Muslim Perspectives on Multiculturalism', *Theory Culture Society*, vol. 24, no. 2, 2007, pp. 187-213.

Modood, T., Berthoud, R., Lakey, J., Nazroo. J., Smith, P., Virdee, S., and Beishon, S. *Ethnic Minorities in Britain: Diversity and Disadvantage*, London: Policy Studies Institute, 1997.

Moore, K., Mason P., & Lewis J. *Images of Islam in the UK: The Representation of British Muslims in the National Print News Media 2000-2008*, Cardiff: Cardiff School of Journalism, Media and Cultural Studies, 2008.

Mujaddidī, Muḥammad. '*al-Qawāʿid al-Fiqhiyya*', in Mujaddidī, M., *Majmūʿat qawāʿid al-fiqh*, Karachi: Mīr Muhammad Kutub Khāna, 1960, pp. 49-144.

Mullah Jewan. See under Abu Saʿīd, Aḥmad b.

Mutairi, Mansour. *Necessity in Islamic Law*, PhD thesis, Edinburgh University, 1997.

Nielsen, Jorgen. *Islamic Surveys: Muslims in Western Europe*, Edinburgh: Edinburgh University Press, 2004.

Nyazee, Imran. 'Introduction', in Marghīnānī, *Al-Hidāyah: The Guidance*, Bristol: Amal Press, 2006, pp. ix-xxxii.

Oliver, Paul. *The Student's Guide to Research Ethics*, Open University Press: Maidenhead, 2003.

Omar, Mohammed. 'Reasoning in Islamic Law: Part One', *Arab Law Quarterly*, vol. 12, 1997, pp. 148-96.
——'Reasoning in Islamic Law: Part Two', *Arab Law Quarterly*, vol. 12, 1997, pp. 353-83.
——'Reasoning in Islamic Law: Part Three', *Arab Law Quarterly*, vol. 23, 1998, pp. 23-60.

Open Society Institute, *Monitoring Minority Protection in the EU: The Situation of Muslims in the UK*, New York: Open Society Institute, 2002.

Othman, Mohammed. 'ʿUrf as a Source of Islamic Law', *Islamic Studies*, vol. 20, 1981, pp. 343-55.

Pālanpūrī, Saʿīd. *Āp Fatwā Kaysay Day?* Karachi: al-Maktaba al-Nuʿmāniyya, 2006.

Parekh Report, The, see, Runnymede Trust, The.

Park, Robert. *Race and Culture*, London: The Free Press of Glencoe, 1950.

Patient UK. *Delaying a Period*, see http://www.patient.co.uk/showdoc/23069068, 2008.

Patterson, Sheila. *Dark Strangers*, Harmondsworth: Penguin, 1965.
——*Immigration and Race Relations in Britain 1960-1967*, London: Oxford University Press, 1969.

Pearl, David. 'The 1995 Noel Coulson Memorial Lecture: The Application of Islamic Law in the English Courts', *Arab Law Quarterly*, vol. 12, 1997, pp. 211-19.

Pearl, D., and Menski, W., *Muslim Family Law*, London: Sweet & Maxwell, 1998.

Pearsall, Judy (ed.). *The Concise Oxford Dictionary*, New York: Oxford University Press Inc., 1999.

Performance and Innovation Unit [PIU]. *Ethnic Minorities and Labour Markets: An Interim Analysis*, London: Cabinet Office, 2002.

Pettit, Philip. 'Liberal/Communitarian: MacIntyre's Mesmeric Dichotomy', in Horton & Mendus (eds.), *After MacIntyre: Critical Perspectives on the Work of Alasdair MacIntyre*, Cambridge: Polity Press, 1994, pp. 176-204.

Phillips, Deborah. 'Experiences and Interpretations of Segregation, Community, and Neighbourhood', in *Housing and Black and Minority Ethnic Communities*, London: Office of the Deputy Prime Minister, 2003, pp. 36-49.

Piscatori, James. *Islam in a World of Nation-States*, Cambridge: Cambridge University Press, 1986.

Porter, Jean. 'Openness and Constraint: Moral Reflection as Tradition-Guided Inquiry in Alasdair MacIntyre's Recent Works', *Journal of Religion*, vol. 73, no. 4, 1993, pp. 514-36.

Poulter, Sebastian. *English Law and Ethnic Minority Customs*, London: Butterworth, 1986.
——*Ethnicity, Law and Human Rights: The English Experience*, Oxford: Oxford University Press, 1998.

Qaraḍāwī, Yūsuf al-. *Fī fiqh al-aqalliyyāt al-muslima: Ḥayāt al-muslimīn wasṭ al-mujtamaʿāt al-ukhrā*, Cairo: Dār al-Shurūq, 2001.

Raḥamānī, Khālid. *Jadīd fiqhī masāʾil*, 5 vols., Karachi: Zam Zam Publishers, 2005.

Rahman, Habib. *A Chronology of Islamic History 570–1000 CE*, London: Ta-Ha Publishers, 2003.

Ramadan, Tariq. *Islam, the West and the Challenges of Modernity*, Leicester: The Islamic Foundation, 2001.

——*Radical Reform: Islamic Ethics and Liberation*, New York: Oxford University Press, 2009.

——*To be a European Muslim*, Leicester: The Islamic Foundation, 1999.

Ramić, Šukrija. *Language and the Interpretation of Islamic Law*, Cambridge: The Islamic Texts Society, 2003.

Ramji, Hasmita. 'Dynamics of Religion and Gender amongst Young British Muslims', *Sociology*, vol. 4, no. 6, 2007, pp. 1171-89.

Raysuni, Ahmad al-. *Imam al-Shatibi's Theory of the Higher Objectives and Intents of Islamic Law*, London: The International Institute of Islamic Thought, 2005.

Reinhart, A. Kevin. 'When Women Went to Mosques', in M. Masud, D. Messick and D. S. Powers (eds.), *Islamic Legal Interpretation: Muftis and their Fatwas*, Pakistan: Oxford University Press, 2005, pp. 116-28.

Reiter, Yitzhak. '*Qāḍīs* and the Implementation of Islamic Law in Present Day Israel', in R. Gleave and E. Kermeli (eds.), *Islamic Law: Theory and Practice*, London: I. B. Tauris, 1997, pp. 205-31.

Robinson, Neal. *Islam: A Concise Introduction*, Surrey: Routledge Curzon Press, 1999.

Rose, Martin. *A Shared Past for a Shared Future: European Muslims and History-Making*, UK: AMSS, 2009.

Runnymede Trust, The. *The Parekh Report, The Future of Multi-Ethnic Britain: Report of the Commission on the Future of Multi-Ethnic Britain*, London: Profile Books, 2000.

Safi, Louay. 'The Creative Mission of Muslim Minorities in the West: Synthesising the Ethos of Islam and Modernity', presented at *Fiqh Today: Muslims as Minorities*, AMSS UK, Westminster University, London, 21 February 2004.

Safi, Omid (ed.). *Progressive Muslims: On Justice, Gender and Pluralism*, Oxford: Oneworld Publications, 2003.

Saʿīd, Asʿad. *Al-Fiqh al-ḥanafī wa-adillatu*, 5 vols., Karachi: Idārat al-Qur'ān wa'l-ʿUlūm al-Islāmiyya, 2003.

Salam, Nawaf. 'The Emergence of Citizenship in Islamdom', *Arab Law Quarterly*, vol. 12, 1997, pp. 125-147.

Sarakhsī, Aḥmad, al-. *Kitāb al-mabsūṭ*, 30 vols., Beirut: Dār Iḥyā' al-Turāth al-ʿArabī, 2002.
——*Uṣūl al-Sarakhsī*, 2 vols., Beirut: Dār al-Kutub al-ʿIlmiyya, 2005.

Schacht, Joseph. *An Introduction to Islamic Law*, Oxford: Oxford University Press, 1982.

Seddon, Mohammed. 'Muslim Communities in Britain', in M. Seddon, D. Hussain and N. Malik (eds.), *British Muslims between Assimilation and Segregation*, Leicester: The Islamic Foundation, 2004, pp. 1-42.

Semmerling, Tim. 'Those "Evil" Muslims! Orientalist Fears in the Narratives of the War on Terror', *Journal Institute of Muslim Minority Affairs*, vol. 28, no. 2, 2008, pp. 207-223.

Serrano, Delfina. 'Legal Practice in an Andalusī-Maghribī Source from the Twelfth Century CE: The *Madhāhib al-ḥukkām fī nawāzil al-aḥkām*', *Islamic Law and Society*, vol. 7, no. 2, 2000, pp. 187-234.

Shadid, Wasif. 'The Integration of Muslim Minorities in the Netherlands', *International Migration Review*, vol. 25, no. 2, 1991, pp. 355-74.

Shadid, W.A.R., and van Koningsveld, P.S. *Religious Freedom and the Position of Islam in Western Europe: Opportunities and Obstacles in the Acquisition of Equal Rights*, Kampen: Kok Pharos Publishing House, 1994.

Shāshī, al-. *Uṣūl al-shāshī maʿ aḥsan al-ḥawāshī*, Karachi: Qadīmī Kutub Khāna, no date.

Shāṭibī, Abū Isḥāq, al-. *Al-Muwāfaqāt fī uṣūl al-sharīʿa*, 4 vols., Beirut: Dār al-Kutub al-ʿIlmiyya, 2003.

Shaw, Alison. *A Pakistani Community in Britain*, Oxford: Basil Blackwell, 1988.

Shaybānī, Muḥammad, al-. *Al-Jāmiʿ al-ṣaghīr maʿ sharḥ al-nāfiʿ al-kabīr*, Karachi: Idārat al-Qur'ān, 2004.
——*The Muwatta of Imam Muhammad*, London: Turath Publishing, 1990.

Ṣiddīqī, Muḥammad. *Rawḍat al-azhār: sharḥ lī kitāb al-āthār*, Karachi: Zam Zam Publishers, 2001.

Sieber, Joan. *Planning Ethically Responsible Research: A Guide for Students and Internal Review Boards*, Sage Publications: California, 1992.

Silvestri, Sara. *Europe's Muslim Women: Potential, Aspirations and Challenges*, Research Report, King Baudouin Foundation, 2008.

Soltan, Salah. 'Methodological Regulations for the Fiqh of Muslim Minorities', see http://www.salahsoltan.com/main/index.php?id=16,64,0,0,1,0, 2005.

Stout, Jeffrey. 'Commitments and Traditions in the Study of Religious Ethics', *Journal of Religious Ethics*, vol. 25, no. 3, 1998, pp. 23-56.

Sulaymān, Muḥammad. *Al-Mu'taṣar al-ḍarūrī: sharḥ lī al-mukhtaṣar al-qudūrī*, Karachi: Idārat al-Qur'ān wa'l-ᶜUlūm al-Islāmiyya, 2004.

Suleiman, Yasir. *Contextualising Islam in Britain: Exploratory Perspectives*, Cambridge: Cambridge University Press, 2009.

Symon, G. and Cassell, C. (eds.). *Qualitative Methods and Analysis in Organizational Research: A practical guide*, Sage: London, 1998.

Thomson, Ahmad. *Dissolution of Marriage: Accommodating the Islamic Dissolution of Marriage Law within English Law*, Regents Park Mosque: Lecture Proceedings, 2006.

Toronto, James. 'Islam *Italiano*: Prospects for Integration of Muslims in Italy's Religious Landscape', *Journal Institute of Muslim Minority Affairs*, vol. 28, no. 1, 2008, pp. 61-82.

Tyser, C. R., Demetriades, D. G. and Effendi, I. H. *The Mejelle: Being an English Translation of Majallah el-Ahkam-l-Adliya and a Complete Code of Islamic Civil Law*, The Other Press: Kuala Lumpur, 2001.

University of Bradford. 'Ethics Policy and Strategy', see, http://www.bradford.ac.uk/rkts/researchsupp.php?content+EthicsPolicyandStrategy, 2008.

ᶜUthmānī, Muḥammad. *Buḥūth fī qaḍāyā fiqhiyya muᶜāṣara*, 2 vols., Karachi: Maktabat Dār al-ᶜUlūm, 2006.

ʿUthmānī, Ẓafar. *Aʿlā al-Sunan*, 22 vols., Karachi: Idārat al-Qur'ān wa'l-ʿUlūm al-Islāmiyya, 1996.

Valakatzi, K. E. *Clash of Civilisations: Islam and the West*, University of Bradford: MA Dissertation, 1999.

Vertovec, Steven. 'Muslims, the State, and the Public Sphere in Britain', in G. Nonneman, T. Niblock and B. Szajkowski (eds.), *Muslim Communities in the New Europe*, Reading: Ithaca Press, 1996, pp. 167-186.

Vikor, Knut S.. *Between God and the Sultan: A History of Islamic Law*, London: C. Hurst & Co (Publishers) Ltd, 2005.

Weiss, Bernard. 'Interpretation in Islamic Law: The Theory of *Ijtihād*', *American Journal of Comparative Law*, vol. 26, 1978, pp. 199-212.
——'Text and Application: Hermeneutical Reflections on Islamic Legal Interpretation', in P. Bearman, W. Heinrichs, and B. G. Weiss (eds.), *The Law Applied: Contextualising the Islamic Shariʿa*, London: I B Tauris, 2008, pp. 374-697.

Williams, Rowan. 'Rome Lecture: 'Secularisation, Faith and Freedom', see http://www.archbishopofcanterbury.org/654, 2006.

Wintle, Michael. 'Cultural Identity in Europe: Shared Experience', in M. Wintle (ed.), *Culture and Identity in Europe: Perceptions of Divergence and Unity in Past and Present*, Aldershot: Avebury, 1996, pp. 9-32.

Wolffe, John. 'Fragmented universality: Islam and Muslims', in G. Parsons (ed.), *The Growth of Religious Diversity: Britain from 1945: Volume 1: Traditions*, vol. 1, London: Open University Press, 1993, pp. 133-72.

Yilmaz, Ihsan. 'The Challenge of Post-Modern Legality and Muslim Legal Pluralism in England', *Journal of Muslim Minority Affairs*, vol. 20, no. 2, 2002, pp. 343-50.
——'Law as Chameleon: The Question of Integration of Muslim Personal Law into English Law', *Journal of Muslim Minority Affairs*, vol. 21, no. 2, 2001, pp. 297-308.
——'Muslim Alternative Dispute Resolution and Neo-*Ijtihad* in England', *Alternatives: Turkish International Relations*, vol. 2, no. 1, 2003, pp. 117-39.
——'Muslim Law in Britain: Reflections in the Socio-Legal Sphere and Differential Legal Treatment', *Journal of Ethnic and Migration Studies*, vol. 28, no. 2, 2000, pp. 343-54.

Yusuf, Abdur Rahman, ibn. *Fiqh al-Imam: Key Proofs in Hanafi Fiqh*, Santa Barbara: White Thread Press, 2003.
——*Imām Abū Ḥanīfa's Al-Fiqh Al-Akbar Explained*, Santa Barbara: White Thread Press, 2007.

Zaman, Muhammad. *The Ulama in Contemporary Islam: Custodians of Change*, Princeton: Princeton University Press, 2002.

Zaylaʿī, ʿUthmān. *Tabyīn al-ḥaqā'iq: sharḥ kanz al-daqā'iq*, 7 vols., Beirut: Dār al-Kutub al-ʿIlmiyya, 2000.

Zhongkai, Zhang, Li, Guoying and Shi, Bi. 'The Physicochemical Properties of Collagen, Gelatine and Collagen Hydrolysate derived from Bovine Limed Split Wastes, *Journal Of the Society of Leather Technologists and Chemists*, vol. 90, 2006, pp. 23-28.

INDEX